RECONCILIATION

TONY PENIKETT

RECONCILIATION

FIRST NATIONS

TREATY MAKING

IN BRITISH COLUMBIA

Λ

Douglas & McIntyre
VANCOUVER/TORONTO/BERKELEY

Douglas & McIntyre Ltd.
2323 Quebec Street, Suite 201
Vancouver, British Columbia
Canada V5T 4S7
www.douglas-mcintyre.com

Library and Archives Canada Cataloguing in Publication
Penikett, Antony, 1945–
Reconciliation : First Nations treaty making in British Columbia / Tony Penikett.
Includes bibliographical references and index.

ISBN-13: 978-1-55365-143-7 · ISBN-10: 1-55365-143-X

1. Indians of North America—British Columbia—Treaties. 2. Indians of North
America—Canada—Government Relations—1951–. I. Title.
E78.B9P46 2006   342.71108'72   C2006-903195-9

Editing by Barbara Pulling
Cover design by Jessica Sullivan
Text design by Lisa Hemingway
Maps by Stuart Daniel/Starshell Maps
Source for maps: *Aboriginal Law: Commentary, Cases and Materials*
by Thomas Isaac. 3rd edition. Purich Publishing, 2004.

Printed and bound in Canada by Friesens
Printed on acid-free paper that is forest friendly
(100% post-consumer recycled paper)
and has been processed chlorine free.

We gratefully acknowledge the financial support of the Canada Council
for the Arts, the British Columbia Arts Council, and the Government
of Canada through the Book Publishing Industry Development
Program (BPIDP) for our publishing activities.

For Tahmoh, Sarah, and Stephanie

CONTENTS

∇

INTRODUCTION

MY INTEREST IN Aboriginal treaties, and my dismay at the time it takes to negotiate the modern versions, began in my Yukon youth at Dawson City, the territory's old capital, where my father was the local doctor in the late 1960s. Back in the Klondike Gold Rush era, the Canadian government had decided that Yukon Indians had no land rights to the territory they had occupied exclusively for thousands of years. Lake Laberge chief Jim Boss petitioned Ottawa for a land settlement in 1902, but not until 1973 did treaty negotiations begin. By then, I was well acquainted with the North's two solitudes: the Aboriginal hunters and trappers in the villages of the Yukon Territory and the Northwest Territories, and the settler community dominated by the merchants and bureaucrats in their respective capitals, Whitehorse and Yellowknife. Most of the Aboriginal people were poor, and most of the poor were Aboriginal. This poverty seemed to result from the Aboriginal peoples being dispossessed of their ancestral lands, which was but one chapter in an oft-repeated story of the colonization of the Americas. My generation of northerners hoped that treaties would bridge the economic and social divide. After twenty years of negotiation, the Yukon treaty became law in 1993. As yet, it is still far too soon to know if it will deliver the social peace and economic prosperity it promised.

As a territorial legislator from 1978 to 1995, I participated in debates about Aboriginal rights in every imaginable venue, from local talk-radio shows to national constitutional conferences. Between 1985 and 1992, I was the minister responsible for Yukon's land-claims and self-government negotiations, and I survived long enough to sign the final agreement. Much tension and anger had accompanied the two-decade process, but during my time in office I learned much about the healing, or decolonizing, effects of negotiating treaties. Even as a minister, I remained a student of treaty making, every day learning from the chiefs and lawyers and negotiators. With a growing appreciation that the Yukon negotiations were part of a bigger historical picture, I began reading colonial documents about conflict and cooperation between indigenous peoples and settler communities across the continent.

In 1995 I moved to Saskatchewan, a province covered by nineteenth-century numbered treaties, to advise Premier Roy Romanow's administration on emerging self-government issues there. Then, in 1997, Glen Clark's New Democratic Party government brought me to British Columbia, initially to negotiate with the province's public sector unions and later to lead a provincial team in negotiations with the federal government and the First Nations Summit. For its first hundred years, the province had denied the existence of Aboriginal title, but a 1973 decision by the Supreme Court of Canada on a case brought by the Nisga'a Nation had reopened the issue. In December 1997 the Supreme Court of Canada's decision in another case, *Delgamuukw v. British Columbia*, affirmed the continuity of Aboriginal title in the province. Over the next few months, in discussions with Ottawa, my Negotiations Project Team in Victoria developed both new tools to expedite negotiations and the province's first unified consultation guidelines, as well as drafting a new model for treaties—the "fast-track" treaty.

Although the new constitution that Canada adopted in 1982 recognized Aboriginal rights, it was not until 1990 that the B.C. government got involved in treaty negotiations. After thirteen years and half a billion dollars in B.C. Treaty Commission expenditures, the process has produced no treaties. While in Opposition, politicians in the current provincial government fought the Nisga'a treaty, filibustering it in the legislature and opposing it in the courts. Now the same people control the treaty-making machinery. Abdicating its responsibilities, the federal government allowed this situation to continue. This book is a plea to both governments to look at what they have done, consider the human and financial costs, and change direction.

For most of my twenty-five years as a legislator and a negotiator, I viewed situations in either political or policy terms. The legislators I most admired combined political principle with strategic brilliance. In politics, I thrived on the partisan struggles. As a negotiator, I was excited by the strategies in play at the table, the camaraderie of the team, the skill of articulate advocates. Over time, however, the nature of my work evolved. Increasingly, it required me to play the role of peacemaker or mediator. Consequently, I have come to appreciate the subtler qualities of the discreet facilitator, the anonymous but effective go-between, and the careful listener. My perspective on Canada's treaty negotiations, as set out in these pages, grew from this appreciation.

The enormous difficulty, the great costs, and the shameful delays in working out just settlements with Aboriginal peoples remain my greatest concern. Although I believe that Aboriginal people have generally had a raw deal, I have never represented anybody other than a provincial or territorial government at negotiating tables. For my sins in this connection, Interior Alliance and Shuswap Nation chief Arthur Manuel once attacked me and my kind of negotiating as a "racist, colonial, log and talk" approach to treaty making.[1] On the other hand, I've received death threats from right-wing Yukoners opposed to any treating with Aboriginal peoples. As a Canadian, I've long believed that, together, the northern treaties negotiated with the Inuvialuit, the Gwich'in, the Labrador Inuit, the Sahtú Dene, Tlicho and Yukon First Nations, and the Nisga'a over the last three decades of the twentieth century represent a remarkable nation-building exercise. When the parties show the will to settle, negotiation works. Much has changed in Canada over the last thirty years. The seventies were a more generous time. These days tougher-minded politicians are in charge, and thousands of "Chrétien's children" are begging on Canada's street corners. Still, if the unloved Brian Mulroney showed us one thing, it was that conviction could get you a deal.

The chapters that follow examine some of the issues around Aboriginal treaty making and suggest low-cost remedies to revitalize the ailing B.C. treaty process. My observations about the current British Columbia Treaty Commission process and my suggestions for improving it are my own, and my perspective may not be shared by the parties at the treaty tables. Nevertheless, I hope that some of what I suggest will prove useful to policy makers. Because certain age-old questions remain unresolved, this book also includes a fair bit of historical information. Reminders of our colonial past are necessary because the settler approaches to land and government that coloured relations with Aboriginal people from the beginning prejudice negotiations even today. Unshackling ourselves from these prejudices is essential if respect and reconciliation are to be achieved at treaty tables.

IN 1492 CHRISTOPHER COLUMBUS sailed across the Atlantic to Haiti, where he met the Taino people and misnamed them "Indians." Over the next forty years Spanish colonists reduced the Taino's numbers almost to extinction. Five hundred years later, after millions of Indian deaths and hundreds of North American treaties, settler governments have yet to make peace with the original inhabitants on Canada's Pacific Coast, in the province Queen Victoria named British Columbia.

For the most part, the British and French settlers of Canada did not enslave the indigenous populations, as did Spain, nor slaughter them, as did the Americans. Yet Canadians are not without sin. Newfoundland settlers shot on sight the Beothuk, the original "red Indians." Colonial-era officials cheated, stole, and expropriated Aboriginal lands. In 1884 Canada's Parliament outlawed vital cultural ceremonies like the ghost dance and the potlatch. The Canadian government undermined Aboriginal families by forcing their children into residential schools. And from 1927 to 1951, Canadian law forbade Aboriginal peoples from hiring lawyers to press their land claims.

To Canada's credit, it officially abandoned the policy of assimilation in 1973. In 1982 it became the first nation state to recognize Aboriginal rights in its constitution. It also opened its colonial history to a searching examination with the 1991–96 Royal Commission on Aboriginal Peoples (RCAP).[2] In the country's northern region, Canada has signed modern treaties that deal honourably with Aboriginal claims to land and demands for self-government. Yet in British Columbia, settler resistance, Aboriginal anxieties, and political indifference have for too long hobbled treaty negotiations.

British Columbia could as easily have become "Spanish" or "American" Columbia. Valdez and other early Spanish mariners explored the continent's northwest coast. In the nineteenth century, Americans cast covetous eyes on the fur, salmon, and gold riches to their north. Captain George Vancouver, and possibly Francis Drake, visited the area, but the British Empire did not secure the province until the completion of a transcontinental railroad and B.C.'s political union with Canada in 1871.

Between 1850 and 1854, James Douglas, the colony's first governor, negotiated fourteen local treaties with tribal groups on Vancouver Island. In 1899 the Dene in the northeast corner of British Columbia signed Treaty 8 with Canada. One hundred years later, at the end of the twentieth century, the Nisga'a Nation on the north coast concluded the province's first modern treaty. But that's it. In common with parts of Quebec, Newfoundland, and the northern territories, British Columbia is still largely without treaties to resolve the great dispute about who owns which lands.

Why scrutinize negotiations in this one province? Beyond the fact that it is larger than the states of California, Oregon, and Washington combined, British Columbia is important for at least three reasons. First, more than 100,000 Indians, representing one-sixth of the country's total, live in this province, and, of all British colonies in North America, only British Columbia refused to extinguish Aboriginal title through treaties. Second, what happens in B.C. over the next decade will show whether Canadians are serious about settling the historic "land question," as it was known until about 1960. Third, the treaty challenge is not unique to Canada; throughout the world, tribal groups are fighting to defend their lands and ways of life. Given their political resolve and court precedents, Aboriginal people at treaty tables in B.C. may well shape the international debate about Aboriginal self-government in the years to come.

Broadly speaking, I see this book as a history in three acts, each marked by critical policy choices in the Aboriginal-settler relationship. In naming these three acts, I have been inspired by game theorist Anatol Rapoport's three stages of conflict: "fight/game/debate."[3] In assembling this content, I have drawn upon both historical and contemporary records, as well as personal conversations, correspondence, and roundtable discussions with many of the key players in the B.C. treaty process.

The three stages I have identified in the long history of treaty making are Legal Slaughter, Assimilation Games, and Reconciliation Debates. The Spanish conquistadors launched the Legal Slaughter stage in 1519; the private war Cortés waged against the Aztec rulers of Mexico led ultimately to the killing of millions of indigenous peoples in Mexico, South America, and, later, the United States. The signing of the Royal Proclamation by the British in 1763 marked the advent of the Assimilation Games in which the United States and Canada dispossessed Indian peoples of their lands and tried to eradicate tribal cultures. In 1973 the Nisga'a Nation went to the Supreme Court of Canada in defence of their Aboriginal title to the Nass Valley in northern British Columbia. The court's decision in that case reopened the question of Aboriginal rights in Canada and marked the beginning of the Reconciliation Debates stage, in Canada's intermittent efforts to turn a deeply conflicted four-hundred-year relationship into a serious dialogue about the land and governance rights of indigenous peoples and the responsibilities of settler states. Although Acts 1 and 2 in the treaty drama each took two hundred years, the country should ensure that the third stage does not take as long.

In 1991 Prime Minister Brian Mulroney referred the unresolved problems of Indian, Inuit, and Métis life in Canada to the Royal Commission on Aboriginal Peoples. The commissioners decided to focus on one overriding question: What are the foundations of a fair and honourable relationship between the Aboriginal and non-Aboriginal people of Canada? Their five-volume report, published in 1996, advocated "an alternative to extinguishment through recognition of Aboriginal and treaty rights and a new treaty making paradigm based on the peaceful and harmonious coexistence of Aboriginal and non-Aboriginal people." It proposed a new Royal Proclamation to codify this new relationship. It even recommended the renegotiation of old treaties, because the extinguishment of Aboriginal title was an alien concept to the Indian parties. The commissioners also recommended increased spending of $2 billion annually over the following fifteen to twenty years to implement the 435 recommendations in their report.

Even before the RCAP report was published, governments were ready to try something new. In 1992, following a series of road blockades, office occupations, and other acts of civil disobedience by Aboriginal protestors in B.C., the governments of British Columbia and Canada, along with the First Nations Summit, an umbrella organization of Aboriginal leaders involved in the treaty process, created the British Columbia Treaty Commission to facilitate treaty making with First Nations other than the Nisga'a, who were already on their way to a settlement. The In-SHUCK-ch First Nation was the first to enter the new process, in 1993. Thirteen years later, about forty tribal groups have come to the commission's treaty tables, and several are at an advanced stage of negotiations. But by May 2006, the process had produced no treaties.

Having treaty negotiations move at a snail's pace may suit some negotiators, but it has led to public criticism of a burgeoning land-claims "industry" in Canada. The pace and the cost of the current process are clearly unsustainable. Aboriginal peoples have long ago found the colonial powers guilty of terrible crimes: genocide, slavery, grand larceny. Today, some First Nations accuse the successor govern-ments of colonial attitudes, land scams, financial misappropriation, bad-faith negotiations, manipulative mandates, hamstrung mediators, and broken promises. They also allege judicial myopia.

One can draw lines from Columbus to British Columbia and from the thinking of Spain's Juan Ginés de Sepúlveda to that of B.C.'s Melvin H. Smith. It's not much of a stretch to connect the dots from the horrors of Haiti's Port au Prince to the misery of Canada's poorest community, Vancouver's Downtown Eastside, where thousands of Aboriginal people reside. The issues of colonial deprivation are deep wounds in New World societies. Inevitably, some people outside the treaty process have asked: Why should anyone care about treaties any more? The answer is that the history of treaty making is alive in British Columbia today. The sins of our forebears against indigenous nations demand a moral reckoning. The rule of law requires that treaty makers address ancient grievances as current events.

The conflicts between peoples of the Old World and the New are very old, but they will not quietly fade away. On city streets, in downtown slums, and in garbage-strewn alleys, the survivors of deci-mated tribes subsist on the margins of settler societies. Aboriginals are overrepresented in federal penitentiaries, on the welfare rolls, and in hospital emergency wards. The sorry consequence of failures at accommodation and reconciliation, these tragedies mark the settler majority's lack of respect for the humanity of those who were here first.

Canada outlawed capital punishment in 1976, but apparently the police in western Canadian cities still have little respect for Aboriginal life. While this book was in progress, Winnipeg constables killed Gordon Dumas in a scuffle, and Saskatoon officers faced accusations of conducting "starlight cruises" in which they dumped Aboriginal men on the outskirts of the city on cold winter nights. On Boxing Day 2004, a few blocks from my home, on Vancouver's Downtown Eastside, two rookie constables with a combined on-the-job experience of fourteen weeks confronted a young Nisga'a man, Gerald Chenery. The incident quickly turned ugly, and the constables fired eleven bullets into Chenery's body. A police sergeant who ran to the scene attempted to resuscitate the victim, but it was too late. For months afterwards, Native people in Vancouver spoke bitterly of "cops killing Indians." The Vancouver police force was already under a cloud for ignoring the plight of more than fifty women, many of them Aboriginal, missing from Downtown Eastside streets, some of whose remains were later found on a farm near the Vancouver suburb of Port Coquitlam.

Such tragedies are haunting reminders of colonial traumas. More hopeful signs are the growing number of Aboriginal graduates from universities, the prosperity of some treaty groups, and the emergence on the national political stage of a new generation of articulate Aboriginal leaders and lawyers. For all their skill, these leaders have not yet achieved their goal of reconciliation with the settler society.

My study flows from a belief that the public interest in social peace, economic prosperity, and simple justice depends on expeditiously negotiating the settlement of long-standing Aboriginal land and governance issues. Left untreated, these will continue to frustrate us at home and embarrass us in the outside world.

A NOTE ON TERMINOLOGY

I AM A PRACTITIONER, not a scholar, and I wrote this book for the general reader. Nevertheless, it may be useful to briefly define some of the words I use throughout.

ABORIGINAL: Section 35 of Canada's *Constitution Act, 1982,* "recognizes and affirms" the "existing" Aboriginal and treaty rights of Indian, Inuit, and Métis peoples, which means that governments can no longer extinguish these rights without Aboriginal consent.

FIRST NATION: A First Nation is an Aboriginal community tracing its ancestry to people living in a particular area prior to European contact. The term was originally used to describe pre-contact Aboriginal linguistic and cultural communities, but after the National Indian Brotherhood changed its name to the Assembly of First Nations in 1982, "First Nation" came to describe the tribal groups or Indian bands that make up the AFN's constituency. Some conservatives object to this use of the word "nation."

INDIAN: This term was coined by Christopher Columbus to describe indigenous or Aboriginal Americans, people he imagined were residents of India.

INDIGENOUS: This adjective is used to describe the original inhabitants of an area. It is often used as a synonym for "Native" or "Aboriginal."

INUIT: This term describes Aboriginal people who live largely above the tree line in northern Canada and who were formerly called "Eskimos."

LAND CLAIMS: Ironically, the original landowners of Canada must now petition the government for settlement of their claims against the settler governments that took over the land. In recent history, the Canadian government has entertained two kinds of claims, "special" and "comprehensive." Specific claims relate to outstanding obligations of the federal government arising from nineteenth-century treaties and the *Indian Act*. Comprehensive claims cover a wide range of social, legal, and economic issues; they can be made only on the basis of an Aboriginal group's traditional use of an area and on occupancy that has not already been extinguished by treaty or other law. Current British Columbia treaty negotiations are "comprehensive" in character.

MÉTIS: The Métis are a people of mixed First Nation and European ancestry who once thrived in a buffalo-hunting society on the Canadian prairies.

NATIVE: This term has been in common use for much of Canada's history to describe any Aboriginal person or group.

NON-STATUS INDIAN: Non-status Indians are persons of Aboriginal ancestry whose names do not appear on federal government lists of "status" or "registered" Indians.

RECONCILIATION: According to the Supreme Court of Canada, "what subsection 35(1) [of the Canadian constitution] does is provide a constitutional framework through which the fact that Aboriginals lived on the land in distinctive societies, with their own practices, traditions and cultures, is acknowledged and reconciled with the sovereignty of the Crown."[1]

SOVEREIGNTY: Dictionaries define sovereignty as pertaining to "independent states" with "self-government." This is highly convenient, since the United Nations recognizes no Aboriginal American nation states.

TREATY: The report of Canada's Royal Commission on Aboriginal Peoples concludes, "Treaties have a long and honourable history as a way of solving disputes between peoples, nations and governments. Although Canada's historical treaties with Aboriginal nations have been ignored and violated over the years, the treaty format is still a powerful way of stating the terms of a relationship."[2]

PART I

LEGAL SLAUGHTER

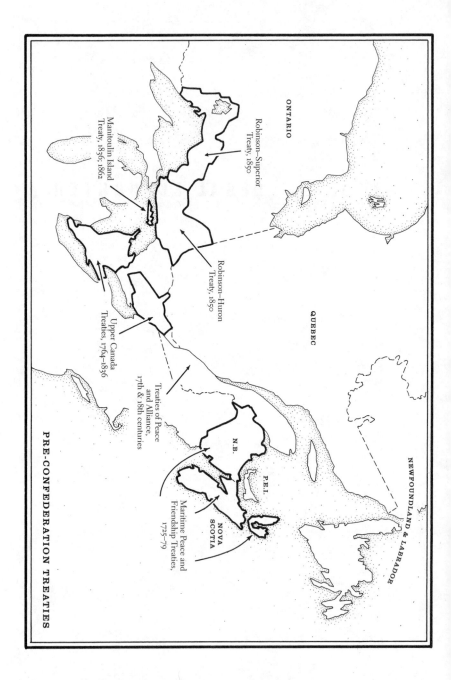

PRE-CONFEDERATION TREATIES

ONTARIO

QUEBEC

NEWFOUNDLAND & LABRADOR

N.B.

P.E.I.

NOVA SCOTIA

Robinson-Superior
Treaty, 1850

Manitoulin Island
Treaty, 1836; 1862

Robinson-Huron
Treaty, 1850

Upper Canada
Treaties, 1764–1836

Treaties of Peace
and Alliance,
17th & 18th centuries

Maritime Peace and
Friendship Treaties,
1725–79

CHAPTER 1

COLONIAL ATTITUDES

IN 2003 THE EUROPEAN media were full of
stories about the discovery of a 13,000-year-old rock
painting in Cresswell, England.[1] Such events have inclined some
people to believe that all humans have a common history and that our
development moves in a straight line from caves to condominiums.
Such beliefs reinforce views that Aboriginal North Americans were
less evolved than European colonists. The great French anthropologist Claude Lévi-Strauss disagreed with his contemporary Jean-Paul
Sartre on exactly this point.[2] There is no single path to human history,
insisted the anthropologist. Progress is an ethnocentric illusion, and
we should respect the wisdom of other cultures.[3]

A central element of the mystery of the missing treaties is this
debate about Aboriginal cultures and Aboriginal capacity for self-
government. Bartolomé de Las Casas, the Spaniard who served as
the first bishop of Mexico's southern province of Chiapas, argued that
all humanity was one, but this was a minority, even radical, opinion
for the time.[4] Spanish, Portuguese, French, Dutch, and English
invaders saw the Indian as an inferior form of life. This attitude enabled colonial authorities to defend the extermination of numerous
Indian nations.

Even today, Spain's exhaustive records of conquest and colonization attract researchers such as the United Nations' special rapporteur on indigenous-treaty questions. These records are astonishing accounts of appalling brutalities inflicted on Amerindians by European invaders. The documents are also remarkable for what they teach us about the moralizing that accompanied the brutality. It is here, in both the legalistic justifications for the enslavement and slaughter of millions and the chorus of protests about the treatment of the Indians, that one discovers the roots of the treaty process.

In October 1492, Columbus's ships stopped at the Bahamas and Cuba before sailing on to another large island, which the admiral named Hispaniola. Believing he was in India, Columbus called the inhabitants Indians. In fact, this "India" was known to the locals as Haiti.

In view of subsequent events, Columbus's account of a meeting with the indigenous people of Isabella Island, on the way to Cuba, is fascinating. Although he would soon kidnap seven Taino and take them forcibly to Spain, Columbus was fairly respectful of both the Indians and their property in his earliest encounters. His diary describes their homeland as a New World Garden of Eden:

> Sunday, 21 OCTOBER... Here and throughout the island the trees and plants are as green as in Andalusia in April. The singing of small birds is so sweet that no one could ever wish to leave this place. Flocks of parrots darken the sun and there is a marvelous variety of large and small birds very different from our own; the trees are of many kinds, each with its own fruit, and all have a marvelous scent. It grieves me extremely that I cannot identify them, for I am certain that they are all valuable and I am bringing samples of them and of the plants also. As I was walking beside one of the lagoons I saw a snake, which we killed. I am bringing the skin to your Highnesses.[5]

As Columbus approached a village near his anchorage, the inhabitants hid their possessions in the bushes and fled. He negotiated with the one Taino man brave enough to stay behind.

> I allowed nothing to be taken, not even to the value of a pin. Afterwards a few of the men approached us and one of them came quite close. I gave him hawk's bells and some glass beads, and he was very pleased and happy. In order to foster this friendship and ask for something from them, I asked them for water, and after I had returned to the ship they came down to the beach with their gourds full and gave it to us with delight. I ordered that they should be given another string of little glass beads and they said they would return the next day.[6]

The Taino people participating in the exchange could not have known that this was as good as it would get. Within forty years, the Taino had been almost wiped out. Today, Taino culture survives only in the slums of the West Indies and in various words for things of the New World: avocado, barbecue, buccaneer, guava, hammock, hurricane, iguana, and maize.

Columbus thought he was in Asia, and the language barrier prevented the indigenous Americans from setting him straight. This was the first of many misunderstandings.[7] In his book *The Imaginary Indian*, historian Daniel Francis muses about the long-term consequences of these misunderstandings: "From the first encounter, Europeans viewed Aboriginal Americans through a screen of their own prejudices and preconceptions. Given the wide gulf separating the cultures, Europeans have tended to imagine the Indian rather than to know Native people, thereby to project onto Native people all the fears and hopes they have for the New World."[8] Columbus imagined his New World "Indian" both as a guileless resident of an earthly paradise and the primitive guardian of fabulous riches. In an instant, he invented both the noble Indian and the Indian savage, stereotypes that persist today in the dream world of Hollywood Westerns and in the blinkered thinking of bureaucrats with assimilationist agendas.

What historian Alfred W. Crosby has called "the Columbian Exchange"[9] involved a massive swap of foods, flora, fauna, cultures, trade goods—and germs. The exchanges would go both ways; once started, they would never stop. Spaniards gave smallpox to the New World; Indians passed on syphilis to the invaders. Spain brought horses and wine; the Americas introduced the Spanish to tobacco and chocolate.

On May 4, 1493, Pope Alexander VI issued an edict awarding the New World to Spain. The Papal Bull drew a north-south line near the Azores. Land west of this line was placed under Spanish dominion; the Portuguese later acquired sovereignty over Brazil to the east. Spain's rulers, Ferdinand and Isabella, had pushed the Muslims out of the Iberian Peninsula, banished Jews, and set up the Inquisition. Now, Columbus's sponsors had discovered a new continent. In rewarding them, the pope expressed his hope that the New World's "barbarous nations be overthrown and brought to the faith itself."[10]

Columbus returned to Hispaniola one year after his first voyage with 1,200 or more Spanish settlers, many of them pardoned criminals. The settlers began immediately to hunt for gold, and their failure to get rich quick caused them to turn on Columbus. To appease them, the Italian admiral granted the Spaniards both lands and Indian slaves. For indigenous Americans, that was how the horror story began.

Almost fifty years later, the Dominican cleric Las Casas, who would become known throughout Latin America as Defender of the Indians, described the decimation of the Taino and Caribs in his book *The Devastation of the Indies: A Brief Account*:

> This large island was perhaps the most densely populated in the world... And of all the infinite universe of humanity, these people are the most guileless, the most devoid of wickedness and duplicity, the most obedient and faithful to their native masters and to the Spanish Christians whom they serve... They have no beds, but sleep on a kind of matting or else in a kind of suspended

net called hamacas. They are very clean in their persons, with
alert, intelligent minds, docile and open to doctrine, very apt to
receive our Holy Catholic faith, to be endowed with virtuous
customs, and to behave in a godly fashion. Yet into this sheepfold,
into this land of meek outcasts there came some Spaniards who
immediately behaved like ravening wild beasts, wolves, tigers, or
lions that had been starved for many days.[11]

In another of his works, *History of the Indies*, Las Casas said of
indigenous peoples, "They own everything in common and share all
they have, especially in matters of food, and they live from day to day
making no provision for the future and amassing no wealth."[12]

In his books, and in dozens of petitions to the Spanish Crown,
Las Casas detailed the atrocities of the settlers. When the Indians
tried to defend themselves, he said, the Spaniards only increased their
cruelties. He wrote of Spanish horsemen: "They attacked the towns
and spared neither the children nor the aged nor pregnant women
nor women in childbed, not only cutting them to pieces as if dealing
with sheep in the slaugher house."[13] In his description of the hunting
dogs the Spaniards used to terrorize the Indians, Las Casas could
barely conceal his horror:

> I saw all these things I have described, and countless others.
>   And because all the people who could do so fled to the moun-
> tains to escape these inhuman, ruthless, and ferocious acts, the
> Spanish captains, enemies of the human race, pursued them with
> fierce dogs they kept which attacked the Indians, tearing them to
> pieces and devouring them. And because on few and far between
> occasions, the Indians justifiably killed some Christians, the
> Spaniards made a rule among themselves that for every Christian
> slain by the Indians, they would slay a hundred Indians.[14]

In response to such protests, the Spanish court created rules
for the conquistadors. The court authorized a lawyer and professor,

Juan López de Palacios Rubios, to draft a declaration known as the Requerimiento, which conquistadors were ordered to read aloud at first contact with any group of Indians. The Requerimiento announced that the Spaniards had arrived on the instructions of the pope, and that in the name of their king and queen they were taking over the land. After the reading, the commanding officer was supposed to have the document notarized. In fact, the declaration was often read out in empty buildings or whispered into the wind. Usually, too, the Requerimiento was proclaimed in Latin or Spanish:

> Wherefore, as best we can, we ask and require you that you consider what we have said to you, and that you take the time that shall be necessary to understand and deliberate upon it, and that you acknowledge the Church as the Ruler and Superior of the whole world, and the high priest called Pope, and in his name the King and Queen Doña Juana our lords, in his place, as superiors and lords and kings of these islands... If you do so, you will do well, and that which you are obliged to do to their Highnesses, and we in their name shall receive you in all love and charity, and shall leave you, your wives, and your children, and your lands, free without servitude...[15]
>
> But, if you do not do this, and maliciously make delay in it, I certify to you that, with the help of God, we shall powerfully enter into your country, and shall make war against you in all ways and manners that we can, and shall subject you to the yoke and obedience of the Church and of their Highnesses; we shall take you and your wives and your children, and shall make slaves of them, and as such shall sell and dispose of them as their Highnesses may command; and we shall take away your goods, and shall do you all the mischief and damage that we can, as to vassals who do not obey, and refuse to receive their lord, and resist and contradict him; and we protest that the deaths and losses which shall accrue from this are your fault, and not

that of their Highnesses, or ours, nor of these cavaliers who come with us.[16]

In 1519 Hernán Cortés, the conqueror of Mexico, wrote to King Charles v of Spain describing the typical effect of the reading of the Requerimiento:

> Seeing therefore that nothing was to be gained by the Requerimiento, we began to defend ourselves as best we could, and so drew us fighting into the midst of more than 100,000 warriors who surrounded us on all sides. We fought all day long until an hour before sunset, when they withdrew; with half a dozen guns and five or six harquebuses and forty crossbowmen and with the thirteen horsemen who remained. I had done them much harm without receiving any except from exhaustion and hunger. And it truly seemed that God was fighting for us, because from such a multitude, such fierce and able warriors and with so many kinds of weapons to harm us, we escaped so lightly.[17]

Cortés was coldly calculating in his use of terror:

> The next day some fifty Indians [Tlaxcalans] who, it seemed, were people of importance among them, came to the camp saying they were bringing food, and began to inspect the entrances and exits and some huts where we were living... I had one of them seized and questioned him... He confessed they had been sent to spy out our camp and to see where it could be entered, and how they might burn the straw huts. Then I took five or six and they all confirmed what I had heard, so I took all fifty and cut off their hands and sent them to tell their chief that by day or by night, or whenever they chose to come, they would see who we were.[18]

At the city of Cholula, home of great temple pyramids, Cortés invited the city's leaders and their entourages to parlay, and then he and his mercenary army of four hundred men slaughtered them all.

In *The Devastation of the Indies,* Las Casas recorded his outrage:

> Among other massacres there was one in a big city of more than thirty thousand inhabitants, which is called Cholula. The people came out... and received them with great respect and reverence, and took them to a lodge in the center of the town, where they would reside in the houses of the most important nobles.
>
> Soon after this the Spanish agreed to carry out a massacre, or as they called it a punitive attack, in order to sow terror and apprehension, and to make a display of their power in every corner of the land. With this aim, therefore, they sent a summons to all the caciques and nobles of the city and in the localities subject to it, and also the head chieftain, and as they arrived to speak with the Spanish captain they were taken prisoner... When they were all placed together they were bound and tied. At the closed doorways armed guards took turns to see that none escaped. Then, at a command, all the Spaniards drew their swords or pikes and while the chiefs looked on, helpless, all those tame sheep were butchered, cut to pieces.[19]

Cortés set his sights next on Tenochtitlán, which later became Mexico City. Historian Hugh Thomas says Mexico's great city was probably larger than any in western Europe at that time.[20] Writer James Wilson describes what the conquistadors saw:

> a vast expanse of canals, plazas, markets, temples and brightly painted houses, shops and schools. An army of a thousand men kept the streets clean; waste was removed by barge to be processed as fertilizer, and the elite, like Moorish nobles, bathed every day.[21]

Encountering the smelly Spaniards, Aztecs held flowers to their noses.

In his written accounts, Cortés glorified his triumphant arrival in Mexico's capital, but Aztec legends say that he entered the city at the rear of his conquistador army and their five thousand Tlaxcala allies. After being welcomed grandly, Cortés kidnapped his host, the Aztec leader Montezuma (Moctezuma). His troops then set about looting the Aztec temples.

After electing a new leader, the Aztecs chased the Spaniards out of Tenochtitlán, but the war was not over. Cortés came back a year later to destroy the city he had once admired, but the smallpox the Spaniards brought with them from Cuba had got there first. In his book *Stolen Continents*, Ronald Wright thinks that perhaps 80 per cent of its citizens died defending the Mexican capital.[22] The Aztecs might have beaten back the Spaniards, but they had no resistance to the disease. According to the Aztec calendar, the tragic day, August 13, 1521, was One Serpent in the year Three House, at the end of a fifty-two-year cycle; each of these cycles was supposed to end with a great crisis. Because he refused to reveal the location of hidden stores of gold, the conquistadors beheaded Cuauhtémoc, the last Aztec ruler. Aztec autonomy and governance died with him. An Aztec poet mourned the loss of their nationhood:

> Now they abandon the city of Mexico
> The smoke rises; the fog is spreading…
> Weep, my friends
> Know that with these disasters   ·
> We have lost our Mexican nation[23]

Cortés's war crimes won the approval of both the Spanish Crown and the country's church hierarchy. But many of the churchmen who had come to the New World vigorously opposed his methods. Starting with Columbus's second voyage, every boatload of settlers included a number of Christian clerics. These preachers spread out across Latin America. Some claimed to have converted Indians in the thousands; others learned Indian languages and translated the Bible. It was Dominican friars who led the first protests against Indian slavery and the wholesale slaughter of the Indian people. Bartolomé de Las Casas was most prominent among them.

Las Casas argued that the Indians had rightful sovereignty over their lands by both natural law and the law of nations. Eventually, he came to see the conquest as illegitimate. He made the hazardous voyage back to Spain fourteen times to petition for the Indians. In 1542, at Las Casas's urging, the Spanish king proclaimed the New Laws of the Indies, making Indian slavery illegal. When settlers and their clerical allies in Mexico and Peru rose in revolt, however, the king backed down.

In 1550 King Charles V summoned a council of fourteen jurists and theologians to Valladolid to inquire into the legitimacy of the Spanish conquest and the treatment of the people Columbus had named "Indians." Pending the council's findings, Charles V ordered a stop to all conquests in the Americas. For Las Casas, now seventy-six years old and retired, the council's determinations represented his last chance to change the king's mind. For the Americas, this was the first royal commission on Aboriginal peoples.

Dr. Juan Ginés de Sepúlveda, a lay jurist and a leading intellectual of the Spanish court, chose to defend the conquest. Standing before the council on opening day, Sepúlveda argued that, according to Aristotle's doctrine of "natural slavery," the Indians were an inferior race whom Spain had every right to Christianize—by force, if necessary. He spoke for three hours.

> The man rules over the woman, the adult over the child, the father over his children. That is to say, the most powerful and most perfect rule over the weakest and most imperfect. This same relationship exists among men, there being some who by nature are masters and others who by nature are slaves… If you know the customs and nature of the two peoples, that with perfect right

the Spaniards rule over these barbarians of the New World and the adjacent islands, who in wisdom, intelligence, virtue, and humanitas are as inferior to the Spaniards as infants to adults and women to men. There is as much difference between them as... between apes and men... In his conquest of the Mexico Indians, Hernán Cortés definitively proved the superiority of the Spaniard. Can there be a greater or stronger testimony how some men surpass others in talent, industry, strength of mind, and valor? Or that such peoples are slaves by nature?[24]

Natural law required that Indians submit to Spanish rule, Sepúlveda insisted. "And if they refuse our rule, they may be compelled by force of arms to accept it. Such a war will be just according to natural law."

Las Casas's rebuttal took five days. His argument must have seemed ragged and repetitive, but it was also passionate and exhaustive. He pleaded that the only legal foundation for the Spanish presence in the Americas was Alexander VI's Bull of 1493. However, since the pope enjoyed no temporal powers, he had no ability to confer those powers on anyone else, even the king of Spain. In the age of the Spanish Inquisition, this was a courageous argument for a priest to make about popes and kings. At heart, Las Casas's philosophy was a conviction about universal human equality. He preached that "all humanity is one" and vigorously defended the Indians' right to self-government.

Las Casas argued that large numbers of Indians lived settled lives; they had great cities, kings, judges, and laws. People engaged in commerce, buying, selling, lending, and committing themselves to contracts. Indians were self-governing peoples before the Spanish invasion, Las Casas said, and no law justified their subjugation or the abolition of their governments.

Sepúlveda either did not know, or did not understand, biblical teachings, Las Casas said, and his misunderstandings would lead to dangerous errors. Las Casas also mocked the absurdity of the Requerimiento. "[W]hat language will the messengers speak so as to be understood by the Indians? Latin, Greek, Spanish, Arabic? The Indians know none of these languages. Perhaps we imagine that the soldiers are so holy that Christ will grant them the gift of tongues so that they will be understood by the Indians?"[25]

The hearing at Valladolid in 1550 was a remarkable event, not least because in a vital debate about their future, the Indians themselves had no voice, only a proxy in Las Casas. Because the Spanish systematically destroyed Indian archives, art, and writings, archaeologists are still struggling to uncover authentically Aboriginal stories of the conquest.

Having heard from Sepúlveda and Las Casas, the council at Valladolid retired to render a decision, but it never came. It was a hung jury. Las Casas may have won a moral victory, but the conquistadors were invincible. In time, the conquest was fully "privatized," and from it emerged the distinct roles of the military and the church in the social and political structures of Central and South America. In Guatemala and other Latin American countries, the conquistador power structure persists today. Powerful landowners, the church establishment, and military authoritarians continue to rule an impoverished indigenous underclass. In 1519 Cortés landed on the beaches of Mexico and founded America's first European-style municipality, Villa Rica de la Veracruz, then declared war on the Aztec confederacy. Thus began the fight against and for Aboriginal self-government.

Rarely did the Spanish negotiate treaties. To their mind, the 1493 Papal Bull obviated the necessity for them. Yet the debate joined in the Spanish court in the sixteenth century echoes down across five centuries to British Columbia today. Should the Aboriginal self-government issue be resolved here in the twenty-first century, models designed for First Nations on the west coast of Canada could inspire peacemakers and indigenous peoples from Chiapas to the southern tip of Chile. The problem of colonial attitudes—in other words, the Aboriginal self-government issue—has always stood at the top of treaty-table agendas, right beside the question of land.

∇

CHAPTER 2

LAND CLAIMS

A FTER THE CONQUEST of Mexico, the European powers—Spain, France, Holland, and England—began to fight for control of the rest of North America. The Spanish moved into what we now call Florida, Georgia, Arizona, New Mexico, Texas, and California. At Gaspé in 1534, Indians objected when Jacques Cartier erected a proprietary cross on their land, but by 1605 France had founded Port Royal in Nova Scotia. The Dutch settled on Manhattan Island and around the Hudson River in 1612. When the English landed on the eastern seaboard in the seventeenth century, they called their settlement New England.

In his influential 1689 essay "Of Property," English philosopher John Locke explained how, by his own labour, a man could earn property from the lands and resources God had given to humanity. According to Locke's theory, a person's labour belonged to no one but himself:

The Fruit, or Venison, which nourishes the wild Indian, who knows no Inclosure, and is still a Tenant in common, must be his and so his, i.e. a part of him, that another can no longer have any right to it, before it can do him any good for the support of

27

his Life ... Thus this Law of reason makes the Deer, that Indian's who hath killed it; 'tis allowed to be his goods who hath bestowed his labour upon it, though before, it was the common right of every one.[1]

Locke's appropriation of the Indian hunter as a metaphor for European-style property rights is rich with irony. Locke had a financial interest in a Carolina colony that traded in Indian slaves and deerskins, but it is unknown if he ever met an Indian. He seemed unaware that tribal economies were based on mutual reciprocity, not individual accumulation. In most tribes, meat harvested by the Indian would be shared not only with the hunter's family but also with all needy members of his community. Today's conservationists would find the idea that the deer had been "improved" by its killing doubly ironic, but Locke's notion of improvement became the cornerstone of English ideas about land and provided European justification for taking "unimproved" land from the Indians of North America.

The thinking went something like this: Improvement is the engine of civilization and progress. Indians waste land, and settlers improve it; therefore, settlers should take Indian lands, by force if necessary. A later, improved version of this reasoning said: Settler governments should take Indian land by treaty, the civilized way of exercising settler sovereignty.

In *The Great Land Rush and the Making of the Modern World, 1650–1900*,[2] John C. Weaver expertly describes how European ideas, attitudes, and acquisitiveness permeated the New World. The English colonists who emigrated to Canada, the United States, Australia, New Zealand, and South Africa had grown up with firm ideas about the importance of progress and the power that comes from land. All classes in England hungered for land—land that was not available in the home country.

The desire to improve themselves drove thousands of ambitious souls to the colonies. Colonial authorities in North America allowed colonists considerable freedom of movement, a policy that created constant tension on the frontiers. American ideas about democracy popularized the ideal of land ownership even for people with little income and few prospects. Although there were some scandalous grants to railways and other corporations, legislators usually favoured individuals rather than companies. The American ideal of the small farm spread as far as to Australia and New Zealand.

Weaver emphasizes the importance of relative political stability and secure property rights to the settlement of British colonies and American frontiers: "Still, apart from the momentous seizure of land from first peoples—a major exception—British and American governments did not divest people of property without some due process; even the dispossession of most first peoples engaged legal processes, though ones manipulated by colonizers."[3] Legal surveys and secure titles were necessary for farmers and creditors alike. This attention to the law in colonial times has, on occasion, facilitated legal action by Aboriginal peoples in the modern day.

Despite occasional efforts by European governments to prevent it, no colonized area escaped the land grab. From the sixteenth century on, colonizers took land aggressively and pushed aside indigenous populations that resisted the takeover. However, for strategic reasons, Europe's rulers also wished to maintain certain relationships with first peoples. They knew that from time to time they might need Indian nations as allies, trading partners, or sources of cheap labour. Spain might be reluctant to regard heathen Indians as human beings, but it appreciated their value as slaves and as tithe payers to both church and state. The French purchased land from the Indians or, like the English, claimed underutilized land as their own. Everywhere, Indian rights to land were underestimated, undermined, and misunderstood.

In English colonies, the doctrine of improvement became the principal technique for the dispossession of Indians. Massachusetts's first governor, John Winthrop, preached that so long as the colony left the Indians land enough for their subsistence, settlers were within their rights to expropriate everything else. Nevertheless, English common law provided a measure of protection to first peoples. Colonial governments knew that, until they had paid the Indian occupants for land, they could not convey clear title to settlers. In North America, therefore, land takings normally involved treaties and, hence, some recognition of Aboriginal title.

In Australia, arguments about *terra nullius* or no man's land, wilderness, and wandering tribes of nomadic Aborigines were used to claim land for settlers. Assertions of terra nullius, like the papal "donation" to Spain, made negotiations with Aboriginals unnecessary; the Australian High Court did not nullify terra nullius until 1992. In Canadian government policy, Aboriginal peoples have long seen elements of this idea of "empty" or no man's land.

Settler views about land ownership were highly convenient and deeply prejudicial. If tribal groups resisted the sale of lands, colonial administrations invariably played the sovereignty card. Crown agents might acknowledge Aboriginal possession, even ownership, but the sovereign could, if necessary, overrule those rights. A reluctant seller of tribal lands could one day find the colonizer had changed the rules. Colonial governments proclaimed their sovereignty by right of discovery, right of conquest, or surrender through treaty. As every conquistador since Hernán Cortés had demonstrated, if you had the guns and the guts, sovereignty worked.

Once the colonial powers assumed the unilateral right to adjudicate any land dispute between settlers and Aboriginals, first peoples never had a chance. The Crown might ban private sales of Aboriginal lands to settlers and justify the ban as a protection of tribal interests. Clearly, however, the ban meant a diminution of Aboriginal sovereignty. Such a ban also increased the pressure on first peoples to sell to the single legitimate purchaser. "This so-called pre-emptive right bared the very sharp edge of sovereignty,"[4] John C. Weaver notes.

The ban on private sales of Indian lands in the American colonies did not stop under-the-table deals. Cunning speculators endorsed arguments for tribal sovereignty to justify their own land deal-ings. In the eighteenth and nineteenth centuries, frontier lawyers prepared speculators' briefs defending the natural right of tribal leaders to freely trade in their lands. Although the Supreme Court of the United States ultimately affirmed the nation's right to ban such sales, that did not stop prominent lawyers like Daniel Webster from making "natural rights" arguments to justify private purchase of Indian lands. Intervening in the celebrated 1823 case of *Johnson v. McIntosh*, Webster claimed that, as proprietors, the members of the Cherokee Nation enjoyed every right to sell their land.

Property rights and sovereignty are different, of course. Sovereignty is about power; property is about wealth. Sovereignty relates to public authority, property to private interests. But in the English colonies, public law and private law worked hand in hand to disempower and dispossess Indian nations. If the colonial government could prevent Indians doing what they wished on their land, they might thereby accelerate the sale of that "property."

On the one hand, the colonizer recognized the Indian interest in frontier lands; on the other, he asserted the colony's exclusive sovereign right to purchase these same lands. Now you see it, now you don't. What the Lord giveth, the Lord taketh away. The colonizer reserved to his lawyers, his courts, and his legislatures all decisions about what was just, fair, and legal in dealings to do with Indian lands. The Europeans wrote the rules according to their conventions and needs.

Indians were often cheated, and not only by white settlers. In 1754 the Iroquois Confederacy sold, to a Connecticut company, land that ac-tually belonged to the Delaware Nation. Similar scams happened else-where. In these cases, the speculators would try to flip the land quickly, because the latest purchasers would be sure, in their own interest, to support the initial speculator's title. On occasion, Aboriginals tried to cheat settlers. The settlers had one advantage, though. The governments and the courts were almost always on their side.

Although operating always from their cultural bias towards improvement, some colonial officers did try to deal honourably with Indians. In negotiations with a particular nation, an officer might try to establish the extent of the nation's territory and to map, if possible, the nation's uses of the land. London's representatives made keen assessments both of the military significance of the area the tribe controlled and of the amount of potentially agricultural land that was being "wasted."[5] Washington's agents were even sharper in assessing the costs and benefits of adding a territory to the national land base. From the 1830s to the 1850s, as Britain grew more cautious, the Americans became fierce, forcibly removing Indians from their hereditary lands and aggressively importing settlers.

There was one other way in which official prejudices came into play against the Indians. American land administrators commonly graded squatters according to how much they planned to improve lands by European standards. Such Lockean assessments had the useful effect of further devaluing the indigenous interest. If the Indians were to survive, they would have to accept less land and become farmers. In this way, the European land grab became a key element of government policies of assimilation.

By the late eighteenth century, a new theory of historical development served this type of appraisal. In his 1766 "Private Law" lectures, the Scottish philosopher Adam Smith proposed a classification of human societies by their stages of development and their degree of sovereignty over their homelands.[6] Smith ranked societies from hunters through pastoralists and farmers up to businessmen. He specifically exempted Indians from the agriculturalist class: "There is only one exception to this order, to wit, some North American nations cultivate a little piece of ground, tho' they have no notion of keeping flocks."[7]

Smith had no idea that Aboriginal hunters might also be farmers or that first peoples might have sophisticated systems of land management. Today, Aboriginal critics would call Smith's perspective "Eurocentric":

> Private property in land never begins till a division be made from common agreement, which is generally when cities begin to be built, as every one would choose that his house, which is a permanent object, should be entirely his own. Moveable property may be occupied in the very first beginnings of society, but lands cannot be occupied without an actual division. An Arab or a Tatar will drive his flocks over an immense country without supposing a single grain of sand in it his own.[8]

It probably never occurred to Smith that there might be complexities beyond his ken in Indian laws or that, for example, neighbouring tribes might enjoy overlapping and mutually agreed-upon land uses. Besides, as David Christian points out in his history *Maps of Time*, Mesoamerican agriculturalists had no large animals, horses, or cattle to domesticate, a major difference from the story of European farmers.[9]

Naturally, European settlers chose the best land for themselves. This provided an ironic counterpoint to Locke's notion that the Indian might make the land and resources his own property by mixing them with his own labour. Aboriginal peoples could never win the debate about improvement. If they were hunters, then settler farmers could claim they would make Indian lands more productive. If the Indians were subsistence farmers, producing native crops like corn for their own communities' consumption, then the prospective European plantation owner could prove that his slaves would produce exportable commodities like cotton.

Each tribal culture may have had a distinctive view of land ownership, but most had one thing in common: their thinking was unlike that of European colonists. In their essay "Canadian History: An Aboriginal Perspective," Georges Erasmus and Joe Sanders describe the way First Nations valued land:

> Land was revered as a mother from which life came, and was to be preserved for future generations as it had been from time immemorial. Land was used for common benefit, with no individual having a right to any more of it than another. A nation's traditional hunting grounds were recognized by its neighbours as "belonging" to that nation, but this was different from the idea of private ownership.[10]

For First Nations, social relations governed land uses. Tribal members did not picture, as Europeans did, a simple legal connection between one person and one single piece of land. Rather, they saw land use as a system of reciprocal obligations. First peoples saw themselves as guardians of lands, not owners of a commodity. Yukon Aboriginals sometimes said they were "part of the land."[11] As Erasmus and Sanders point out, First Nations also understood there to be a spiritual relationship between a people and a place.

This was a concept foreign to many Europeans. In *The Law of the Land*, Henry Reynolds quotes from a missionary's 1821 letter explaining the Australian Aborigines to people in Britain: "[T]hey are so senselessly bigoted to this particular spot, that when you would persuade them to settle in any place, they will not understand you, no more if you discoursed to them in Latin or Greek.[12]

The doctrine of improvement has long ago completed its dirty work in the Americas. It legitimized the great land rush, settled the continent, and displaced its original inhabitants. The taking of Indian lands made the Americas rich and the Indians poor. Some writers have argued that, although murderous and larcenous, the continent-wide conversion of Indian hunting grounds and cornfields into settler farms and plantations was inevitable and necessary to the development of America's unprecedented prosperity and power. According to economist John Richards,

> hunting societies inevitably would yield in time to the superior economic productivity of settled agricultural and industrial society. Aboriginals had no choice but to abandon their economic and cultural traditions, and adopt those of European settlers. Admittedly, this would entail cultural loss, psychological distress, and disruption of extended family links.[13]

But many contemporary critics have questioned this view. In his 2002 essay "1491," published in *Atlantic* magazine, Charles Mann asserts that most Indians at the time of contact were farmers. In an interview published alongside his essay, Katie Bacon explained:

> For years the standard view of North America before Columbus's arrival was as a vast, grassy expanse teeming with game and all but empty of people. Those who did live here were nomads who left few marks on the land. South America, too, or at least the Amazon rain forest, was thought of as almost an untouched Eden, now suffering from modern depredations.[14]

More and more anthropologists, Mann said, have come to see this old image as mistaken. Such scholars estimate 100 million people lived in fifteenth-century America, with cities and towns surrounded by cultivated land. The Europeans arrived not to find wilderness or terra nullius, but a landscape already transformed by Aboriginal agriculturalists. Native peoples used fire to create the midwestern prairie, perfect for herds of buffalo. They also cultivated at least part of the rain forest, living on crops of fruits and nuts.[15] American Plains tribes had cultivated and worshipped corn for five centuries before Europeans arrived. The people of Canada's northernmost Indian community, the Vuntut Gwitchin at Old Crow, Yukon, cultivated medicinal herbs.

Before the iconic Sioux discovered horses and the buffalo hunt, many of them were sedentary farmers.[16] Before colonization, B.C. First Nations managed pine forests with controlled burns.

Others have questioned the long-held stereotypes of "nomadic" hunters and "settled" farmers. In his book *The Other Side of Eden*, Hugh Brody argues, "It is agricultural societies that tend to move; hunting peoples are far more firmly settled. This fact is evident when we look at the two ways of being in the world over a long time span—when we screen the movie of human history, as it were, rather than relying on a photograph." [17]

When farmers and hunters find themselves in conflict, the farmers usually win. Not only are they more numerous; they enjoy more political power. "The farmers have it in their power to overwhelm hunter-gatherers, and they continue to do so in the few regions of the world where this domination is not already complete," Brody writes.

Remarkably, some critics now wonder about the sustainability of European-style agriculture on the North American continent. In his book *The Earth Shall Weep: A History of Native America*, James Wilson questions whether the dispossession of Indians to make room for dry-land farming ever made economic sense.[18] He cites research showing that vast areas of the Great Plains with small settler populations survived only because of substantial federal subsidies. He goes on to suggest that the settler experiment of the last 150 years should simply be abandoned, and that these areas should be returned to the herds of bison that occupied them before colonization.

Another possibility is that First Nations reacquire agricultural land, establish urban reserves, and build prosperous futures for their children. However, even that kind of outcome would not disguise the bitter irony that the original owners must file "land claims" with settler governments that made their countries rich with land either appropriated or bought for next to nothing.

PONTIAC'S PROCLAMATION

MANY INDIAN NATIONS fought for their land, some more successfully than others. But disease devastated and demoralized the Indian population. Frenchman Jacques Cartier sailed into the St. Lawrence River in 1535. In *One Vast Winter Count*, Colin Calloway writes: "Cartier saw crops and orchards covering the banks of the St. Lawrence. Seventy years later, when Samuel de Champlain traveled the same route, villages were abandoned, and the river banks were overgrown."[1] Epidemics had depopulated the area.

In Massachusetts the Plymouth colonists moved into recently vacated Indian cabins in 1620 and took over Indian farmland.[2] At "Thanksgiving" the colonists dined on turkey, corn, pumpkin, and potatoes—all American Indian foods. The Indians may have provided the early settlers with corn and fish, but it was never enough. The settlers kept coming, and soon they were waging bloody war against the Indians. Disease and war took less than two hundred years to destroy most of the eastern tribes.

Spaniards coveted gold. The English craved land, yet England's "conquistadors" copied their Iberian predecessors.[3] The colonial leader

Captain John Smith, for example, modelled himself consciously on Cortés in his use of terror to exploit and control Virginia's Indians.[4] By the same token, English Protestants were delighted to justify their colonization in the Americas by using the criticisms of a Spanish Catholic; Oliver Cromwell and his co-religionists loved to quote Bartolomé de Las Casas in their propaganda. How perfect it was to have Las Casas providing proof of the New World's need for the improvement of English law, rights, and freedoms. In Mexico, Spain made no treaties with the Aztec or the Maya. It did sign treaties with the Chickasaw and the Choctaw in 1784, however, in an effort to find allies in an ongoing struggle with the United States. Until their conquest was complete, all of the colonial powers needed Indian allies. Indian nations were too weak to fight off the invaders but too strong to be ignored; hence, they were forced to choose sides in fights between European competitors. In the first decade of the seventeenth century, the French armed the Huron and the Algonquin against the Mohawk. This made the Mohawk allies in the Iroquois Confederacy, deadly enemies of the French. The Iroquois alliance with the English may have given the eventual victor a crucial advantage in the struggle for North America.

The French and Indian wars were part of a worldwide struggle that raged from 1689 until 1763. At first, the North American theatre was just a sideshow, but settlers in the colonies came to see the battle in terms of eastern ports and western forts, coloured by constant threats of Indian attack. Those living in what became the United States began to think of themselves as Americans rather than as English colonists. For Canadians, the wars would decide whether colonies were to be English or French. The aftermath of these wars also saw the dawning of a new relationship between colonizing powers and Indian nations.

After English and Iroquois forces defeated the French army at the Plains of Abraham in 1759, France ceded all land east of the Mississippi to the English. The Europeans did not bother to consult the Indian nations, like the Cherokee, who would be affected by this partition. Tribes that had tried to maintain good relations with both the English and the French were apprehensive. From the Indians allied with the French, such as the Ottawa, there was anger at English encroachments on their lands.

When the English and the French began their contest for control of North America in 1754, the Ottawa fought on the French side. In battle, the Ottawa were fierce and took no prisoners—not even settler women or children—so the English came to hate and fear them. This enmity eventually focused on the most remarkable of the Ottawa warriors, Pontiac.

Pontiac had grown up in an Ottawa village near Fort Detroit, where the tribes gathered to trade each spring. As a young man, he proved himself in the Ottawa's summer battles with the Shawnee and Iroquois tribes, which had been shifting westward as English settlers pushed them off their ancestral lands. He quickly earned a reputation as a brave, shrewd, and eloquent war chief.

With victory at the Plains of Abraham, England's troops began to occupy French forts around the Great Lakes and to flood their area with new settlers. All of this Pontiac watched from the edge of the forests on the frontier. England sent envoys to negotiate with the Ottawa and the neighbouring tribes. They promised the Indians that all would be well, but the settlers kept coming, and the indigenous communities grew more and more restive.

Financially challenged after the war with France, England cut back on the gifts the Indians had come to expect as incidence of diplomacy. In 1761 Sir Jeffrey Amherst, the English commander in North America, worsened relations by limiting the ammunition Indians could buy from western traders. Sir William Johnson, a wealthy fur trader and mediator known to the Mohawk as Warraghiyagey,[5] warned that this policy alienated Indians and put English settlers at risk.[6] Amherst's arrogance demonstrated to Indian leaders like Pontiac that the English had come to take their land.

According to nineteenth-century historian Francis Parkman, the Indian, as a child of the wilderness, could neither adapt nor accept defeat:

> Unhappily for the strength and harmony of the Indian race, each tribe is prone to regard itself, not as a member of a great whole, but as a sovereign and independent nation, often arrogating to itself an importance superior to all the rest of mankind; and... whose petty horde might muster a few scores of half-starved fighting men.[7]

Many of Parkman's persuasion might have shared this assessment, but Pontiac could not be so easily dismissed. He began to organize an effective Indian army of resistance. He travelled to all the tribes in the western Great Lakes and persuaded them to unite against the English invaders. Together, he argued, they could defeat their common enemy. He sent a red wampum war belt, symbolizing intertribal unity, all the way down the Ohio Valley to the Mississippi River.

In April of 1763, Pontiac called a war council on the banks of the Ecorse River near Detroit. At the council fire, he conveyed a message to a fellow chief from the Great Spirit:

> I am the Maker of heaven and earth, the trees, lakes, rivers and all things else. I am the Maker of mankind; and because I love you, you must do my will. The land on which you live I have made for you, and not for others. Why do you suffer the white men to dwell among you? My children, you have forgotten the customs and traditions of your forefathers. Why do you not clothe yourselves in skins, as they did, and use the bows and arrows, and the stone-pointed lances, which they used? You have bought guns, knives, kettles and blankets from the white men, until you can no longer do without them; and, what is worse, you have drunk

the poison firewater, which turns you into fools. Fling all these
things away; live as your wise forefathers lived before you. And as
for these English—these dogs dressed in red, who have come to
rob you of your hunting grounds and drive away the game—you
must lift the hatchet against them. Wipe them from the face of
the earth, and then you will win my favor back again and once
more be happy and prosperous.[8]

On May 7, 1763, Pontiac attacked. Supported by the Huron and
the Potwawtomi, the Ottawa stormed Fort Detroit. Their allies took
forts Sandusky, Saint Joseph, Miami, Ouiatenon, and Presque Isle.
The Ottawa and the Ojibwe staged a lacrosse game outside Fort
Michilimackinac, then sneaked into the fort after a "lost" ball. From
the start, Pontiac's strategy was an extraordinary success.

Other tribes joined in the uprising until only forts Detroit, Pitt,
and Niagara remained in British hands. There were no reserves left
to assist the troops in Fort Edward Augustus at Green Bay, so they,
too, surrendered. Then the Delaware took up arms against settlers
around Fort Pitt. The Seneca torched Fort Venango and threw the
British out of Fort LeBoeuf. After only six weeks, Pontiac's Indian
armies had taken nine British forts.

Receiving a report of Pontiac's military genius, General Amherst
responded by suggesting a historical first, the use of germ warfare:
"Could it not be contrived to send Small Pox among those disaffected
tribes of Indians? We must on this occasion use every stratagem in our
power to reduce them."[9] Amherst's field commander, Colonel Henry
Bouquet, replied: "I will try to inoculate… some blankets that may
fall in their hands, and take care not to get the disease myself. As it
is a pity to expose good men against them, I wish we could make use
of the Spanish method, to hunt them with English dogs."[10]

Amherst and Bouquet need not have dirtied their hands, because
Pontiac's attack was stalled at Detroit. Thanks to a spy in the Indian

camp, the English detachment there had been warned, and it held off Pontiac's warriors. The Ottawa chief fell back, regrouped, and then laid siege to the fort.

The British navy sailed up the river and bombarded Pontiac's camp with cannon fire. Pontiac floated fire rafts towards the warships. Then fresh troops arrived to relieve the British fort. On July 31 the English troops tried to surprise Pontiac's camp. They lost many men in the assault. Pontiac won that battle, against a numerically superior force, but Fort Detroit held.

Pontiac had hoped that the Ottawa's old allies, the French, would send help, but they did not. In October the French sent Pontiac a message advising him that Britain and France had ended hostilities. France had surrendered North America. So Pontiac abandoned his campaign. The English army tried to capture him, but he escaped to Illinois.

The French trading centre of Cahokia, near the Mississippi River in southern Illinois, had once been the greatest Indian metropolis north of Mexico. The city was home to the Illinois Nation. In its glory days, five hundred years before Europeans arrived in America, Cahokia was six square miles in area and filled with hundreds of dwellings lined up around a great plaza. Nineteenth-century visitors to the site would be awed by a hundred-foot-high central mound, which Charles Mann described as "vaster than the Great Pyramid at Giza,"[11] and by the desolation. By then, the place was almost empty of people. Today, Cahokia Mounds is a United Nations world heritage site. In retreat, it was to this haunted place that Pontiac came.[12]

Admitting final defeat in 1766, Pontiac sent a peace pipe to Sir William Johnson and received a pardon from the British Crown. His vision of a united Indian resistance to the European invasion crumbled like autumn leaves. Some of his followers hated him for giving up, and in 1769 the Peoria sent an assassin to knife him in the back. Pontiac died, defeated and alone, at Cahokia. Yet his influence endures in ways he could not have imagined.

The British had been shocked by what they called "Pontiac's Conspiracy." Settlers from Pennsylvania to Maryland to Virginia had been terrified; two thousand of them had died in the conflict. At Westminster, members of Parliament could hardly comprehend the rage exemplified by Pontiac's uprising. Following its hard-won military victory, the British Crown realized belatedly that it had to repair the relationship with the Indians.

Thanks to Sir William Johnson's diplomacy, the Iroquois Confederacy had stayed out of Pontiac's war. However, Johnson had long warned England that the government's neglect of the injustices wrought by its abusive soldiers, dissolute traders, and demanding settlers was turning the Indians into determined foes. The solution, Johnson and his deputy George Croghan proposed, was the setting aside of large tracts of western land as Indian hunting grounds.

With Pontiac in mind, the British took Johnson's advice and issued the Royal Proclamation of 1763, which contained new instructions to the military commanders and colonial governors in North America:

> George III, Royal Proclamation, Given at our Court at St. James the 7th Day of October 1763… And whereas it is just and reasonable, and the Security of our Colonies, that the several Nations or Tribes of Indians with whom We are connected, and who live under our Protection, should not be molested or disturbed in the Possession of… their Hunting Grounds…
>
> In order, therefore, to prevent such Irregularities for the future, and to the End that the Indians may be convinced of Our Justice, and determined Resolution to remove all reasonable Cause of Discontent, We do, with the Advice of Our Privy Council, strictly enjoin and require, that no private Person do presume to make any Purchase from the said Indians of any Lands reserved to the said Indians, within those Parts of Our Colonies where We have thought proper to allow Settlement; but that if, at any Time, any

of the said Indians should be inclined to dispose of the said Lands,
the same shall be Purchased only for Us, in Our Name, at some
publick Meeting or Assembly of the said Indians to be held for that
Purpose by the Governor or Commander in Chief of our Colony
respectively, within which they shall lie; and in case they shall lie
within the Limits of any Proprietary Government, they shall be
purchased only for the Use and in the name of such Proprietaries,
conformable to such Directions and Instructions as We or they
shall think proper to give for that Purpose.[13]

The proclamation's main purpose may have been to organize
the governance of England's new colonies in North America, but its
more enduring impact was on treaty making. In effect, England had
recognized Indian governments and their Aboriginal title to ancestral
lands. To reduce tensions, the Crown would now obtain lands required
for settlement only through treaties negotiated in public with Indian
nations. This was the crucial idea behind the proclamation.

It was not an entirely new idea. John C. Weaver points out in *The
Great Land Rush and the Making of the Modern World, 1650–1900* that
there were plenty of precedents for it. Since 1629 in New Netherlands,
the Dutch West India Company had inspected property sales in
accordance with Dutch and Roman laws that required such transac-
tions be approved by a magistrate. Similar approvals were mandated
in seventeenth-century Massachusetts, Connecticut, Rhode Island,
New Jersey, Virginia, Maryland, Pennsylvania, New York, and North
and South Carolina. From 1761 to 1763, the laws of the Northwest
and Canada also reflected "[e]ffective sovereignty in property rights:
assertions of the government right to exercise an exclusive right to
purchase."[14]

One no doubt unintended consequence of the 1763 edict was the
triggering of a century of frantic treaty making in the United States.
Initially, George Washington, who was contemplating investments in

western land, was annoyed at the proclamation, but he saw it as only a temporary pacifier of the Indians. In a letter to a friend, he wrote:

> I can never look upon that Proclamation in any other light (but this I may say between ourselves) than as a temporary expedient to quiet the Minds of the Indians & [one that] must fall of course in a few years especially when those Indians are consenting to our Occupying the Lands. Any person therefore who neglects the present opportunity of hunting out good Lands & in some Measure & distinguishing them for their own (in order to keep others from settling them) will never regain it.[15]

America's founding fathers often praised the Iroquois Longhouse as the oldest parliament in North America, and Thomas Jefferson had frequently cited the Great Law of Peace of the Iroquois Confederacy as the model for the U.S. constitution. However, in the 1776 Declaration of Independence, Jefferson raged against the Royal Proclamation, the English, and the Indians:

> [T]he English King... has excited domestic insurrections among us, and has endeavoured to bring on the inhabitants of our frontiers, the merciless Indian Savages whose known rule of warfare is an undistinguished destruction of all ages, sexes, and conditions.[16]

America's first peoples saw things differently. The proclamation recognized their title and their governments and articulated clear rules for selling lands through treaties. In the ten years following the proclamation, the English signed a dozen or more treaties with Indian nations. For Indians, despite the limitations it put on their sovereignty, the Royal Proclamation of 1763 was a veritable Magna Carta, defining a relationship with the British—and subsequently the Canadian—Crown that even today colours negotiations between First Nations and the national government. Until the American Revolution, the proclamation also reserved for the Indians lands west of the Appalachian heights.

In 1700 Indians were still a majority in North America, but by the end of the century they had become a minority. Throughout the eighteenth century, Indians from Quebec to California "fought their own wars against empires to defend their lands, resources, and ways of life."[17] Pontiac lost his battle, but he won the First Nations some time. His resistance and the proclamation it produced slowed the European takeover. This proclamation has informed every major judicial intervention on Aboriginal rights from the Cherokee cases to the Nisga'a and *Delgamuukw* rulings in British Columbia more than two centuries later. It crystallized colonial policy. Most importantly, Pontiac's war forced the English, the Americans, and the Canadians to make treaties. For years to come, the principles in the proclamation would provide some protection for the Indian way of life in the West and the North and slow the juggernaut of assimilation.

PART II

ASSIMILATION GAMES

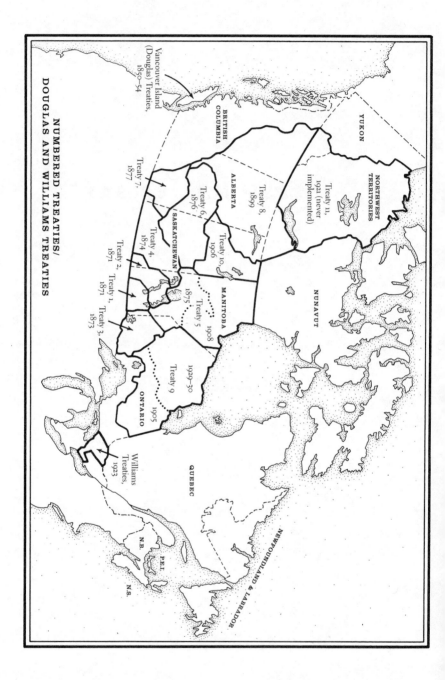

NUMBERED TREATIES/
DOUGLAS AND WILLIAMS TREATIES

Vancouver Island
(Douglas) Treaties,
1850–54

BRITISH
COLUMBIA

YUKON

Treaty 7,
1877

ALBERTA

Treaty 8,
1899

Treaty 11,
1921 (never
implemented)

NORTHWEST
TERRITORIES

Treaty 6,
1876

SASKATCHEWAN

Treaty 10,
1906

Treaty 4,
1874

Treaty 2,
1871

MANITOBA

NUNAVUT

Treaty 1,
1871

Treaty 5
1875

Treaty 3,
1873

Treaty 5
1908

1929–30

Treaty 9

ONTARIO

1905

Williams
Treaties,
1923

QUEBEC

N.B.

P.E.I.

N.S.

NEWFOUNDLAND & LABRADOR

CHAPTER 4

CHEROKEE SELFISHNESS

L AWYER AND ABORIGINAL-RIGHTS advocate Thomas Berger has defined assimilation this way: "Always, assuming our goal was not extermination by deadly force, our object has been to transform the Indians, to make them like ourselves. But if they become like ourselves, if they assimilate, they will no longer be Indians, and there will be no Indian languages, no Indian view of the world, no Indian political communities nor Indian land."[1]

Many stories tell of Aboriginal defeat, dispossession, and assimilation into the American mainstream; Dee Brown's *Bury My Heart at Wounded Knee* and Vine Deloria's *Custer Died for Your Sins*,[2] among other books, recount some of them. None serves as a better lesson in the workings of assimilation than the story of the Cherokee, as it appears in Angie Debo's *A History of the Indians of the United States*.[3]

The Cherokee Nation's lands once covered a 124,000-square-mile area now included in eight states: Alabama, Georgia, Kentucky, North Carolina, South Carolina, Tennessee, Virginia, and West Virginia. In 1539 Hernando de Soto's conquistadors raped and pillaged their way across Florida and into Cherokee territory, but Cherokee chiefs steered the Spaniards away from Cherokee women and community corn warehouses with promises of gold to the north. In 1663 England's

Charles II granted a large estate of Indian lands in the Carolinas to eight royal favourites, who began to trade in deerskins and Indian slaves. English traders from Virginia reached the Cherokee ancestral lands in the Carolinas in 1673 and quickly established a commercial relationship. During the American Revolution, both sides tried to bind the Cherokee as allies, and Cherokee warriors found themselves fighting on the Virginia, Carolina, and Georgia frontiers. At Augusta in 1763 and 1773, the Cherokee signed land-surrender treaties to cover trading debts with Georgia's English merchants.[4]

In 1778, at Fort Pitt, the United States signed its first Indian treaty, an accord that allowed American troops passage through Delaware lands near the Great Lakes and guaranteed the Delaware people a seat in Congress. This guarantee became the first broken promise in the history of United States Indian treaties. In 1785, at Hopewell, South Carolina, the Cherokee reached their first treaty with the American government. They acknowledged the sovereignty of the United States and signed over land already lost to settlers. In return, the United States promised to honour the boundaries of Cherokee lands and to restrain American citizens from "further trespass." The Cherokee were invited to send a delegate to Congress, but that promise also became "inoperative."

The Cherokee adapted to their new situation and adopted the farming methods of neighbouring settlers, but land surveyors soon arrived to violate the treaty of Hopewell. In 1791 President George Washington called the Cherokee to a treaty council at the Holston River near Knoxville, Tennessee. Forty chiefs signed a new treaty that entrenched their land losses since Hopewell but guaranteed no further loss. The treaty also contained a provision—one common in future American treaties—that the government would supply agricultural implements. The Cherokee fenced their farms and planted orchards. Although they never received the promised plows, they prospered. However, faced with the growing settler invasion, early in the 1800s the Cherokee began to migrate westward.

In 1789 President Washington had made assimilation the official policy of the United States. Initially, President Thomas Jefferson (1801–9) saw the Indian way of life as a barrier to progress, and he favoured teaching Indians to survive on less and less land. After acquiring the vast Louisiana Territory in 1803, however, Jefferson perceived an alternative: the removal of the Indians to the lands west of the Mississippi River. Tennessee land speculator, slaveholder, and congressman Andrew Jackson was the greatest promoter of removal.

In an 1817 letter to President James Monroe, Jackson wrote, "I have long viewed treaties with the Indians as an absurdity."[5] Jackson felt that Washington had made treaties with Indians for temporary strategic considerations. Now that the Indians' allies among the European nations had withdrawn, treaties were no longer even a tactical necessity. After the War of 1812, treaty making became largely an exercise in extinguishing Aboriginal title to huge areas of the West.

As a militia major general, Jackson had led armies into Louisiana, Florida, Mississippi, and Alabama to clear Indians off these frontier lands in preparation for settlement and statehood. The general's troops killed thousands of Seminole, Chickasaw, Choctaw, Creek, and Cherokee. As president, Jackson used his first Message to Congress in 1829 to advocate removal. In 1833 he indicated to Congress how much he hated Indians:

> They have neither the intelligence, the industry, the moral habits, nor the desire of improvement. Established in the midst of another and superior race, they must necessarily yield and ere long disappear.[6]

The Cherokee warrior Januluska had saved Jackson's life in 1814, at the Battle of Horseshoe Bend, but that did not spare the Cherokee from Jackson's murderous invasions. As his Tennessee troops marched home through Cherokee lands, he let them terrorize Indian women and children. Jackson bullied the tribe into giving up a million acres in northern Alabama. He even tried to talk them into exchanging all their lands for territory in the West. Still the Cherokee people clung to whatever remained of their inheritance.

If any group of American Indians embraced both economic assimilation and the Christian religion, it was the Georgia-based Cherokee. By the time Jackson was elected president in 1828, the Cherokee had become model citizens. Private ownership of land was still an alien concept to them, but they had established schools and farms, a national constitution, and a supreme court. In 1821, after twelve years' work, Sequoyah, a warrior-genius from Tennessee, invented a Cherokee alphabet, and by 1828 the nation was publishing the Cherokee Nation newspaper. The Cherokee had become wealthy and self-reliant, but that was not good enough. Indeed, it was an insult to the Jacksonian idea of the Indian.

Land-hungry Georgia settlers petitioned the United States government to remove the Cherokee from their homes and farms. By what right did a few thousand Cherokee control millions of acres of prime farmland and timberlands in Georgia, the settlers asked? The state legislature responded by outlawing the Cherokee Nation and banning the Cherokee parliament from meeting within state boundaries. Settler agitation peaked after the discovery of gold. Georgia forbade the Cherokee from mining gold on their own lands, then started surveys of Cherokee properties. More than ever, President Jackson was bent on removing the Cherokee to the far side of the Mississippi. Although he told Congress, "This emigration should be voluntary; for it would be as cruel [and] unjust to compel the aborigines to abandon the graves of their fathers, and seek a home in a distant land,"[7] such sentiments did not stop Jackson from using force when the Cherokee resisted removal.

Jackson believed in the God-given right of Anglo-Saxon Protestants to create a homogeneous society in America. He was also attempting to enact the terms of the fraudulent Treaty of New Echota. Signed in 1835 by one hundred Cherokee acting without tribal approval, the treaty exchanged all tribal lands east of the Mississippi for lands in a new

Indian territory. The majority of Cherokee strongly opposed the treaty and their relocation, and they sought legal redress. Eventually, their fight with the governments of Georgia and the United States reached the Supreme Court and the attention of Chief Justice John Marshall.

In his resonant work *Inventing a Nation: Washington, Adams, Jefferson*, Gore Vidal describes John Marshall, the inventor of judicial review, as a principal "inventor" of the nation.[8] Raised in a Virginia family of fifteen children, Marshall was a cousin of Thomas Jefferson. Marshall's father was a close friend of George Washington. As a captain of the Virginia Militia, John Marshall wintered with General Washington at Valley Forge and later wrote a biography of the man who became America's first president.

During Virginia's debate on ratification of the United States constitution, Marshall led the Federalist side in arguing for a judicial role in defending the constitution. Opponents predicted a "consolidated government" and tyranny. Marshall proposed that judges should void any law that exceeded the powers delegated by the constitution.

Jefferson, for his part, saw the states as protectors of individual rights against the growing power of the federal government. He penned the words in the Declaration of Independence that would later inspire Confederate secession:

> When in the course of human events, it becomes necessary for one people to dissolve the political bonds which have connected them with another, and to assume, among the powers of the earth, the separate and equal station to which the laws of nature and of nature's God entitled them, a decent respect to the opinion of mankind requires that they should declare the causes which impel them to the separation.[9]

Of course, Jefferson overlooked the fact that African-American slaves and Indian nations did not enjoy these rights. As Vidal points out, America has ever after lived with this "great contradiction."[10]

Marshall served one term in the House of Representatives. Then, in 1801, John Adams, a lame-duck president, appointed the young Virginian chief justice of the Supreme Court. On his way out of the White House, Adams packed the judiciary with patronage appointments. Jefferson, the new president, sought to "disappoint" many of these "midnight judges."[11]

The judges of the Supreme Court assembled at their Washington boarding house in 1801 to consider the case of *Marbury v. Madison*. The issue was whether Adams's last-minute appointments should stand. For Marshall, one thing was clear: it was up to the courts to interpret the law. With that one ruling, Marshall made judicial review a cornerstone of American law. Rather than Jefferson's secessionist option, judicial review became the instrument to undo the errors of cabinets and legislatures. *Marbury v. Madison* established the United States Supreme Court's right to arbitrate constitutional questions.

Marshall reigned as chief justice of the Supreme Court until 1835, and his judicial review of questions about Indian sovereignty and Aboriginal title had a huge impact on the future of the United States. In the 1823 Cherokee-lands case, *Johnson v. McIntosh*, Marshall accepted that Euro-Americans had taken Indian land. Consistent with the 1763 Royal Proclamation and a 1783 congressional commitment, Marshall ruled that only the federal government, through treaties, could buy that land. Marshall saw that England had recognized Indians as the original occupants of the Americas, retaining an interest in, or "Indian title" to, their homelands and hunting grounds. The United States had inherited from England both its sovereignty and its obligations. Crafting a careful compromise, Marshall found that both the Indian and the colonizer had legitimate interests in the land.

When, as president, Andrew Jackson signed the *Indian Removal Act* in 1830, the Cherokee Nation hired former U.S. attorney general William Wirt and went to the Supreme Court for an injunction. As the first tribal group to petition the Supreme Court, the Cherokee tried to get standing as a "foreign state." On March 5, 1831, the Supreme

Court delivered its judgment in *Cherokee Nation v. Georgia*. "If courts were permitted to indulge their sympathies, a case better calculated to excite them can scarcely be imagined," Marshall wrote. A once-proud people in "uncontrolled possession of an ample domain" had submitted to the superior arms of the United States and surrendered their lands by treaties:

> Though the Indians are acknowledged to have an unquestion-able, and therefore, unquestioned right to the lands they occupy, until that right shall be extinguished by a voluntary cession to our government; yet it may well be doubted whether those tribes which reside within the acknowledged boundaries of the United States can, with strict accuracy, be denominated foreign nations. They may, more correctly, perhaps be denominated domestic dependent nations... Their relation to the United States resembles that of a ward to his guardian.[12]

Marshall concluded that the Cherokee Nation was neither a state like Georgia nor a foreign power. The implications of designating the Cherokee Nation a "domestic dependent nation" were enormous. If the Cherokee were not sovereign, then the title to their lands might be at risk. The judgment in *Cherokee Nation v. Georgia* deeply disap-pointed the Cherokee, but they did not quit. Later that year, Georgia jailed two missionaries, Samuel Austin Worcester and Elihu Butler, for "Residing in the Cherokee Nation without License." This time the Cherokee won. In his ruling on *Worcester v. Georgia*, the seventy-seven-year-old chief justice wrote that the treaties of Holston and Hopewell both recognized the Cherokee Nation's government:

> The Indian nations had always been considered as distinct, in-dependent political communities, retaining their original rights, as the undisputed possessors of the soil, from time immemorial, with the single exception of that imposed by irresistible power,

which excluded them from intercourse with any other European potentate than the first discoverer of the particular region claimed... The Cherokee nation then is a distinct community, occupying its own territory, with boundaries accurately described, in which the laws of Georgia can have no force.[13]

Jackson was having none of it. "What good man would prefer a country covered with forests, and ranged by a few thousand savages to our extensive republic, studded with cities, towns, and prosperous farms; embellished with all the improvements, which art can devise, or industry execute," he said in defence of the removal legislation.[14] Legend has it that the president responded to the chief justice by saying, "Marshall has rendered his decision; now let him enforce it." Apparently, Jackson had no qualms about defying the Supreme Court. In 1838 the president ordered General Winfield Scott and seven thousand soldiers to round up the Cherokee and herd them into stockades. From these internment camps, the tribe's members were taken westward in detachments. Four thousand Cherokee died of hunger and disease on their "Trail of Tears."[15]

As a warrior-politician in the Napoleonic mode, Jackson cared little for Marshall's legal recognition of Indian rights, and the populist president's policies prevailed. The settlers kept coming; the Indians kept retreating. As the new country manifested its westward destiny between 1815 and 1860, American presidents signed, then violated, almost four hundred treaties.

The United States established reserves for Aboriginal peoples and then expropriated much of the land. Nevertheless, Marshall's thinking eventually influenced judicial opinion throughout the English-speaking world. In *Johnson v. McIntosh*, his court established the Indians' right to land; *Cherokee Nation v. Georgia* defined the trust relationship with the federal government. *Worcester v. Georgia* affirmed the Indian right to self-government.

Although Indian title continued, the United States had a sovereign

right to take it, Marshall decided. *Worcester* inhibited settler theft
of Aboriginal lands, but *Cherokee* promoted assimilation. Indian
sovereignists came to regard Marshall's "Indian title" and "domestic
dependent nation" as somewhat hypocritical "political" statements.
On the one hand, Indians had a right to land and self-government,
but on the other, another government could extinguish those rights
whenever it wanted.

The idea of "manifest destiny" drove the army created by the Civil
War to extend American "freedom" across the continent. By the late
nineteenth century, the Indians had lost most of their lands, even in
the West. In 1871 the United States quit making Indian treaties.

At the end of their Trail of Tears, twelve thousand Cherokee survivors landed in Indian Territory in northeastern Oklahoma. They
reunified their nation, built schools, educated women, published
a newspaper in their own language, and graced their capital city,
Talequah, with fine public buildings, courts, and a bicameral legislature. Then another disaster struck.

In 1885 Senator Henry Dawes of Massachusetts visited the Cherokee
Nation at their new home. Dawes was impressed, but he had an idea:

> There is not a pauper in that nation, and the nation does not owe
> a dollar. It built its own capitol... its schools and its hospital. Yet
> the defect of their system was apparent. They have got as far as
> they can go, because they own their land in common. There is
> no enterprise to make your home any better than your neighbors.
> There is no selfishness, which is at the bottom of civilization. Till
> this people will consent to give up their lands and divide them
> among their citizens so that each can own the land he cultivates,
> they will not make much more progress.[16]

So, in 1887, the United States Congress passed the *General
Allotment Act*, also known as the *Dawes Act*. The government could
now allot tribal lands to individuals. Each head of a family would

receive 160 acres (a quarter section). However, as historian Angie Debo writes, "The Indians expressed so much opposition to this alien 'head of family' concept—in their society married women and children had property rights—that in 1891 the Act was amended to provide equal shares to all—80 acres of agricultural, 160 acres of grazing land."[17] The *Dawes Act* required that the majority of Indian reservation lands be transferred to individual Indians, and U.S. marshals jailed the Cherokee "irreconcilables" who insisted on their treaty rights instead.[18]

Theodore Roosevelt praised the *Dawes Act* as "a mighty pulverizing engine to break up the tribal mass."[19] Through foreclosures and state tax collections, settlers soon grabbed all the best land. In less than a lifetime, Indians had lost half of their remaining lands in the United States. According to Chris Stainbrook, executive director of the Indian Land Tenure Foundation, prior to 1887 the United States had 138 million acres reserved for Indians. By 1934 approximately 48 million acres remained in Indian hands.[20]

Over the course of the nineteenth century, the United States government removed Cherokee, Apache, Catawba, Cheyenne, Chickasaw, Choctaw, Comanche, Creek, Delaware, Natchez, Osage, Pawnee, Seminole, Seneca, Shawnee, and Wichita nations to the Indian Territory. Each nation received legal title to a new homeland. Yet no sooner had they re-established themselves than the United States opened the Indian Territory to settlement. In 1907 the territory was made part of Oklahoma.[21]

A *New York Times* correspondent described the last great land rush into the Indian Territory in 1889. Under the headline "Into Oklahoma at Last—Thousands Wildly Dashing in for Homes—The Scramble of Settlers, Boomers and Speculators—Reports of Disturbance and Quarrels," the *Times* story captured all the insanity of the lust for land in the American West:

> Purcell, Indian Territory, April 22—A great change has come over this town. Yesterday it was a metropolis, to-night it is a hamlet in point of population. The metamorphosis was effected at 12 o'clock

to-day, when several thousand men, women, and children crossed the Canadian River and entered upon a wild struggle for homes in the promised land.[22]

Telescope in hand, the *Times* correspondent watched from high ground overlooking the river. He observed Lieutenant Samuel E. Adair of the Fifth Cavalry acting as starter and referee of the race for land. Determined to prevent anyone from jumping the gun, Adair had ordered dozens of wagons to halt on the Purcell side of the river. One hour ahead of the rush, Adair and his men forded the river and took up posts on the far banks.

> Lieut. Adair could be seen calmly sitting watching, and all eyes were centered on him. Suddenly he is seen to motion to the soldier near him, and the next moment the cheerful strains of the recall are sounded. In an instant the scene changes. There is a mighty shout, and the advance guard of the invading army is racing like mad across the sands toward the narrow expanse of water... Within thirty minutes Purcell had resumed its normal aspect.[23]

The *Times* noted that several Purcell businessmen and a number of deputy United States marshals had illegally joined the land rush.

One year later, the Wounded Knee massacre finalized the genocidal separation of Indian tribes from their American lands. The U.S. government had banned the ghost dance, a religious ceremony, and the military arrived at the Lakota reservations in South Dakota to enforce the ban. Colonel James Forsyth ordered the Seventh Calvary to surround a ghost-dance encampment of 350 traditionalists, two-thirds of them women and children. Forsyth set up four cannons around the perimeter. On December 29, five hundred of his soldiers entered the camp. When a soldier tried to wrestle an elderly Indian's rifle from his hands, the gun went off. Forsyth's artillery responded; in minutes 150 Lakota and twenty-five of the cavalry lay dead in the snow. The Indian Wars were over. The American frontier was settled, the West won.[24]

CHAPTER 5

MONEY MATTERS

IN A NOSTALGIC presentation to the Treasury Board in Ottawa on June 25, 1992, Indian Affairs Deputy Minister Harry Swain described his department's work as living history:

> I think of treaty days on the Prairies, when all the endless bickering over bucks stops for a day, and departmental staff and community members join together for the immensely symbolic paying of treaty... The day starts with prayers and speeches, with the invocation of the sacred relation between the Crown and the First Nations, and proceeds to a table, set up outdoors, with DIAND [Department of Indian Affairs and Northern Development] officers scrubbed, in shirt and tie or tailored dress—jeans and boots, the normal uniform of our field staff of both sexes, simply will not do for an occasion of such joy and solemnity—and a Mountie, in full-dress red serge. There is a strongbox on the table full of brand new five-dollar bills, and there is a box of ammunition, too. The whole community lines up, joking and gossiping in the bright Prairie sun, behind the Chief. One by one their names are formally checked against the pay list, solemn-eyed young

additions to the list in tow, and the payment required by treaty is passed to the senior officer present, who passes it over the flag, a Union Jack laid out on the table, to the recipient. Heads of families get ammunition—a box of .22s these days, restraint being what it is—and every third year the chief gets a special payment for a new treaty suit. Then everybody goes to the community hall for a meal and another speech or two.[1]

In the last treaty negotiated by the Indian Affairs ministry, the Nisga'a received approximately $200 million—a capital transfer of approximately $33,000 per person. The beneficiaries of the numbered Prairie treaties each receive $5 annually. The Nisga'a treaty took decades to negotiate; the Prairie treaties took merely days. There's a world of difference in the scope and magnitude of the late nineteenth- and the late twentieth-century treaties, but there are some things that never change. Consider the following accounts of the negotiation of Treaty 6 with the Cree and Salteaux nations at Fort Carlton, Saskatchewan, in 1876.

From Canada's earliest days, France and England had signed "peace and friendship" treaties to consolidate trading alliances with first peoples on the East Coast. For example, the Iroquois, who occupied strategic lands between French outposts on the St. Lawrence River and the English colonies on the East Coast, had linked themselves to European powers in a "Covenant Chain," which the colonizers saw not so much as sacred covenants but rather as short-term contracts. The British Crown signed hunting and fishing treaties with the Mi'kmaq and Maliseet in 1760 and 1761, but by the nineteenth century, British interests had become more focused on land acquisition. Treaties of cession and purchase added something like 50 million acres to the country. Between 1871 and 1899, Canada acquired ten times as much land again on the Prairies, from both the Hudson's Bay Company and the signing of new treaties with Plains tribes. By 1885 the fur trade was dying, the railroad had connected the country, and the Hudson's

Bay Company had begun selling agricultural plots to immigrants who, after the turn of the century, were arriving by the million.

The Crown negotiated the 1850 Robinson Treaties with the Indians of lakes Superior and Huron after the Ojibwe objected to miners exploring their lands. The Robinson Treaties created the model of Indian reserves for individual First Nations. On the Pacific Coast, from 1850 to 1854, Governor James Douglas negotiated 14 treaties and "postage stamp" reserves before Britain withdrew its support. The Royal Proclamation of 1763 had limited the surrender of Indian land to treaties publicly negotiated with Crown representatives. Treaties covering parts of Ontario, Manitoba, Saskatchewan, Alberta, Northwest Territories, and British Columbia followed this model.

A trans-Canada railway construction project triggered the negotiation of the eleven numbered treaties. Canada signed Treaties 1 and 2 with the Ojibwe and Cree of Manitoba in 1871, and Treaty 3, signed in 1873, settled with the Ojibwe of northwestern Ontario. That year, Treaty 4 covered Ojibwe, Cree, and Assiniboine lands in southern Saskatchewan. Treaty 5, signed in 1875, encompassed Ojibwe and Cree territories in what is now northern Manitoba. Treaty 6 took in areas in the middle of Saskatchewan and Alberta. The Blackfoot Confederacy and allies in southern Alberta accepted Treaty 7 in 1877. Treaty 8 covers northern Alberta, northwest Saskatchewan, and the northeast corner of British Columbia. Indian Affairs official Duncan Campbell Scott negotiated Treaty 9 with the Ojibwe and Cree of northern Ontario in 1905 and 1906. Nations in northern Saskatchewan and Alberta signed Treaty 10 in 1906. In 1921 Canada made Treaty 11 with tribes in the Northwest Territories. By then, however, treaties were no longer a government priority, and Treaty 11 was never implemented.

In these numbered treaties, the Canadian government, in Queen Victoria's name, promised certain ongoing benefits to the members of signatory tribes, including small annuities. All of these benefits became known as treaty rights. Based on its population, a tribe would receive a specified amount of reserve land. In exchange, the tribe agreed, in the language of the treaty, to "cede, release and surrender" all other lands in its territory for settlement and development.

Deanna Christensen's book *Ahtahkakoop* wonderfully describes events around the negotiation of Treaty 6, which occurred from August 18 to 23, 1876. Lieutenant Governor Alexander Morris headed the treaty commission, and William J. Christie and James McKay joined him as commissioners. A.G. Jackes, a medical doctor, acted as secretary. As the commission travelled from Winnipeg to Fort Carlton, two thousand Cree also began to converge on the site. The Cree leaders present included Ahtahkakoop (Starblanket), Kamiyestawesit (or Beardy, as he was also known), Mistawasis (Big Child), Mistahimaskwa (Big Bear), and Pitihkwahkew, or Poundmaker, as he has become famously known.

Sergeant Major Samuel Steele's autobiography, *Forty Years in Canada: Reminiscences of the Great North-West*, describes the encampment, composed of buffalo-hide lodges, each with room enough for thirty people. "On the outside of the lodge Indians had painted the figures of birds, beasts or reptiles representing their totems. Like the rest of their race on the Plains, the Indians had many thousands of horses, the hills and prairie being covered with them, each family having its own herd and band of ponies."[2]

In his book *Buffalo Days and Nights*, Métis guide and interpreter Peter Erasmus writes: "It was an impressive sight. I had never seen so many teepees in one locality before. There were hundreds of horses feeding on the flats, some picketed close by their owners' teepee with the usual assortment of dogs which appeared to have barked themselves to exhaustion as they lay before each teepee."[3]

Arriving at Fort Carlton, the treaty commissioners took to the comforts of the fort. Beardy was camped nearby and waiting for the lieutenant governor. After being introduced, Beardy asked that the negotiations be held at a hill near Duck Lake in accordance with a vision that had come to him. Morris agreed.

A majority of Cree chiefs had already decided there was no alternative to a treaty. At a pre-negotiation caucus of chiefs, Ahtahkakoop
had said:

> We have always lived and received our needs in clothing, shelter,
> and food from the countless multitudes of buffalo that have been
> with us since the earliest memory of our people. No one with
> open eyes and open minds can doubt that the buffalo will soon
> be a thing of the past.[4]

Given the international character of the formalities involved in
translating Indian hunting grounds into settler farmland, it should
have been no surprise to the treaty commissioners that the first
issue in the negotiation turned out to be one of interpreters. Chief
Mistawasis advised the commissioners that the Cree had hired their
own interpreter, Peter Erasmus. Lieutenant Governor Morris argued
that this was not necessary, but Mistawasis insisted: "Our man will
interpret as well as yours. I can speak Blackfoot, and I know what it
takes to interpret. If you do not want the arrangement, there will be
no talks. We did not send for you. You sent for us."[5]

The next day, Morris awoke in a better mood and acknowledged
that the site selected by the Indians for their negotiations "had been
most judiciously chosen."[6] Erasmus later observed that the mounted
policemen in scarlet uniforms impressed the Indians. "Though small
in number, the Police were to be an important factor in establishing
in the minds of the tribes the fairness of justice of government for
all the people regardless of colour or creed—something they had no
concept of in its broader sense."[7] Morris's predecessor, Lieutenant
Governor Adams G. Archibald, had expressed an illiberal version
of the same idea: "Military display has always had a great effect
on savages and the presence of even a few troops would have a
good tendency."[8]

In Morris's *Treaties of Canada with the Indians of Manitoba and
the North-West Territories*, commission secretary Jackes described

the chief's approach: "In about half an hour they [the Cree] were about ready to advance and meet the Governor; this they did in a large semi-circle; in their front were about twenty braves on horseback, galloping about in circles, shouting, singing and going through various picturesque performances."[9] The semi-circle closed around Morris's tent, and a chief stepped forward holding high a decorated pipestem.

Morris understood the pipestem ceremony as a gesture of friendship. For the Cree, the ceremony had a deeper meaning. "According to Indian traditions, in the presence of the sacred pipestem only the truth could be spoken," Christensen writes in her book. "Thus, for Ahtahkakoop, Mistawasis, and the other leading men, the promises made during the treaty negotiations at Fort Carlton would be considered as binding as those that appeared in the written document."[10] The tribes gathered at Fort Carlton believed that everything said in the negotiation of a treaty formed part of the understanding. The treaty was a covenant.

Erasmus's telling captures the moments following the opening ceremonies: "We were finally seated on the grass in a large semi-circle in front of the Governor's tent crossed-legged, a position that seems to be the most restful and relaxed manner of listening to speech. I have seen quite old men rise to their feet to speak from this position without the use of their hands or arms to assist them, all with apparently effortless ease."[11] Then, before the negotiations had really begun, they almost broke down over interpreters and interpretation.

Before Morris spoke, James McKay made a major faux pas: he called on Erasmus to interpret the lieutenant governor's speech. Mistawasis stood, and the Cree fell silent. The chief lifted his finger so that Morris could see it. "Already you have broken your word on what you have agreed." At that moment, all the Indians got to their feet and stood behind their chief. Erasmus said it was "like a forest as a gathering storm of words rolled forward." The police moved forward to protect the treaty commissioners. After staring down Morris long enough to provide a warning to the lieutenant governor, Mistawasis signalled that his followers should resume their seats.

Morris stood to make his opening statement. He had come to Fort Carlton, he said, representing Queen Victoria.[12] Morris explained that he was a treaty maker, not a trader. After hearing him out, the chiefs requested an adjournment for the day.

The next day, August 19, Morris met all the chiefs at the council tent. The treaty commissioners well knew that the buffalo had been hunted almost to extinction—horses and guns had made the hunter's life easier, but they also speeded the buffalo's destruction. Also, in the years before the treaty talks, smallpox had devastated the Aboriginal populations in the area. For the government, the answer was assimilation into the immigrant agricultural economy. Like his American counterparts, Morris urged the Indians to take up farming on the reserves they would get as part of a treaty.

> I do not want to interfere with your hunting and fishing. I want you to pursue it through the country, as you have heretofore done; but I would like your children to be able to find food for themselves and their children that come after them. Sometimes when you go to hunt you can leave your wives and children at home to take care of your gardens.[13]

In other treaties, Ottawa had generally reserved areas for each Indian band, based on a formula of one square mile for every family of five. Once the chiefs had chosen a site, government surveyors would arrive to mark the boundaries of the reserve. Morris described the tools, implements, livestock, seed, and other items that the government would provide as part of Treaty 6. He also talked about the importance of chiefs. Chiefs would be paid an annual salary of $25; headmen, "not exceeding four for each band," would get $15.[14]

Nearing the end of his remarks, Morris told the tribal leaders that after Treaty 6 was signed, he would "make a present to every man, woman and child, of $12." The money was to be paid "to the head of a family for his wife, and children not married." He added something he had forgotten to mention earlier: "[I]f a treaty is made here and at Fort Pitt, we will give every year to the Indians included in it, one thousand five hundred dollars' worth of ammunition and twine."

Morris stressed that the treaty "was not for to-day or to-morrow only but should continue as long as the sun shone and the river flowed." Finally, he said, "The Queen will agree to pay yearly five dollars per head for every man, woman and child."[15] This was not generosity. The government had already calculated that revenues from developments on the surrendered lands would more than offset the cost of treaty annuities.

Erasmus's account records, but Morris's does not, that Poundmaker objected to the treaty's terms: "The governor mentions how much land is to be given to us. He says 640 acres, one mile square for each family, he will give us." In a loud voice Poundmaker shouted, "This is our land! It isn't a piece of pemmican to be cut off and given in little pieces back to us. It is ours and we will take what we want."[16]

After Morris's offer was complete, the serious bargaining started. One concession Morris made was the inclusion of some Métis in the treaty: "The small class of Half-breeds who live as Indians with the Indians, can be regarded as Indians by the Commissioners."[17] Those Métis eligible for lands in the Red River Valley would not be included. In the winter of 1869–70, Louis Riel had led an uprising that forced the Government of Canada to create a new province, Manitoba, on terms acceptable to the Métis, French-speaking descendants of fur traders and Cree or Ojibwe Indians.

On August 23, 1876, interpreters read and translated the text of Treaty 6 aloud for the Indians assembled at Fort Carlton. Lieutenant Governor Morris signed on behalf of Canada. The majority of chiefs affixed their names to the document. But Poundmaker refused to sign, as did Big Bear.

By 1879 Mistawasis and other Cree chiefs were complaining that Canada was not keeping its treaty promises. The Métis were no happier. When government surveyors arrived to parcel off their lands, the Métis in Saskatchewan called back Louis Riel from exile in Montana. Riel tried unsuccessfully to petition the government, then mounted another armed revolt. On March 26, 1885, a Métis force led by Gabriel Dumont fought the North West Mounted Police at Duck Lake and won the day. Mistawasis's son, Ayimisis, and a war chief, Kapapamahchakwew, killed nine settlers at Frog Lake on April 2, before burning Fort Pitt. The Canadian government ordered out the army, the North West Mounted Police, and the militia, and at the Battle of Batoche, the Métis lost to a much larger force. Together, these battles became known as the Northwest Rebellion.

Louis Riel surrendered on May 15. Although he had not fought in any of the battles, Mistawasis turned himself in at Fort Carlton in July and, after fifteen minutes' deliberation, a jury sentenced him to three years at Stony Mountain Penitentiary. Poundmaker also went to jail. The government jailed forty-four men and hanged eight for treason, including Wandering Spirit and the Métis leader, Louis Riel.

Treaties 1 to 7 were negotiated quickly, according to pre-determined government formulas and usually with government interpreters. Not surprisingly, issues of interpretation surround them to the present day.

Among the clauses contained in Treaty 6 is the community "medicine chest" provision:

> That in the event hereafter of the Indians comprised within this treaty being overtaken by any pestilence, or by a general famine, the Queen, on being satisfied and certified thereof by Her Indian Agent or Agents, will grant to the Indians assistance of such character and to such extent as Her Chief Superintendent of Indian Affairs shall deem necessary and sufficient to relieve the Indians from the calamity that shall have befallen them.

Yet although the federal government has for forty-some years paid the cost of basic health services to treaty Indians, it has always refused to recognize this benefit as a treaty right.[18]

Some tribal groups remember "outside promises" made by negotiators that were not written into the text of the treaty. For example, Treaty 8 First Nations were promised tax freedom. Indeed, the treaty commissioners reported this commitment to Ottawa: "We assured them [the chiefs negotiating Treaty 8] that the treaty would not lead to any forced interference with their mode of life, that it did not open the way to the imposition of any tax, and there was no fear of enforced military service."[19]

Because the federal government believed it might owe a constitutional duty to protect reserve lands from erosion due to forced tax sales, it later included the tax exemption in the *Indian Act*. In 1992 Gordon Benoit, an Aboriginal entrepreneur, went to court to claim the exemption for all Treaty 8 beneficiaries, even if they live off-reserve. In 2006 the *Benoit* case was still before the courts, and the Indian taxation question remains one of the most controversial issues arising from the numbered treaties.

All numbered treaties also contain commitments to create reserves of land, with land allocation based on pre-determined formulas. Government surveyors determined how much land went into each reserve. The allocation was based on a band list that also governed payment of the annual annuities. The system had plenty of flaws, and in the 1980s and 1990s the federal government was forced to create a process called Treaty Land Entitlement to fix the allocation errors. Sometimes this involved transfers of cash so that the First Nation could purchase lands on the open market.

Until the nineteenth century, it was accepted that certain indigenous nations controlled large, well-defined territories, and the European powers that negotiated alliances with indigenous leaders learned not to underestimate indigenous peoples' abilities as warriors and diplomats. By the time the Canadian government began the negotiation of Treaty 6, the capacities of the Cree, Assiniboine, and Saulteaux nations had been reduced by hunger. Regardless, the oral histories of the tribes who negotiated the numbered treaties show that these people firmly believed in the treaties' "international" character. The Canadian government demonstrated its contrary view with the *Indian Act*, a piece of legislation it tabled the same year it negotiated Treaty 6.

Canada's *Constitution Act, 1867*, granted Parliament legislative authority over "Indians, and Lands reserved for the Indians." In 1876 Parliament adopted the *Indian Act* to consolidate federal control over Indians and Indian lands. Borrowing Chief Justice Marshall's words, Canadian Indians were to become "dependent" nations. Long acknowledged as a paternalistic piece of legislation, the *Indian Act* has nevertheless been resistant to reform. Successful amendments have often increased, rather than decreased, the bureaucratic oversight of Indian bands and their assets. There has always been a financial element to the debates about the *Indian Act*, too. Bill C-31, for example, passed in 1985, returned to band lists Indian women who had been unjustly delisted for marrying non-Indians. However, the bill provided inadequate funding to reserves to house these new band members.

Canadians have learned to equate the numbered treaties and the reserves they created with poverty and despair. The Department of Indian Affairs spends billions of dollars annually, but much of it is eaten up in administration and welfare; too little gets spent on reducing poverty. Late in 2001, Ottawa introduced legislation that would have allowed Indian reserve governments to raise money for economic development in international capital markets. Ottawa entitled the legislative initiative the *First Nations Governance Act*. Despite its name, critics claimed the act was more about accounting than accountability.

Some conservative politicians see the Third World conditions of Indian reserves as a breeding ground for nepotism, corruption, and irresponsible financial management. Right-wing MPs routinely fume about "chiefs flying first class" and accuse Indian bands of lacking financial accountability. Band governments receive federal funds for education, housing, and social services, but, according to these conservatives, all-powerful chiefs and councillors control every spending decision. Auditor General Sheila Fraser has countered that, "[A]ccountability must flow two ways—from First Nations to the federal government, and from the federal government to First Nations."[20]

The rushed negotiation of the numbered treaties in the late 1800s left many hugely costly matters unresolved, including issues of investment, health, housing, and taxation. These issues remain for the courts or negotiators to sort out in the twenty-first century.

▼

CHAPTER 6

THE BERGER-SMITH DEBATE

EXPLORERS DID NOT cross the Pacific region west of the Rocky Mountains until late in the eighteenth century, but by the twentieth century British Columbia had become Canada's third largest and third richest province. For a century after it joined Canada in 1871, British Columbia was also a province in deep denial about Aboriginal rights. Between long periods of indifference, dramatic Aboriginal-rights issues occasionally captured public attention: road blockades, court decisions, political crises in the fishery, or disputes between First Nations and their tenants. For all their efforts, the parties to the Nisga'a settlement—B.C.'s only modern treaty—were never able to convince much more than half the B.C. public that it was "affordable," "equal," and "open."[1] Politicians from the B.C. Liberal Party even took that deal to court. When they lost the case, they used a provincial referendum to ensure that some of the settlement's provisions would never be repeated.

None of this was surprising. For at least a generation, the province's political class had been polarized on Aboriginal issues. Two books published in the 1990s illustrate the 120-year history of that polarity. One is written by an Aboriginal-rights lawyer, jurist, and, in his youth, a New Democratic Party politician; the second author was a deputy minister in the provincial Social Credit administration. Both books tell the story of treaty making in the province, but the authors held deeply divergent views. For several years, these books contributed to a lively public debate. Examining the views of these two prominent lawyers, as they cover the period from the nineteenth century to 1973, provides important clues about the mystery of the missing treaties in British Columbia.

Thomas Berger, the Aboriginal-rights advocate, published *A Long and Terrible Shadow* in 1991.[2] Melvin Smith, the redoubtable provincial bureaucrat and conservative polemicist, issued *Our Home or Native Land* four years later.[3] Berger thinks the treatment of Indians by settlers was, and is, a crime. Smith thinks that modern treaty settlements with Indians are an even greater crime.

In 1792 when Captain George Vancouver first saw the place that came to bear his name, he said it required "only to be enriched by man to render it the most lovely country that can be imagined."[4] When B.C. Lieutenant Governor Garde Gardom quoted Vancouver at a ceremony in February 2000, First Nations Summit chiefs Joe Mathias and Ed John demanded a public apology. Vancouver's statement was not only a classic invocation of the colonial doctrine of "improvement"; as Grand Chief John observed, it also implied that the land was Vancouver's for the taking.

In his book, Berger picks up the story with the Hudson's Bay Company's establishment of Fort Victoria on Vancouver Island, in 1841, and the settlement that followed once Vancouver Island was made a Crown colony in 1849.[5] As usual, the European power asserted sovereignty upon arrival. Aboriginal people generally welcomed the visitors and traded with them, but when outsiders took liberties with their lands, they reacted badly. On Vancouver Island, the Kwakiutl tried to chase off Scottish coal miners. When that failed, they impaled the miners' heads on spikes and stuck them on the beach.

Hudson's Bay Company chief factor James Douglas asked HBC headquarters in London for instructions on the purchase of Indian land. In reply, the company took up John Locke's thesis of improvement, ordering Douglas to treat with Indian chiefs only under certain conditions: "[I]n your negotiations with them you are to consider the natives as the rightful possessors of such lands only as they are occupied by cultivation, or had houses built on, at the time the island came under the undivided sovereignty of Great Britain in 1846." The company considered all remaining lands in the colony "the entire property of the white people for ever,"[6] hence open for settlement. Aboriginal people could continue to hunt and fish on unoccupied Crown land, but only on their community lands would they enjoy property rights.

Melvin Smith's version of the story has a different focus. Douglas, still the HBC's chief factor, was appointed governor of the colony of Vancouver Island in 1851. "No doubt to ensure friendly relations with the natives, who far outnumbered the handful of white settlers," Smith writes, "Douglas went beyond his instructions and began to purchase the 'native interest' in certain lands around Victoria, Saanich, Fort Rupert and Nanaimo."[7] During debate on the establishment of the colony, the House of Commons heard that the British government had appointed Governor Douglas "because, as a fur trader, he would protect the Indians from the 'mere caprice of ordinary settlers."[8]

But Douglas was no bleeding-heart liberal. In 1852 two Indians killed a shepherd in the Cowichan Valley. Douglas ordered the hanging of the accused, although he did not blame their tribes, the Nanaimo and the Cowichan, as a settler government might have done.[9] When a sailor wounded a Stikine Indian, Douglas arranged for the payment of blood money to the victim's relatives.[10] In 1855, when Indians in the State of Washington were suffering casual slaughter at the hands of settler volunteers, Douglas supplied arms to the Americans to block, in Jefferson's words, the "merciless savages."[11]

Over the next six years Douglas negotiated the fourteen agreements that later became known as the Douglas Treaties.[12] Smith sees Douglas's initiative as merely unwarranted statecraft. Berger takes the view that Douglas rightly adopted a policy of treaty making on Vancouver Island. On August 2, 1858, the British government established direct rule on the mainland, and New Caledonia became British Columbia. Once Douglas left the HBC to also become governor of this new, separate colony, Smith points out, his "requests to London for funds to enter into still more agreements of this kind were rebuffed."[13]

After Douglas retired in 1864, the colony's legislature began to undo his policies. It first removed the Indians' right to acquire "Crown" land, and then claimed that Douglas had never really recognized Aboriginal title. No longer would the colony compensate Indians for lost lands or resources, certainly not from local government coffers. Berger notes that the colonial House of Assembly changed its tune only once London stopped underwriting the treaties. The mainland colony followed the same policy, as did the united colony of British Columbia after 1866.

London's stand against funding treaties did not stop the governor, Smith complains. "Although abandoning treaty making as such, Douglas by no means foresook dealing with the native interest. As an alternative, he embarked upon a vigorous policy of establishing Indian reserves."[14] (Although Smith deplores Douglas's treaty initiative, he finds the reserve alternative to be a useful precedent.)

Berger quotes a letter written in 1867 by Joseph Trutch, the chief commissioner of lands and works of the newly united colony. "The Indians have really no right to the lands they claim, nor are they of any actual value or utility to them, and I cannot see why they should either retain these lands to the prejudice of the general interests of the Colony or be allowed to make a market of them either to the Government or to Individuals."[15] Ironically, although the peoples of the West Coast had the most advanced systems of property rights of all Canadian Aboriginal people, B.C.'s colonial administrators would accord them none. Berger writes that the question of Aboriginal rights therefore continued to be unresolved, because the Douglas Treaties "covered less than one per cent of the new province."

As the colony was joining Canada in 1871, disputes about the cost of further treaties complicated negotiations. Lieutenant Governor Trutch, as he had now become, wrote to Prime Minister John A. Macdonald: "If you now commence to buy out Indian title to the lands of B.C. you would go back on all that has been done here for 30 years past and would be equitably bound to compensate the tribes who inhabited the districts now settled (and) farmed by white people equally with those in the more remote and uncultivated portions."[16]

In the years that followed, Indian nations in British Columbia began to question the terms of the province's union with Canada. Trutch might have mastery of public lands, but he couldn't escape questions about Aboriginal title. Berger notes that Canada's minister of justice, Télesphore Fournier, mentioned British Columbia's Aboriginal-rights question in writing an opinion recommending disallowance of the province's 1874 *Land Act*. Referring to the policy exemplified by the 1763 proclamation, Fournier wrote: "There is not a shadow of doubt, that from the earliest times, England has always felt it imperative to meet the Indians in council, and to obtain surrenders of tracts of Canada, as from time to time such were required for the purposes of settlement."[17] Government had secured no land surrender from Indians in B.C.

In his book, Smith counters that when British Columbia entered Confederation, Ottawa assumed constitutional responsibility for "Indians and lands reserved for Indians." He notes that Article 13 of B.C.'s Terms of Union with Canada reads, "The charge of the Indians and the trusteeship and management of the lands reserved for their use and benefit, shall be assumed by the Dominion Government and a policy as liberal as that hitherto pursued by the British Columbia Government, shall be continued by the Dominion Government after the Union."[18]

According to Smith, the terms of union did not cover "Indian title"—and this was no accident. One year before, the legislation establishing the province of Manitoba had directly addressed Indian-title issues.

> It is inconceivable that the question of Indian title, fresh in the mind of federal authorities in 1870 in respect of Manitoba would be overlooked only one year later when B.C.'s entry to Canada was under consideration. The better view is that there was recognition by federal authorities in 1871 that B.C. was dealing with the Indian matter differently... by the establishment of reserves.[19]

Governor Douglas replaced treaties with reserves as a matter of financial necessity, but for Smith reserve creation was inspired public policy: "Today, of 2,323 Indian reserves throughout the whole of Canada, 1,634 of them are located in B.C. The practice of establishing Indian reserves without entering into treaties sets B.C. apart from the rest of Canada in dealing with the Indian interest."[20] The reserves surveyed for Treaty 8 signatories in the northeast corner of British Columbia in 1899 came from federal lands in the region. The province was not involved in those negotiations.

For Smith and his followers, British Columbia inherited no obligation to First Nations other than to convey "tracts of land" to Canada for the use of the Indians, consistent with the policy of the colonial government. B.C. met that obligation long ago, the argument goes, and Canada acknowledged that by a 1924 federal order-in-council. Yet, as early as August 3, 1877, David Mills, minister of the interior, had written to Gilbert Malcolm Sproat, Indian land commissioner in Kamloops, clearly stating a contrary view: "It is obvious that the discontent of the Indians is wholly due to the Policy which has been pursued toward them by the local authorities. The government of British Columbia have all along assumed that the Indians have no rights in the soil to extinguish, and they have acted toward the Indian population upon this assumption. This policy is wholly at variance with that which has hitherto been pursued by the Crown in dealing with the aboriginal population of the Continent."[21]

Distinct Aboriginal voices began to be heard in provincial debates about Aboriginal rights. Berger quotes Nisga'a chief David Mackay: "What we don't like about the Government is their saying this: 'We will give you this much land.' How can they give it when it is our own? We cannot understand it. They have never bought it from us or our forefathers."[22]

Throughout this period, chiefs lobbied government to recognize Aboriginal title but without success, Berger notes. B.C. premier Richard McBride said in 1909: "Of course it would be madness to think of conceding to the Indians' demands. It is too late to discuss the equity of dispossessing the Red man in America." As many others would in the years to follow, McBride blamed agitation about Aboriginal title on the "pernicious advice of some unscrupulous Whites" and pressed for reductions in the land base of B.C. Indian reserves.[23]

The federal and provincial governments eventually agreed to form a joint royal commission to make an "adjustment" of Indian lands in British Columbia. Berger cites Nisga'a leader Gideon Minesque's statement to the commission when it came to the Nass Valley in 1915. Minesque had heard that some white men thought the Nisga'a were dreaming when they claimed title to the land. "It is not a dream," he said. "We are certain that this land belongs to us. Right up to this day the government never made any treaty, not even to our grandfathers or our great-grandfathers."[24]

Minesque spoke pointedly to the outstanding Indian-title question, but as Berger observes, government turned a deaf ear to his message: "The Commission, however, restricted itself to the allotment of land for reserves. In British Columbia as a whole the Commission confirmed some of the existing reserves, and it added about 35,000 hectares of new reserve land. But the Commission removed from the reserves some 20,000 hectares of land the Indians held. These 'cut-off' lands were far more valuable than the lands given to the Indians to replace them."[25]

Smith, naturally, holds a different view: "The Province considered the establishment of reserves to more than satisfy any claims which the Indians might have over their traditional territories in British Columbia."[26] Nevertheless, Smith complains, B.C.'s Indians refused to accept defeat. For example, the Nisga'a filed a formal claim to the Nass Valley in 1913. "Fed up with persistent lobbying by B.C. Indians and satisfied the Parliamentary Committee had given the final word, in 1927, the federal government amended the *Indian Act* to prohibit the collection of funds for pro-land claims activities. This effectively terminated political activity on land claims until the law was repealed in 1951."[27]

At the same time, Ottawa outlawed the great institution of West Coast First Nations, the potlatch. The government took children from their families and put them into church residential schools, where they were subject to shocking physical and sexual abuse and punished for speaking their own Aboriginal language. Years later, these people returned to their communities as emotionally damaged and institutionally dependent adults. Yet far from ending Aboriginal peoples' legal and political demands for their rights, governments would soon learn that the demands were just beginning.

In 1967 Nisga'a chiefs called on Thomas Berger at his law office. "They wanted to go to court to establish that their Indian title—their Aboriginal title—had never been extinguished," Berger writes. "The Nisga'a case was to open the way for Native land claims in Canada."[28] *Calder v. The Attorney General of British Columbia*, named for a Nisga'a chief, reached the Supreme Court of Canada in 1973. The Nisga'a sought recognition of their Aboriginal title to the Nass River Valley, which they have fished and hunted for thousands of years.

Lawyers for the B.C. government argued that Aboriginal title had been extinguished in the province. Berger argued that the Nisga'a had a common-law interest in their lands based on their traditional use and occupancy. In English common law, property rights arise from continued use and occupancy, especially if the Crown has erected no legal barrier to that right. Ironically, an Aboriginal advocate was now borrowing a version of Locke's idea.

The judges were divided, but important ground had been gained. As Berger later summed it up: "In February 1973 when the Court handed down its judgment, the Nisga'a appeared to have lost, four to three. But six judges held that Aboriginal rights were recognized under Canadian law. Three held that they had never been extinguished, three that they had. The seventh judge held against the Nisga'a on a technicality. Although technically the Nisga'a lost their case, in fact they won a moral victory. Moral victories are often just that, but this was a moral victory which changed federal policy forever."[29]

What had happened was that the Supreme Court had recognized the importance of Aboriginal rights in law. The decision reopened the political debate on Aboriginal title in Canada. In August 1973, the federal government announced an intention to settle land claims in the parts of Canada where no treaties had yet been made: the Yukon and the Northwest Territories, Quebec, and British Columbia. The moment marked the beginning of the end of the assimilation games. The third act of the treaty-making drama was about to open.

In 1969 Prime Minister Pierre Trudeau and his Indian Affairs minister, Jean Chrétien, had published a white paper designed to as-similate Indians into mainstream Canada. In a speech in Vancouver on August 8 of that year, Trudeau said:

> If we think of restoring Aboriginal rights to the Indians, well, what about the French who were defeated at the Plains of Abraham? Shouldn't we restore rights to them? And what about the Acadians

who were deported—shouldn't we compensate for this? And what about the other Canadians, the immigrants? What about the Japanese Canadians who were badly treated at the end or during the last war? What can we do to reform the past? I can only say as President Kennedy said when he was asked about what he would do to compensate for the injustices that the Negroes had received in American society. We will be just in our time. This is all we can do. We must be just today.[30]

After the *Calder* ruling, though, Trudeau observed that perhaps Aboriginal peoples had more rights than he and his government had previously thought.

Mel Smith's book expresses indignation at the prime minister's reversal. "In result, the Supreme Court of Canada in the Calder case did NOT decide that Aboriginal title exists in Canada today. The Nisga'a appeal was dismissed. There was NO finding of present-day Aboriginal title."[31]

Smith had been one of the Trudeau/Chrétien white paper's strongest supporters, and he hated the new federal policy. "In 1976," he writes, "Ottawa went ahead and opened talks with the Nisga'a on its own. The Social Credit government of Bill Bennett, which won the 1975 election, maintained B.C.'s long-standing resistance to being drawn into land-claim negotiations." Smith quotes a Bennett statement Smith himself might have drafted: "The position of the province is that if any Aboriginal title or interest may once have existed, that title or interest was extinguished prior to the union of British Columbia with Canada in 1871."[32]

Berger thought otherwise: "Where Native people are asserting land claims, they do so on the basis of their rights as Aboriginal peoples. In the United States and Canada this has given rise to a well-developed theory of Aboriginal rights. These rights are unique because at the time of contact Aboriginal peoples were present in self-governing, organized political communities, in use and occupation of the land."[33]

Melvin Smith would have none of that. "The term 'land claim' itself is a misnomer. The native interest must be recognized and discharged by government, because the Courts have said so. But, as we have seen, the entitlement is much more modest than a claim to the ownership of land."[34] Over the next three decades, Smith and his ideological allies lost important legal battles, but they would continue to win political wars.

PART III

RECONCILIATION DEBATES

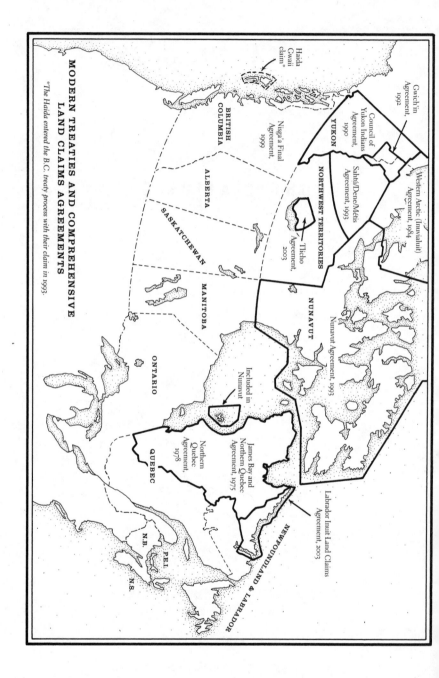

MODERN TREATIES AND COMPREHENSIVE LAND CLAIMS AGREEMENTS

The Haida entered the B.C. treaty process with their claim in 1993.

Haida Gwaii claim*

Council of Yukon Indians Agreement, 1990

Gwich'in Agreement, 1992

Western Arctic (Inuvialuit) Agreement, 1984

Sahtu/Dene/Métis Agreement, 1993

Nisga'a Final Agreement, 1999

BRITISH COLUMBIA

YUKON

NORTHWEST TERRITORIES

ALBERTA

Tlicho Agreement, 2003

SASKATCHEWAN

MANITOBA

NUNAVUT

Nunavut Agreement, 1993

ONTARIO

Included in Nunavut

Northern Quebec Agreement, 1978

James Bay and Northern Quebec Agreement, 1975

QUEBEC

Labrador Inuit Land Claims Agreement, 2003

NEWFOUNDLAND & LABRADOR

N.B.

P.E.I.

N.S.

CHAPTER 7

CROSSROADS

Tables, Commissions, and Courts

TABLES

ASSEMBLED ALONG THREE sides of a long conference room table in a tall government building are the treaty-negotiating teams for First Nations and for the federal and territorial governments. City lights burn in the winter sky outside, and the surrounding corporate towers stand watch over the negotiations. After years of protracted bargaining, the parties have reached a crucial decision point, and both federal and territorial ministers have arrived to speak for their governments. What happens next will determine if the parties can reach a final agreement.

From the chair, the federal minister calls the session to order, then invites the territorial minister to make an offer for a final land settlement. The territorial politician tables an offer of several thousand square kilometres,[1] then watches for reactions from the chiefs and councillors across the table. After a couple of clarifying questions, their chief negotiator asks for an adjournment so that the First Nations side can caucus in a breakout room down the hall.

After an excruciating wait, the chiefs return, and their negotiator accepts the offer. The parties shake hands. The lawyers convene to craft the language of the agreement as the federal minister rushes off to catch a plane for Europe.

As in the Yukon, treaty negotiations in British Columbia occur at three-sided tables. Some negotiating sessions require journeys to the nation's capital, some take place in Victoria or Vancouver, and others happen in Aboriginal communities around the province. Wherever government negotiators go, there will be something familiar about the venues. In a community hall, collapsible trestle tables are aligned in a U shape. The tables are loaded with three-ring binders, briefing notes, and coffee cups.

The First Nations side includes chiefs, councillors, staff, and elders in ball caps and jeans, one of whom has given the opening prayer. Against the wall behind them, on benches, sit observers from the bands represented at the table. Federal and provincial officials in smart casual wear from L.L. Bean or Mountain Equipment Co-op listen without betraying any emotion. A representative of the British Columbia Treaty Commission facilitates at the butt of the U.

Whoever is talking, there is always someone recording his or her thoughts on a laptop computer, and someone else at a side table filling a Styrofoam cup from a Bunn coffee urn. In one form or another, these treaty talks may have been ongoing for a decade, so nobody in the room exudes any sense of urgency. The high drama of an Ottawa closing remains a distant prospect.

In the early days of B.C. treaty talks, the trust levels were so low that the parties could not meet without a treaty commission facilitator in the room. On occasion, elders and hereditary chiefs gave long speeches. Sometimes a negotiating session was interrupted by the return of salmon to a nearby river or the arrival of a bear. More recently, at the handful of tables close to a treaty, the parties have brought disciplined teams and skilled negotiators to focus on the three or four outstanding issues. Speeches are short, caucuses frequent. Trade-offs are offered, along with hourly ministerial consultations.

Even the professional negotiators pace the floor, and chiefs fret in the hallways. When a handshake comes and an issue appears to be resolved, everyone in the room applauds.

In contrast to the nineteenth-century's "numbered" treaties, modern treaties are complicated packages. The definitions chapter alone of the Nisga'a final agreement runs to fourteen pages. Modern treaty negotiation involves settling issues as varied as land, funding, taxation, language, culture, heritage, resources (including hunting and fishing questions), forestry, mining, oil and gas development, health, education and social programs, eligibility and enrolment, legal certainty or finality, and self-government. A proposal on any one of these issues requires a considered response. Each party will find it necessary to caucus with its team and consult its principals before coming back to the table.

Most First Nations in Canada have treaties; most in British Columbia do not. Of two hundred First Nations in the province, only three regional groups have treaties: Treaty 8 First Nations in the northeast corner, Douglas Treaty First Nations on Vancouver Island, and the Nisga'a Nation in the Nass Valley. Since 1992, dozens of First Nations groups have joined the treaty process, and some have left it. Currently, the following First Nations have voluntarily entered the B.C. Treaty Commission negotiation process: Acho Dene Koe First Nation, Cariboo Tribal Council, Carcross-Tagish First Nation, Carrier Sekani Tribal Council, Champagne and Aishihik First Nations, Cheslatta Carrier Nation, Council of the Haida Nation, Da'naxda'xw Awaetlatla Nation (formerly Tanakteuk First Nation), Ditidaht First Nation, Esketemc First Nation (formerly Alkali Lake Indian Band), Gitanyow Hereditary Chiefs, Gitksan Hereditary Chiefs, Gwa'Sala-'Nakwaxda'xw Nation, Haisla Nation, Heiltsuk Nation, Homalco Indian Band, Hul'qumi'num Treaty Group, Hupacasath First Nation, In-SHUCK-ch Council, Kaska Dena Council, Katzie Indian Band, Klahoose Indian Band, Ktunaxa/Kinbasket Treaty Council, Kwakiutl

Nation, Laich-Kwil-Tach K'omoks Tlowitsis Council of Chiefs
(Hamatla Treaty Society), Lake Babine Nation, Liard First Nation,
Lheidli T'enneh Band, Maa-nulth First Nations, McLeod Lake
Indian Band, Musqueam Nation, 'Namgis Nation, Nazko Indian
Band, Nuu-chah-nulth Tribal Council, Pacheedaht Band, Quatsino
First Nation, Ross River Dena Council, Sechelt Indian Band,
Sliammon Indian Band, Snuneymuxw First Nation (formerly
Nanaimo First Nation), Squamish Nation, Stó:lô Nation, Taku
River Tlingit First Nation, Te'Mexw Treaty Association, Teslin
Tlingit Council, Tlatlasikwala Nation, Tsawwassen First Nation,
Tsay Keh Dene Band, Tsimshian First Nations, Tsleil-Waututh
Nation, Westbank First Nation, Wet'suwet'en Nation, Wuikinuxv
Nation (formerly known as Oweekeno Nation), Yale First Nation,
and Yekooche Nation.

Of the 198 First Nations in British Columbia, fifty-seven groups
are involved with the treaty process at forty-six tables; almost a quarter of these are not currently active, however. Some First Nations in
negotiations also have headquarters in the Yukon or the Northwest
Territories.

Canada's 1986 Comprehensive Land Claims Policy and 1995
Inherent Rights Policy guide B.C. treaty negotiations, but the process
has no specific legislative underpinning. Canada and British Columbia
each share roughly half the costs.

COMMISSIONS

CONVINCED THAT NEGOTIATING the Nisga'a treaty would be quick
and easy, then B.C. premier Bill Vander Zalm sent provincial negotiators to the table in 1990. In December of that year, Ottawa, Victoria,
and B.C.'s First Nations set up the tripartite British Columbia Claims
Task Force to recommend ways the three parties could begin treaty
negotiations encompassing the whole province.

The task force report, released in 1991, recommended six stages
for the negotiation process:

1. A First Nation submits to the British Columbia Treaty Commission (BCTC) its statement of intention to negotiate a treaty.

2. BCTC responds by meeting with the First Nation to name negotiators, give the negotiators mandates, and identify processes for addressing the overlapping claims of other First Nations.

3. The three parties—the federal government, the B.C. government, and the First Nation—arrive at a framework agreement, which sets out an agenda and a timetable for negotiations.

4. Substantive negotiations of the identified issues start, continuing until the three parties arrive at an agreement in principle.

5. Final-agreement negotiations are undertaken to complete the treaty.

6. The treaty is implemented over the years that follow.

A few months later, after the B.C. Claims Task Force report was published, Prime Minister Brian Mulroney, newly elected B.C. premier Mike Harcourt, their responsible ministers, and First Nations Summit leaders Edward John, Joe Mathias, and Miles Richardson signed the British Columbia Treaty Commission Agreement. The agreement set out details for the composition of the BCTC, the body that would act on the task force's recommendations. The agreement stipulated that the federal and provincial governments would each nominate a commissioner and the summit would nominate two; the three parties would collectively nominate a full-time chief commissioner. All nominees would be appointed for fixed terms, the full-time chief commissioner for three years and the part-time commissioners for two.

According to the BCTC agreement, the commission was to encourage "timely negotiations" and assist the three parties, where necessary, "to obtain dispute resolution services."[2] Consistent with the recommendations of the task force, the commission was to have three main roles: "facilitation, funding, and public information and education." In later chapters, I will examine how effectively the commission plays each of these roles.

COURTS

PRIOR TO THE completion of the Nisga'a and the Yukon settlements in the 1990s, treaties required Aboriginal parties to agree that, upon signing, all their Aboriginal rights would be extinguished. After ratification of their treaty, however, Yukon First Nations defiantly insisted that Aboriginal title would continue to exist on their settlement lands. During the Nisga'a negotiations, the parties spent much time arguing about the traditional "cede, release, surrender" language. For government, "certainty" required extinguishment.

According to government policy, First Nations in treaty negotiations also forgo their right to litigate any issue on the table. In Canadian public policy, this requirement is an anomaly, one that can actually frustrate negotiations. In 2004 B.C. treaty commissioner Jack Weisgerber observed, "The conundrum is this: First Nations may feel they are forced to take legal action to protect their rights. And then they cannot negotiate a resolution of their rights because they have taken legal action. It seems like a catch-22 situation."[3]

In defiance of this prohibition, over the last thirty years Aboriginal peoples have regularly sought the guidance of Canadian courts on questions of Aboriginal law, and the courts have not hesitated to redefine the boundaries of treaty negotiations. Despite a handful of high-profile constitutional victories, however, Aboriginal claimants in the Canadian courts have lost most of their cases.

Aboriginal peoples believe with every bone in their bodies that settlers stole their homelands and suppressed their governments. The descendants of settlers, for their part, frequently believe that colonization made the Americas a better place for the majority of residents. If their forebears were cruel or exploitative, they were simply creatures of their time. Besides, they argue, settler governments have long since paid for earlier sins by providing free housing, education, and medical care for Aboriginal people, plus billions in welfare payments. It is time for Natives to forget the past, proponents of this view say, to move on, join the mainstream, assimilate, and prosper.

Whatever injustices they may have inflicted on indigenous peoples, colonizers knew they were acting according to the rule of law. The two Spanish clerics who argued before the council at Valladolid in 1550 focused their representations on the meaning of the law of nations, which we today call international law. For the European takeover of the Americas, the law of nations provided four rationalizations: conquest, discovery, papal donation, and land cessions or treaties. Hernán Cortés took Mexico in a conquest emboldened by papal donation. Discovery was a "finders keepers" rule that enabled the original European occupants to deny later European claims—except, of course, those advanced by conquest. Britain's 1763 proclamation and the United States Supreme Court both sanctioned land cessions through treaties.[4]

Treaties signed by England, France, and Holland with the Mi'kmaq, Mohegan (Mohican), Iroquois, and Cherokee nations provide ample proof that indigenous peoples were once recognized as nations under international law, but the Supreme Court of Canada now rejects that history. Seminal nineteenth-century United States Supreme Court judgments skilfully juggled contradictions in recognizing both the doctrine of discovery and the validity of Indian nations. However, the key cases involving the Cherokee Nation decided early in the nineteenth century, at U.S. Chief Justice John Marshall's court, further shaped the future of Indian law in both the United States and Canada.

In the *Cherokee Nation v. Georgia* (1831) case, the court declared that Indian tribes were not "foreign nations" but "domestic dependent nations" under the "pupilage" of the United States. In her book *The Cherokee Cases: Two Landmark Federal Decisions in the Fight for Sovereignty*, Jill Norgren argues that Marshall's rulings complicated things as much as clarified them:

> That federal Indian law today is deeply flawed cannot be questioned. To a considerable extent the *Cherokee Nation* and

Worcester decisions are to blame. The equivocating language
of each decision—in particular, the assertion of an undefined
ward-guardian relationship, the denial of foreign nation status,
and the declaration of federal authority over Indian affairs—has
left much room for judicial interpretation.[5]

Although it was heard in England at the Judicial Committee
of the Privy Council, Canadian lawyers often cite *St. Catherine's
Milling Co. v. Regina* (1888)[6] as the country's first Aboriginal-law
case. The Privy Council declared that the Indian interest in lands
was dependent on the goodwill of the Crown, but the ruling also
indicated that provincial authorities could not alienate Indian lands
until a treaty had been negotiated and Aboriginal title extinguished
by the federal government.

The 1973 Nisga'a case heard by Canada's Supreme Court marked
the turning point from the assimilation-game stage of treaty making
to the reconciliation-debates stage. Justice Emmett Hall, who sided
with the Nisga'a, urged his colleagues to reject colonial and assimilationist attitudes. The "evidence is that the [Nisga'a] in fact are and
were from time immemorial a distinctive cultural entity with concepts
of ownership indigenous to their culture and capable of articulation
under the common law,"[7] Hall wrote.

In 1982, in Section 35 (1), first ministers added to the Canadian
constitution language that recognized existing Aboriginal and treaty
rights (Aboriginal peoples being defined as Indian, Inuit, and Métis)
and safeguarded these rights from legislative abrogation. Canada
thus became the first country in the world to constitutionally affirm
Aboriginal rights. This recognition seemed to assure continuity of
First Nations cultures, customs, and traditions. However, government retained the right to "infringe" treaty rights for "justifiable"
reasons. Since then, and particularly since the 1990 Supreme Court
of Canada decision in *Regina v. Sparrow*, Canadian courts have been
busy clarifying the meaning and import of the new constitutional

language, adjudicating numerous cases on Aboriginal rights, title, and self-government, and slowly redefining the legal relationship between governments and Aboriginal peoples. In *Sparrow*, the court said that Aboriginal rights should receive a "generous, liberal interpretation." It rejected the "frozen rights" concept in favour of a notion of evolving interpretations; it stated too that "existing" rights meant "unextinguished" rights, and it stipulated that, in future, governments should broadcast in advance any intent to extinguish these.[8]

In the *R. v. Van der Peet* (1996) decision,[9] the presiding justices established four factors to consider in establishing whether a First Nation's custom might qualify as an Aboriginal right. The custom had to be integral to the distinct culture of that particular society, must have pre-dated European contact, and could not be common to all societies; the scope of the right would depend on the traditions of the community claiming the right.[10] Writing in the *McGill Law Journal*, Russell Lawrence Barsh and James Youngblood Henderson questioned the wisdom of a Canadian court trying to determine the centrality of Aboriginal cultural practices, not least because the *Van der Peet* decision tightened the *Sparrow* test for the existence of Aboriginal rights: "Activities in which First Nations have engaged continuously for centuries may therefore be extinguished judicially, notwithstanding section 35 of the Constitution Act, 1982."[11]

The *R. v. Gladstone* (1996) ruling demonstrated the vulnerability of the First Nations position as well as the power of the courts to affect it. Where *Sparrow* had required that governments provide compelling legislative reasons for their infringement of constitutionally protected Aboriginal rights, *Gladstone* expanded the list of legitimate legislative objectives to encompass historic resource uses by settlers and regional economic imperatives.[12]

From the beginning, Canada's treaty making explicitly recognized an Aboriginal interest in land. What we today refer to as "Aboriginal title" colonial authorities called "Indian title," and that title depended on a tribe's exclusive use of an area.[13] Aboriginal title includes rights

to practise specific activities, some of which, such as hunting and fishing, may also be Aboriginal rights, and others, such as contemporary
economic pursuits, which are not. Not all judges have been impressed
by Aboriginal-title claims. In his infamous *Delgamuukw* ruling in
1991, B.C. Supreme Court chief justice Allan McEachern opined:
"The plaintiffs' [Gitksan and Wet'suwet'en] ancestors had no written
language, no horses or wheeled vehicles, slavery and starvation was
[*sic*] not uncommon, wars with neighbouring peoples were common,
and there is no doubt, to quote Hobbs [*sic*] that Aboriginal life in the
territory was, at best, 'nasty, brutish and short'."[14]

The Supreme Court of Canada was more judicious, but even
its ruling in *Delgamuukw* cut the baby in half. The court perceived
a spectrum of Aboriginal rights, with Aboriginal title at one end,
land-based customs and site-specific activities in the middle, and
at the other end practices integral to a culture but not so deeply in-
terconnected. Infringement justifications for Aboriginal rights were
to be different from those for Aboriginal title. The Supreme Court
ruling set out criteria for proving Aboriginal title to guide governments in dealing with claimant groups. Merely asserting Aboriginal
title did not lead to any presumption of its existence, the court said.
Aboriginal title is a right to exclusive use and occupation of land. It
is a communal property interest, which only the federal government
can alienate. But Aboriginal title was not absolute, according to the
Supreme Court judges; rather, it amounted to a "burden" on Crown
title. With proper justification, both the federal and the provincial
governments could infringe upon it. Where Aboriginal title had
been proved, the *Delgamuukw* ruling said compensation might be
due the First Nation as a component of the Crown's justification. As
of this writing, no court has recognized the Aboriginal title of any
First Nation in British Columbia.

In the *Delgamuukw* decision, Supreme Court of Canada chief justice Antonio Lamer tried to balance Aboriginal and Crown interests:

The development of agriculture, forestry, mining and hydroelectric power; the general economic development of the interior of British Columbia; protection of the environment or endangered species; the building of infrastructure and the settlement of foreign populations to support those aims, are the kinds of objectives that are consistent with this purpose and, in principle, can justify the infringement of Aboriginal title.[15]

In strongly worded dissent, Justice Beverley McLachlin questioned the constitutionality of infringement for such purposes. In her opinion, reconciliation could best be achieved through negotiation and the time-honoured process of treaty making.[16]

Delgamuukw, like so many judicial findings before and since, is a conundrum. *Sparrow* reaffirmed the government's trust-like duty towards First Nations. *Delgamuukw* reiterated the duty of fairness. Again and again, the court has observed that government "must uphold the honour of the Crown and must be in keeping with the unique contemporary relationship, grounded in history and policy, between the Crown and Canada's Aboriginal peoples."

Where treaties exist, the lands and rights of the First Nation in question are specified therein, and Section 35 of the *Constitution Act* now protects "existing" Aboriginal and treaty rights. In a number of cases, the court has further defined aboriginal and treaty rights. *R. v. Badger* (1996) dealt with the right to hunt on undeveloped private land. *R. v. N.T.C. Smokehouse Ltd.* (1996) concerned the right to sell or barter fish, and *R. v. Powley* (2005) addressed Métis hunting rights.

A B.C. Supreme Court case, *Campbell et al. v. British Columbia* (2000), addressed the Nisga'a treaty right to self-government. A lawyer for the losing side in that case still insists that *R. v. Pamajewon* (1996) remains the leading Supreme Court ruling on this question, because that court has not yet provided a definition of self-government.[17] First Nations naturally prefer the *Campbell* decision and fiercely oppose provincial intrusion into federal or Indian jurisdiction. As Nisga'a Nation lawyer Jim Aldridge puts it:

> In accordance with the principles set out in *Campbell*, there is an inherent right of self-government, and [that right] in its entirety is properly set out in treaties under the *Campbell* principle that a Section 35 provides the framework within which self-government can be given contemporary content and definition.[18]

By giving more precise meanings to the concepts of Aboriginal rights and Aboriginal title, Canadian courts have shaped the issues under discussion at treaty tables. Treaty tables themselves have gradually replaced vaguely defined Aboriginal rights with clear delineations. Some Aboriginal leaders have exceedingly high expectations of the courts. In the *Sparrow, Badger, Delgamuukw,* and *Haida Nation v. British Columbia* decisions, they see an affirmation of Aboriginal rights, fishing and hunting rights, Aboriginal title, and the requirements for consultation and accommodation. Others examining the same decisions find the trump card of Canadian sovereignty and the legitimization of government infringements and accommodation with compensation.

Court battles can be extremely costly. Presiding justice Mary Southin questioned whether the legal fees involved in the Nemiah Valley Aboriginal-title case brought by the Xeni Gwet'in First Nation might exceed the value of the land involved.[19] In Canada, the judges who decide these matters are federal appointees. Despite this, most Canadians accept that the courts are independent institutions. By contrast, Bruce Clark, a scholar of jurisprudence and Aboriginal law, not only accuses Aboriginal negotiators of "collaboration" but also declares that the Canadian courts have no jurisdiction in Indian-law matters.[20]

Clark bases his views on his discovery of the 1704 case *Mohegan Indians v. Connecticut* in *Appeals to the Privy Council from the*

American Plantations.[21] The Mohegan, or Mohican, petitioned Queen Anne to appoint a third-party court to hear the outstanding treaty-interpretation issue. England's attorney general, Lord Northey, recommended the creation of a permanent third-party court, and a committee of the Privy Council accepted his advice. According to Clark, this order-in-council of March 9, 1704, carries the same constitutional weight and force as the Royal Proclamation of 1763.[22] No Canadian judge has come close to endorsing this view.

As Russell Lawrence Barsh once wrote: "Justice, like beauty, is largely in the eye of the beholder."[23] With its 1973 Nisga'a ruling, the Supreme Court of Canada opened the third stage of treaty making. Nine years later, Canada adopted a new constitution that recognized "existing" Aboriginal rights. Ever since, the courts have been busy defining those rights, while continually urging governments and Aboriginal peoples to negotiate rather than litigate their issues. The Supreme Court, in particular, has taken this box of rights and wrapped the package more tightly—some would say more brightly—with each judicial season. At treaty tables, negotiators slowly unwrap the package and re-gift the rights into settlements.

By reopening the question of Aboriginal title and interpreting the "Aboriginal rights" language in Canada's new constitution, the courts cleared the way for the third stage of treaty making in this country and the world beyond.

CHAPTER 8

NORTHERN TREATIES

SOME CANADIANS, AND more than a few
British Columbians, would be surprised to learn
that the model for the Nisga'a Nation's treaty, the first modern treaty
in B.C., was designed and built in the northern territories, particularly
the Yukon.

In the final twenty years of the twentieth century, politics in the
Western world apparently turned cold and bloodless. In Canada's
big cities, the children of cutbacks started panhandling on street corners—something unimaginable only a generation earlier. Everywhere
governments were privatizing public services and getting out of the
equality business. New trade pacts embedded neoliberal economics
and outlawed alternatives. In this cruel world, markets were supposed
to have the answer for everything.

In the Canadian North, though, it was another story. Over the
same period, there was plenty of evidence that people still believed
in government and democracy, albeit of new varieties, as the northern territories began to undergo a profound political transformation.
Until two decades ago, federally appointed commissioners ruled the
North like colonial governors. Territorial legislatures were practically
powerless, and Aboriginal people had little involvement in public life.

All of that changed within a generation. Aboriginal, environmental, and women's organizations became active. Political parties organized conventions. Responsible government, Aboriginal land-claim settlements, and sustainable economics became the subjects of widespread debate. For a number of years, rather than being turned off politics, northerners were hyper-democrats.

Although the experts now believe that Asia sent successive waves of immigrants to the Americas, the most common story about the population of North America has the first arrivals traversing a land bridge across the Bering Strait to Alaska and the Yukon. In this sense, the United States and Canada were born in the North thousands of years ago.[1] Ever since, the North's indigenous peoples have hunted and fished over huge territories. At least once a year, hunting parties would gather in a large meeting of members of the same language group. Trade among the different groups included foodstuffs and other materials, including precious metals.

Today, Canada's North contains 40 per cent of the country's land mass and less than three-tenths of 1 per cent of the population. The Aboriginal populations of the three northern territories differ considerably. Nunavut, in the eastern Arctic, is predominantly an Inuit territory. In the Northwest Territories, Dene communities dot maps of the Mackenzie Valley. In the northwestern corner, Yukon's fourteen First Nations, cousins of the NWT's Dene and Alaskan Athabascans, make up half the territory's rural population. The North is covered in snow and ice for much of the year, but it enjoys short, hot summers with many hours of golden daylight. Global warming has already taken a toll on renewable-resource economies, and Pacific salmon are now appearing in rivers previously populated by Arctic char. The history of non-renewable resources in the North is a story of gold, silver, lead, zinc, iron, and, more recently, oil, gas, and diamonds.

In 1867 the British Parliament gave birth to the Canadian nation state by enacting the *British North America Act* and establishing the Canadian Confederation. It then transferred the vast region known as the Northwest Territories to this new political entity. At that time, the Northwest Territories included most of what is today Western Canada. Following the first Riel rebellion in 1870, the Canadian government carved the province of Manitoba out of the NWT's eastern flank; years later, it added northern lands to the province. During the Klondike Gold Rush of 1898, Canada established the Yukon Territory in the northwest corner of the Northwest Territories. Then, in 1905, Canada created two new provinces, Alberta and Saskatchewan, from what remained of the southern portion of the NWT. Not until 1967 did the capital of the Northwest Territories relocate from Ottawa to Yellowknife. Following the settlement of a land-claim agreement with the Inuit of the eastern and central Arctic in 1999, the Canadian Parliament established the new territory of Nunavut in the vast north and eastern regions of the Northwest Territories.

In 1968 explorers found oil at Prudhoe Bay, Alaska, and by 1971 the U.S. Congress had settled Alaska Native land claims with almost a billion dollars and 178,000 square kilometres of land.[2] As would be true in the Canadian North, the treaty was the product of a twenty-year struggle.[3] The United States had purchased Alaska from Russia in 1867, but Alaskan Natives had long asked when and how the tsar acquired title to the area. Russia had never conquered Alaska, occupied it in its entirety, or made any treaties with the Natives. Although the Tlingit Nation recorded their protest, indigenous people at the time were presumed to have no say in the matter.

Until the 1970s, Canadian southerners made all the decisions affecting the NWT. The turning point arrived with the Mackenzie Valley gas pipeline debate and the election in 1972 of Wally Firth, the NWT's first indigenous member of Parliament, who campaigned against the implementation of the multibillion-dollar pipeline megaproject until Aboriginal land claims had been settled. Firth's election victory startled both the energy industry and the Ottawa mandarins who were championing the 3,860-kilometre pipeline, which was meant to run from Prudhoe Bay through northern Yukon and down the Mackenzie

Valley to southern markets. After the election, the Canadian government appointed B.C. justice Thomas Berger to head a commission of inquiry into the pipeline megaproject. For the first time in Canada, the North would talk and the nation would listen.

In the decade before Firth's election, settler politicians in the Yukon and the Northwest Territories had begun to push for responsible government. During the same period, Indian, Inuit, and Métis leaders mounted a struggle for Aboriginal self-government. When First Nations near Fort St. John in northeastern British Columbia tried to block miners heading for the Yukon gold fields in 1898, Canada signed an extension of Treaty 8 with them. However, when Yukon's Lake Laberge chief Jim Boss sought a land settlement in 1902, the federal government refused negotiations, stating, "There is no Indian title to be extinguished in the Yukon."[4] Treaty 11, the last of the numbered treaties, was never implemented in either the Northwest Territories or Yukon, a fact acknowledged in the text of twentieth-century northern treaties. As did the Klondike Gold Rush, the 1942 construction of the Alaska Highway left permanent environmental and social scars in the North, and in 1968 Whitehorse chief Elijah Smith tried again with a petition to Indian Affairs Minister Jean Chrétien for a treaty. He objected to being treated like a squatter on his own land. But it was not until the Supreme Court of Canada's reflections on the Aboriginal title question in the 1973 Nisga'a case that the Government of Canada accepted the Yukon Indians' land claim.[5] Within a few years, there were other land claims from the Aboriginal peoples in the 3.4-million-square-kilometre area that was then the Northwest Territories.

After much hard bargaining, the three parties (federal, territorial, and Aboriginal) reached an agreement in principle for the Yukon Indians in 1988. In 1992 a final agreement recognized Aboriginal title to 41,595 square kilometres, a land base sufficient to support traditional harvesting activities and the economic development of Aboriginal communities.[6] (As a point of interest, this area exceeds the total of all land on existing Indian reserves in Canada.)

On 26,000 square kilometres of this land, the seven thousand Yukon Indian beneficiaries own all mineral rights. The Yukon settlement also provides for $243 million (in 1989 dollars) in compensation and territorial and Aboriginal co-management of wildlife resources. Companion self-government agreements would eventually replace the *Indian Act* with fourteen individual tribal constitutions. These constitutions describe each First Nation's citizenship code, its local-government powers, and the province-like services it will provide. Parliament passed the necessary legislation in 1993, and the Yukon agreement became an appendix to the Canadian constitution under the provisions of Section 35. The self-government agreements also honour Yukon Aboriginal traditions. For example, the Teslin Tlingit built their government institutions on the foundation of the tribe's five clans.

The Yukon treaty broke new ground in several ways. For the first time in Canada, a treaty did not completely extinguish Aboriginal title. Never before had an aboriginal or "third order" of government been so firmly established in Canadian law. Other innovative provisions include:

· A tripartite, community-based negotiating process that emphasized continuing communication with third-party interests;
· The inclusion of non-status members of the Aboriginal community as beneficiaries;
· The establishment of fish-and-wildlife co-management boards in each First Nation's traditional territory to allocate harvest quotas, with Aboriginal subsistence hunters and fishers getting top priority, and all users agreeing to respect the needs of conservation;
· Guarantees of seats on many government boards, including public-utility boards; and
· Three kinds of self-government powers: internal control of community institutions; local-government powers over land, zoning, and taxation; and shared jurisdiction in education, economic development, health,

and social services. Under the Yukon model, for example, the territory (or province) shares jurisdiction with the tribal government, while the federal government finances governmental institutions.

THESE SELF-GOVERNMENT POWERS did not meet the highest expectations of the Royal Commission on Aboriginal Peoples, but they were nevertheless superior to those in agreements made elsewhere in Canada. Yukon treaty negotiations experienced numerous difficulties, ministerial shuffles, changes of government, and dozens of attendant political crises, even debates about official languages.[7] But the parties were resolute and the treaty was made, the first ever not driven by some development imperative. Political scientist Joyce Green has spoken of the Yukon government's difficulty in negotiating the umbrella final agreement, at the same time educating the white community and building more equitable relations with Aboriginal leaders: "It wasn't easy, it wasn't fast, and it took vision, commitment, and leadership. And it took the courage to take a principled political position that was a political liability for the governing party."[8]

Within a few years of the Nisga'a decision, there were other land claims from Aboriginal peoples in the Northwest Territories. Canada's northernmost First Nation, the Gwich'in, settled in 1992 for 22,332 square kilometres of land, $75 million, and resource-revenue sharing. The Déline community of the Sahtú Dene still suffers the effects of their men being used as the carriers of radioactive materials mined from the Great Bear Lake area for the Second World War's Manhattan Project. In 1993 the Sahtú Dene and the Métis won title to 41,437 square kilometres and similar compensation and revenue-sharing arrangements. The 1993 Nunavut land-claims agreement, Canada's largest, established a huge new territory that the Inuit majority will govern, and in which the Inuit will collectively own 350,000 square kilometres of the land.

While northern Aboriginal peoples pursued their dreams at treaty tables, non-Aboriginal northerners also pressed the Canadian government for more local control of their communities. Parallel to treaty negotiations, an interrelated process of political maturation worked its way through the settler community. In the final years of the twentieth century, Ottawa devolved most of the administrative powers of provinces to the territorial governments. Increasingly, Yellowknife, Whitehorse, and Iqaluit now recruit local people rather than outsiders for their territorial public services. For thirty years, Yukon branches of the Conservative, Liberal, and New Democratic parties have contested seats in the legislature, and each party has governed the territory at least once.

Aboriginal peoples have long criticized the confrontational behaviour of European institutions, legislatures, and courts, which are foreign to the consensus-building circles of their community discussions. From the 1970s on, harking back to their traditions with a form of "consensus politics," the Aboriginal majority in the Northwest Territories legislature has chosen a different path from the more partisan Yukon parliament. And from the start, the Inuit built consensus into the institutions of their new public government for the 350,000 square kilometres of their homeland of Nunavut. The Government of Nunavut, which came into being on April 1, 1999, is truly a unique creation since, historically, the governments of Canada and the United States have permitted the establishment of a new state or regional government only when the settler population had attained a majority. But Nunavut will have an Inuit majority for the foreseeable future.

The NWT and Nunavut legislatures are far from being conflict-free zones, however, and some of the Aboriginal activists elected found legislative life disappointing. As backbenchers, they often felt powerless, and as ministers, they frequently found themselves doing the bidding of colonial bureaucrats. After the 1985 election, a new Yukon government, faced with a deeply divided society—the result of a breakdown in land-claims negotiations and an economy in a slump following a series of mine closures—developed a bottom-up planning exercise called Yukon 2000. For two years, Yukon 2000 moved towards a broad consensus through a series of public conferences, sector workshops for forestry, fishing, mining, tourism, and agricultural interests, and community meetings. In a territory where the Aboriginal tradition of consensus politics lives on, this constructive and sensible form of communication seemed natural. After a while, the verbal violence of parliamentary conflict came to be seen as a perversion, not the norm.

THE YUKON 2000 PROCESS and Yukon land-claim negotiations ran on parallel tracks from 1985 to 1986, and the two activities influenced each other significantly. For example, the Development Assessment Process, which guarantees communities a voice and developers a hearing, emerged as a proposal from both Yukon 2000 discussions and treaty negotiations, although it has still not been fully implemented. The Yukon treaty also enshrines sustainable-development values in the law.

At land-claim negotiating tables, in territorial legislatures, in public consultations, and in the justice system (with ideas like "circle sentencing," which incorporates the advice of community elders in judicial decisions), northerners have been experimenting. A new northern consciousness has awakened. Many current leaders of both Aboriginal and public governments came of age in the 1960s and 1970s. The American civil-rights movement no doubt inspired them, and they have felt the need to respect the traditions of indigenous peoples. Through land-claim settlements, human-rights codes, and environmental laws, northern politicians have tried to marry Aboriginal traditions with the ideals of progressive social movements.

Lockean opponents of the Nisga'a treaty have complained that the treaty created no "private property rights,"[9] but, contrary to popular belief, the market does not provide a solution for every problem. In the sub-Arctic Aboriginal community, the remote company town, and the "isolated post"–style civil-service compound, there existed no such thing as a housing market. The Indian agent, the mining company, or the federal department supplied housing according to need, rank, or seniority. Nor did the North have much of a food or clothing market. First Nation co-ops often did not earn a profit, and the company store commonly subsidized so-called essentials. Many Aboriginal people still harvest much of the meat, fish, and berries they eat, and even today the federal employee may enjoy a northern cost-of-living allowance.

Until recently, there was little British-parliamentary-style democracy in the North. In the old company towns, democracy began and ended at meetings of the miners' local union, if one existed. The company was the law, the mine manager a feudal lord. Who worked, who was housed, what they ate: these were management decisions. The Indian villages down the road lived under the yoke of the *Indian Act*, which treated Indians like children and turned a minor federal official, the Indian agent, into a great white father. All this has now changed, but the market had almost nothing to do with it.

In his 1977 report on the Mackenzie Valley Pipeline Inquiry, *Northern Frontier, Northern Homeland*, Thomas Berger contrasted the settlers' frontier and the Aboriginal homeland.[10] The influential American historian Frederick Jackson saw frontiers as creative, democratic environments with their mixed populations of outcasts, entrepreneurs, individualists, lawmakers, young radicals, and older conservatives.[11] What held for the American West of the nineteenth century also applied to the Canadian North for most of the twentieth century.

But the notion of the North as the last frontier has little current relevance. Nowadays, northern communities are deeply concerned about the social and environmental impacts of major developments. In October 2003, the major oil companies signed a deal promising northern Aboriginal groups ownership, employment, and business opportunities in the latest Mackenzie Valley gas pipeline project, plus a voice in the environmental-assessment process. The Aboriginal Pipeline Group, chaired by Nellie Cournoyea, of the Inuvialuit Development Corporation, and Fred Carmichael, president of the Gwich'in Tribal Council, has become a major equity holder in the project. At the southern end of the proposed pipeline route, however, the Deh Cho Dene community is pursuing litigation to block the pipeline. Northerners are not immune to the glitter of the casino economy, but they know that even in a church-run bingo there are usually more losers than winners.

The best kind of treaty enables First Nations to build strong private and public sectors. Treaties empower Aboriginal peoples, but they do not automatically bring prosperity. To facilitate the massive James Bay hydro project, Canada signed its first modern treaty, the James Bay and Northern Quebec Agreement, in 1975. The Grand Council of the Crees (of Quebec), the Northern Quebec Inuit Association of Canada, and the governments of Quebec and Canada all signed the treaty, which gave the Cree and the Inuit $225 million as compensation. The agreement borrows the "cede, release, surrender" language from the numbered treaties, and in the years since, these "extinguishment" clauses have become the subject of great controversy.

At the "Redefining Relationships" conference in Ottawa in November 2003, Grand Chief Ted Moses of the Council of the Crees (Eeyou Istchee) spoke about frustrations with the 1975 James Bay treaty.[12] Despite the treaty, and an economic study that showed the James Bay development had benefited Canada and Quebec to the tune of $2 billion annually, the Cree were excluded from developments in their territory. "We had less than one per cent of the permanent jobs in hydroelectric development, less than five per cent of the forestry jobs and fewer than ten per cent of the mining jobs. The James Bay Agreement was not working to get us into development," Moses said.[13] When Quebec Hydro started to contemplate a new project, the Cree demanded a "modernized" agreement.

The result was the Paix des Braves Agreement, signed in 2002, which contains, among other things, the following benefits:

- A new Quebec Nation–Cree Nation relationship;
- Sustainable development "compatible with the Cree way of life";
- A Cree-Quebec Forestry Board to review all cutting plans and oversee Cree hunter–Quebec Hydro consultations;
- An extra 350,000 cubic metres annually of harvestable wood;
- Jobs and contracts in the forestry industry;
- $105 million over fifteen years for training and employment; and
- $24 million to combat mercury contamination.

"Fundamentally with this agreement the Crees assume the responsibility for many of Québec's obligations to the Cree Nation under the 1975 agreement," Moses told the conference. "At least in regards to Québec, we now have a new approach to Cree development." In passing, he commented on the nature of the two accords: "The James Bay and Northern Québec Agreement is clearly a treaty, but it is not a land-claim agreement in the sense that this is now meant."[14]

Others noted a curious fact: because Quebec is a provincial administration, and not a nation state, the new "nation-to-nation" agreement is, strictly speaking, not a treaty. However, it certainly looks like one, which probably serves the national aspirations of both the Cree and Quebec.

In 2003 Canada recognized Tli Cho (Dogrib) title to 39,000 square kilometres of land in a treaty and self-government agreement. The Deh Cho have bypassed the existing treaty process to follow a different path in seeking to "implement" their interpretation of Treaty 11. The latest northern treaty is with the Labrador Inuit. The beneficiaries will own 15,800 square kilometres of land in northwest Labrador, an area the Inuit call Nunatsiavut. The Inuit will also enjoy management rights in a larger, 56,700-square-kilometre settlement area. (Labrador Métis, who are descended from Inuit and settlers, have protested that the treaty will extinguish their Aboriginal rights.) Despite concerns about the eventual impact of North American Free Trade Agreement rules, the principles of sustainable development are well served by new northern treaties. The texts of the Yukon, Sahtú Dene, Gwich'in, Nunavut, and Paix des Braves agreements all embody ideas of sustainable development.

Before the Foreign Affairs Committee of the Canadian House of Commons in 1997, American scholar Oran Young articulated certain principles of sustainable development, including subsistence preference, co-management, and subsidiarity. It is worth noting that the only place these principles have found expression in Canadian constitutional law is in the land-claim treaties worked out over the last few decades with northern Aboriginal groups.

Northern ideas about sustainable communities have significantly influenced Canada's foreign policy. The Inuit have certainly influenced Canadian positions for treaties on the law of the sea and on persistent organic pollutants. Canadian parliamentarians have urged the Arctic Council, established in 1996, to develop a new understanding of "soft" (non-military) security questions that incorporate "human and environmental dimensions." Subsequently, Foreign Minister Lloyd Axworthy incorporated these ideas into a "northern dimension" to Canada's foreign policy.[15]

Northern and Aboriginal communities have also for some time been pursuing their own foreign policies, with or without the sanction of national governments. The Porcupine Caribou Management Board, a novel instrument established in 1985, is an international wildlife co-management body. Northern government leaders from several countries met in Anchorage in September 1990 to form the Northern Forum. Canadian government leaders at the forum met Russian officials hungry for information about treaty making and sustainable development. Ever since, circumpolar initiatives have flourished, with conferences on everything from agriculture to education and health. Northerners are keen to establish east-west links that will counter the domination of the North by the South. New institutions reflect this growing feeling of community across the North. The Norway-based Saami Council had its beginnings in 1956. The Inuit Circumpolar Conference was established in 1977 and the University of the Arctic, a network of existing universities in the eight Arctic nation states, in 1998.

The Yukon and Nunavut treaties are important for another reason. As René Fumoleau has observed, national economic objectives drive Aboriginal policy.[16] The 1984 settlement with the Inuvialuit of Canada's western Arctic, like the Alaska and the James Bay treaties, was negotiated for economic reasons. Alaska and Inuvialuit paved the way for Arctic oil developments, and James Bay for massive hydro-electric projects in northern Quebec. The possibility of a gas pipeline along the Alaska Highway triggered Yukon treaty negotiations, but the pipeline project never came to pass, and over time negotiating a fair treaty became an end unto itself. In other words, the policy objective was social as much as economic. For some, including church leaders, justice for Aboriginal peoples by way of "generous" northern treaties had become a moral imperative.

Just as the Alaska Native settlement influenced the Yukon treaty, so did the Yukon treaty influence the treaties negotiated in the Northwest Territories and the Nisga'a treaty in northern British Columbia. Greenland Home Rule, a scheme that leaves most important decision making to local parliaments, has inspired the Inuit in Canada, Alaska, and Russia, and lawyers in the Nordic countries are studying the jurisprudence on Aboriginal law emerging from the Canadian courts. On questions of land, extinguishment, fish and wildlife, self-government, and taxation, the northern treaties have broken new ground; on issues of consultation, dispute resolution, financing, forests, implementation, mandates, and negotiating timetables, northern precedents may be less applicable. Nonetheless, British Columbia First Nations are looking north when considering what treaties should offer.

CHAPTER 9

HUNTING GROUNDS

ENGLAND'S ROYAL PROCLAMATION of 1763 recognized a huge area of North America as Indian "hunting grounds." One enduring effect of that document has been settler governments' acceptance that harvesting fish and game are central features of the Aboriginal way of life. For Aboriginals, the implication is much stronger; for them, the proclamation and the treaties it inspired not only recognized but also protected their hunting and fishing privileges. Regardless, fierce disputes between Aboriginal and non-Aboriginal fishers and hunters continue to the present day, and these disputes cloud the political environment for treaty making.

The fur trade in Canada started on the East Coast in 1534 when Jacques Cartier exchanged some French ironware for a few Mi'kmaq furs.[1] Once the Hudson's Bay Company was established in 1670, trapping became the backbone of Canada's Aboriginal cash economy.[2] In 1778 Captain James Cook anchored at Nootka Sound, on the west coast of what we now call Vancouver Island, where his crew purchased sea-otter pelts and started the west coast fur trade. By 1805 overland explorer Simon Fraser had arrived to establish a fur-trading post on behalf of the Hudson's Bay Company's rival, the North West Company, of Montreal. Early in the nineteenth century, Hudson's Bay Company governor George Simpson decided to forestall American immigration to the Oregon coast by destructively overtrapping the area. By this extreme measure, Simpson succeeded in delaying settlement of that territory for two decades. In 1846 Britain and the United States established the 49th parallel as the international boundary, and the Hudson's Bay Company decamped to Vancouver Island, where James Douglas set up headquarters in Victoria.

As Western Canada became settled, Aboriginal hunters and trappers increasingly ran headlong into government efforts to regulate them. Although Indians believed their treaty rights protected their traplines, provincial officials often took a different view, even to the point of claiming that the 1763 proclamation was no longer in force. Generally, government game officers claimed they were treating all trappers alike. In fact, they usually treated the Indians worse. One ally the Indians could count on was their commercial ally, the Hudson's Bay Company, which even financed litigation over the treaty right to trap.

After the First World War, fur prices exploded, and many young men from the farm and the city started traplines seeking quick riches. The federal government tried to protect existing Indian traplines, but as they increased federal regulation of trappers, the provinces came to prefer the licence-paying non-Aboriginal harvesters of fur. British Columbia seems to have favoured newcomers, although most of the province was covered with Aboriginal trapping areas allocated by tribal custom. Only Quebec and the Northwest Territories reserved separate areas for Aboriginal harvesters.

In the 1940s, when provincial game departments demanded that trappers register their lines, Aboriginal leaders responded politically. Aboriginal war veterans had returned home to find themselves losing their lines to non-Aboriginals. This was the final indignity. Indians had been encouraged to trap as a healthy alternative to welfare dependency. As the cities crept towards the bush, even this option for Indians began to evaporate. The continuing threat to traditional activities became a key issue in negotiations wherever treaties had yet to be settled.

Yukon was a prime example. The Klondike Gold Rush had been largely fuelled by meat from the Fortymile Caribou Herd; for decades afterwards, the herd was in decline. Before 1920, big-game guides required no licence, and many bush-wise Aboriginal people worked in the industry. But growing revenues spawned increased regulation. In 1923 territorial legislators banned Indians from positions as chief guides. In *Yukon Wildlife: A Social History,* Robert McCandless reports that some chief guides gave up their Indian status in order to keep their jobs.[3] At the time, "enfranchisement" was the key to federal policy to eradicate the Indian and turn him into a "civilized" Canadian who could vote, work, and drink legally. An Indian who chose this path made an irrevocable decision not only for himself but also for his spouse, children, and grandchildren.

During construction of the Alaska Highway in 1942, Canadian authorities gave carte blanche hunting rights to American army officers, with calamitous results for big-game populations. After the war, a handful of Aboriginal hunters became big-game guides for American tourist hunters. Over the years, as these operations became heavily capitalized, non-Natives acquired control. Other hunting controversies involved periodic territorial wolf kills, popular with outfitters but opposed by conservationists. Following the Second World War, the Yukon Fish and Game Association, a hunters' lobby, began to press for the importation of bison and elk, along with wolf-poisoning programs to help the imports survive.

Only with the final settlement of the Yukon land claim in 1992 and the establishment of local renewable-resource councils did community control of significant game-policy decisions become a reality. With their land claims secured, some First Nations sought to buy out local outfitting concessions, for reasons of commerce and conservation.

In the 1980s, when Barry Stuart, Yukon's chief land-claims negotiator, and I were presenting the fish-and-wildlife chapter of the
Yukon land-claim settlement at public meetings, we had to provide
a persuasive rationale for the proposed management structure. The
problem was that we had inherited a two-headed system. One section of the *Yukon Act* gave the territorial government the authority to
regulate hunting and fishing. Echoing the 1763 proclamation, another
section gave Indians the right to hunt for food on unoccupied Crown
land.[4] Given that 90 per cent of the jurisdiction then qualified as
"unoccupied Crown land," this meant that our territory and its small
population had two competing regimes for hunting, fishing, and
wildlife management.

The solution, we argued, was a unified system of wildlife management. In return for surrendering their unfettered right to hunt and
fish for food, First Nations would agree to a co-management model.
In each tribal area there would be a co-management board, called
the renewable-resource council, with an equal number of local appointees from the territorial government and the First Nation. These
boards would make harvest allocations or hunting quotas based on
strict criteria, the recommendations of government biologists, and
the traditional knowledge of Aboriginal elders.

The proposal was that nobody—Indian or non-Indian—could
hunt below conservation levels. However, First Nations would have
priority in the food harvest. The food needs of other resident hunters
and fishers would come next. Commercial users would have the last
claim on the resource—a major change, but one easy to effect since
most big-game hunting outfits were controlled by, and for, outsiders.
Recommendations for local harvest allocations would be forwarded
to a Yukon-wide body—the Yukon Fish and Wildlife Management
Board—which would give advice to the responsible minister. Should
the territorial minister not accept the board's recommendation, he
or she would have to give reasons in writing, which would normally
trigger a public debate.

The model was in some ways revolutionary. So before entrenching it in a Yukon-wide agreement, we tested it in one community, Mayo. Critics were sure that cooperative management would never work there. However, the First Nation surprised everyone by appointing a non-Aboriginal person to the joint board. That one action calmed the fears of local opponents, and the board became a great success.

At first, the Yukon hunters' lobby strongly objected to the Aboriginal-preference provision. However, when the Supreme Court reconfirmed this principle in the 1990 *Sparrow* decision, the opposition evaporated. In fact, the people most affected by the co-management model were those who had previously enjoyed all the authority—the game officers, who, in the Yukon, were frequently retired Mounties. Suddenly they became the secretariats or servants of co-management boards composed of local people, Aboriginal and non-Aboriginal. This represented a major transformation in their traditional gamekeeper role.

The co-management arrangements were eventually encoded in Chapter 16 of the Yukon treaty. Chapter 16 also mandates a salmon co-management board for affected First Nations and federal fisheries representatives. There continue to be funding, training, and capacity issues as these measures are implemented, but co-management bodies have become highly popular instruments. Because the minister still has the ultimate authority, they do not constitute co-jurisdiction, but they do effectively limit a government's power. One other benefit of these bodies has been to demonstrate the validity of traditional knowledge. Based on their extensive backcountry experience, Aboriginal elders often have a longer-term perspective about game populations in an area than do young government biologists. Subsequent legislation in the territories, including the *Nunavut Wildlife Act* and the *Yukon Environmental and Socio-Economic Assessment Act*, also reference such knowledge.

The Yukon treaty changed some licensing procedures related to the fall moose hunt, an annual ritual, but less so than some hunters feared. As before, people have to purchase licences, but now these are obtained either from the territorial government or from a First Nation. Under the treaty, there are two classes of First Nation land. Non-Aboriginal Yukoners can hunt Class B land without permission, but First Nations must consent to hunts by others on their Class A land. After a hunt, Class A–land hunters must complete a questionnaire indicating where they hunted, the duration of the hunt, and the condition of any animals they took. This information is incorporated into the local renewable-resource council's recommendations about future harvest levels.

Following the Yukon example, co-management boards have become more common across Canada. On the west coast of Vancouver Island, the Clayoquot Sound Management Board manages lands cooperatively on a double-majority basis, which requires both First Nation and government approval for a decision. The management agreement for Indian Arm Provincial Park near Vancouver creates a cooperative relationship between the provincial government and the First Nation to conserve natural resources and integrate "traditional and scientific knowledge." For Tatshenshini-Alsek Park in the far northwest corner of B.C., the park-management board consists of two representatives from the Champagne-Aishihik First Nations in Yukon as well as B.C.'s district parks manager and the director of lands and resources.

The 1991 B.C. Claims Task Force report affirmed the importance of hunting, fishing, and the harvesting of natural resources for both the traditional economies of Aboriginal peoples and the livelihoods of other provincial citizens, especially in rural areas.[5] First Nations often refer to stewardship of natural resources as a "sacred trust," and they view land, sea, and resources as fundamental components of modern treaties, not only for traditional reasons but also for the new economic opportunities these resources provide.

Because of fishing's economic importance to British Columbia life, fisheries management has long been controversial. As an issue, it has frequently landed in the courts. The 1990 *Sparrow* case was the first in which the Supreme Court of Canada weighed the import of the "existing aboriginal rights" section of the 1982 *Constitution Act*. Federal fisheries officers had charged Ron Sparrow, a Musqueam from the Vancouver area, for using an illegally sized drift net. Sparrow pleaded that the constitution guaranteed his Aboriginal right to fish. The Supreme Court accepted Sparrow's defence and nullified his original conviction. However, the court made it clear that the rights affirmed by Section 35 were not absolute and in subsequent cases outlined certain rules for Aboriginal fishers.

The court's judgments have precipitated vigorous debate. Those favouring the Aboriginal right to a commercial fishery and those opposed have both broadcast their judicial triumphs. So far, though, judges have only laid down a framework for assessing future issues, not decided them. For example, in *Gladstone*, the court recognized that there may be an Aboriginal right to fish commercially but stressed that the claimants would need convincing proof they had engaged in such activities prior to first contact with Europeans. The courts have invalidated First Nation fishing bylaws that applied to public waters, but the Supreme Court has also found that the federal government does not have an unfettered right to manage the fisheries, because it also has historic and legal obligations to Aboriginal people.

The *Globe and Mail*'s Jeffrey Simpson waded into these troubled waters on July 30, 2003. Simpson complained that, since the Supreme Court had recognized an Aboriginal right to fish for food in the *Sparrow* decision, the Government of Canada had mistakenly extended this right by creating a limited commercial fishery for Aboriginals. "First, some aboriginals read the Supreme Court's ruling about a 'food' fishery to mean not just that they could catch salmon to eat, but to earn income from harvested salmon in order to buy other kinds of foods. Salmon for peanut butter, if you like. They didn't accept, in other words, the more limited definition of 'food.'"[6]

As Simpson noted, the fishing industry had immediately attacked this policy, and in B.C., eleven years after the *Sparrow* decision, Provincial Court judge William Kitchen struck down the new federal Aboriginal-fisheries strategy as inconsistent with Canada's Charter of Rights "because it expressly favoured one group (aboriginals) over another (non-aboriginal commercial licence-holders)."[7]

Also in 2001, Cheam First Nation member Francesca Chey-Ann Leon was arrested near Yale, B.C., about 100 kilometres up the Fraser River. Asked why she had salmon in the trunk of her car, Leon asserted her Aboriginal right to fish for food. In court, she asked that the case be dismissed. Judge Wendy Young sent Leon to trial for illegal fishing. On April 28, 2003, another Provincial Court judge heard the case of 40 commercial fishermen in B.C. who defied a government conservation closure and caught 5,412 sockeye salmon. Judge Brian Sanderson ruled that the commercial fishermen were engaged in an act of "civil disobedience" against the incompetence of the federal Department of Fisheries and Oceans (DFO). Sanderson gave the boat owners an absolute discharge, saying that a "race-based" fishery unfairly advantaged Indians.

Under the heading "A Double Standard on Salmon," Stephen Hume wrote about the two cases in the *Vancouver Sun* on June 26, 2003:

> Let's get this straight—members of the Cheam band catch 40 fish to protest a closure they believe infringes their constitutionally guaranteed aboriginal rights and are immediately charged...
>
> But when 40 commercial fishermen take more than 5,000 fish to protest a closure they believe infringed their rights, a judge rules that they deserve an absolute discharge because the Indians have an unfair advantage in access to salmon. Now, just to put this in context, the commercial fleet already gets about 93 per cent of the total allowable catch. So all this resentment is over the five per cent that DFO sets aside for native Indians under its aboriginal fisheries strategy.[8]

Fisheries issues have proved no less challenging on Canada's East Coast. Donald Marshall, the Nova Scotia Mi'kmaq man who served eleven years in jail after being wrongly convicted of murder, was charged after his release from jail with catching 210 kilograms of eels in violation of federal fishing regulations. He lent his name to an Atlantic Coast fisheries case that tested the validity of 1760–1 Mi'kmaq treaties. In their 1999 ruling on the *R. v. Marshall* case, the Supreme Court of Canada decided that the Mi'kmaq treaties enjoyed constitutional protection. Acquitting Marshall, the court said, "would uphold the honour and integrity of the Crown." The ruling affirmed Aboriginal peoples' right to a moderate living from the Atlantic fishery, but it triggered more conflicts on that coast. In September 2000, Ottawa appointed former Ontario premier Bob Rae to mediate a dispute between Mi'kmaq of Burnt Church, New Brunswick, the union representing non-Native fishermen, and the Department of Fisheries and Oceans. The dispute centred on whether the department's limit on the number of lobster traps was justifiable. Both the Mi'kmaq and the department thought they were right.

Lawyer Thomas Isaac wrote about the dispute in the *Globe and Mail* on September 19, 2000. Government justification to override Aboriginal harvesting rights requires a compelling and substantive legislative objective, Isaac argued, such as the conservation of a natural resource. The Burnt Church Mi'kmaq's aim was to regulate their own fishing, but neither the court nor their treaty had given them this authority.

> Other observers have suggested that a resolution to the Burnt Church conflict could be found in replacing the 1760 treaty by negotiating a modern one. Ottawa tends to like the option of negotiating modern treaties, but First Nations that haven't yet exhausted other legal remedies may be reluctant to go this route. By turning too soon to negotiation, many First Nations believe they run the risk of fettering their rights.[9]

A 1974 Washington State court decision offers a possible direction in the substantial resolution of the Aboriginal fisheries issue in British Columbia and the rest of Canada. In that year, federal judge George H. Boldt heard a major case concerning the treaty rights of northwest tribal fishermen to harvest salmon and steelhead. The Boldt decision gave a half share of the annual catch to western Washington tribes who had signed treaties in 1854 and 1855. Over time, the commercial fishing industry and its political allies in the state capital had outmuscled the tribal fishery, and Boldt sought to honour federal promises and restore balance. The United States Supreme Court later upheld his allocation. For a decade after its handing down, Boldt's decision remained controversial. Thirty years on, it seems like nothing more than common sense. Many British Columbians like the Boldt formula, or at least the instrument.

For the last ten years, the global media have carried numerous stories about declining fisheries. According to many experts, the planet is in danger of being fished out. Most of the world's fishing areas and fish species are at or beyond their sustainable yield, and the power of modern trawlers to scoop up everything from salmon to sponges has alarmed policy makers everywhere. Of B.C.'s six salmon species—chinook, chum, coho, pink, sockeye, and steelhead—none is assured of survival.

While the Supreme Court of Canada seeks to balance competing interests by restricting an Aboriginal commercial fishery to those First Nations that traded in fish before colonization, federal policy is a political balancing act that seeks to placate Aboriginal, commercial, and sports fishers. Ironically, though, First Nations are finally getting a share of forest and fish opportunities just as corporations seek to replace B.C.'s forests with tree plantations and to supplant indigenous species of wild salmon with farmed fish.

Some First Nations support fish farming; most are strongly opposed. Both environmentalists and First Nations have expressed concern about farmed Atlantic salmon escaping and displacing the wild species indigenous to the Pacific Coast. When the Norwegian multinational Omega Salmon Group built a huge fish hatchery at Ocean Falls, B.C., the Heiltsuk First Nation fought the project. The Heiltsuk, who claim rights to 33,000 square kilometres of land and water in an area that includes the Omega fish-farm site, launched a lawsuit against the province and the company. In August 2003, the B.C. Supreme Court ruled that Omega's proposed project did not infringe on the Aboriginal rights of the Heiltsuk First Nation. The court said that the Heiltsuk could not veto the project. The court, however, could stop Omega if the company failed to fully "consult and accommodate" the Heiltsuk.

On May 5, 2004, Ottawa and Victoria jointly released an expert report, "Treaties and Transition," on what the West Coast fishery could look like after treaties are concluded.[10] The authors, B.C. resource economist Peter Pearse and Ottawa law professor Donald McRae, advocate the integration of the commercial, recreational, and Aboriginal fisheries. Their report states, "[A]ll sectors of the fishery should play an equal role in determining allowable catches and all... sectors within the commercial fishery [should] operate under the same rules." Pearse and McRae also predict that, after treaties, First Nations will take a third of any commercial catch.

Pearse and McRae begin this 2004 report by facing what they see as some hard facts:

> Prices for salmon declined for the ninth consecutive year. Sales of herring roe in Japan were the worst on record. Coastal communities suffered the closure of more processors. Recent shifts in exchange rates have cut prices across the board. And seafood producers in other fishing countries have been reorganizing themselves, increasing the competition in foreign markets.[11]

Change and uncertainty appear to be constants in the West Coast fishery, the report says, and government policies have contributed to that uncertainty. In the interests of conservation, governments and stakeholders should cooperate more. Pearse and McRae note that, in one decade, the value of the West Coast salmon catch fell by 80 per cent and the herring catch lost a third of its value.

Aboriginal fishers harvest everything from salmon to shellfish, the report says, but the Fraser River sockeye fishery is the most valuable part of the catch. Aboriginal people are well represented in the commercial fishery, too, according to Pearse and McRae with "27 per cent of the licences issued for commercial fishing in 2003."[12] Geoff Meggs, former editor of the United Fishermen and Allied Workers Union newspaper and author of a book on salmon, counts himself a skeptic: "That 27 per cent Indian share of the commercial fishery is worthless under today's management regime, which allows most harvesters a few days of access a year, at most. It's 27 per cent of nothing."[13] Of course, what Pearse and McRae propose does constitute a new regime.

Notwithstanding the Nisga'a view that fish entitlements are a treaty right, Chapter 8 of their treaty describes their allocations as a percentage of the total allowable catch under federal and provincial laws and licences, which means the Nisga'a do not govern the fishery. People opposed to an Aboriginal preference in the fisheries and fearful of further reductions in the portions of a shrinking pie attacked the kind of harvest agreement contained in the Nisga'a treaty, but Pearse and McRae think those critics were mistaken:

> In our view, the concern that Harvest Agreements provide better rights than those of existing commercial fishers should be addressed not by reducing one group's rights but by ensuring that all groups have rights appropriate for the conduct of a fishery. The objective should be a fully integrated commercial fishery based on long-term security for all fishers. And in our view, the long-term rights provided by Harvest Agreements are well suited to commercial fisheries generally.[14]

The idea of individual quotas—something long opposed by most conservationists, who dislike the "privatization" of natural resources— may be timely, writer and fisheries expert Terry Glavin argued on the *Vancouver Sun's* editorial page on May 2, 2005: "In 1991, the halibut fleet agreed to an experimental system of individual quotas; now the season lasts all year, and the fishery is enormously profitable. Halibut stocks are healthy, and conservation concerns, such as the fleet's bycatch of troubled rockfish stocks, are being addressed in sensible ways."[15] Glavin contrasted this situation with that of the subsidized, overcapitalized salmon fleet chasing dwindling stocks. He suggested that individual quotas could facilitate equitable treaty deals by allowing Ottawa to purchase quotas that could then be transferred to First Nations. Like McRae and Pearse, Glavin believes the fishery needs clear rules that apply to everybody. Skeptics argue that privatizing fishery resources removes any public obligation to protect habitat, surely a concern for species at some risk of extinction. Nevertheless, Turning Point First Nations will support the Pearse and McRae regime so long as they have some access to commercial quotas.

Treaties cannot instantly fix federal mismanagement of the ocean fisheries, but the Boldt, Yukon, and Nisga'a experiences suggest that treaties can serve the ends of intersocietal accommodation, sustainable economies, and resource conservation. For a politically vulnerable Aboriginal population, a treaty guarantees some security of access to a resource. For non-Native fishers, a treaty provides legal certainty and clear rules for allocating harvests. For the general public, which worries about conservation, treaties offer a partial solution.

Pontiac's proclamation protected Indian hunting grounds. The spirit of that proclamation, if not the treaties it inspired, is accommodation, not assimilation; reconciliation rather than conquest. That is, or should now be, the Canadian way.

CHAPTER 10

THE NISGA'A REFERENDUM

THE NISGA'A NATION trod a long road to their treaty, persisting with this quest through federal indifference, provincial resistance, and the thick forests of paper planted by negotiators on all three sides.

Nisga'a chiefs first pressed their land question in 1885, when they met with Prime Minister John A. Macdonald. Two years later, the Nisga'a travelled to Victoria to advance their claims, but B.C. premier William Smithe rejected their petition. In 1913 the Nisga'a Land Committee unsuccessfully petitioned the British Privy Council, and in 1967, after decades of frustrated lobbying, the Nisga'a hired Vancouver lawyer Thomas Berger. Once the Supreme Court of Canada's 1973 *Calder* decision reopened the Aboriginal-title issue, the path forward became clearer. Formal negotiations with Canada began in 1976; the province finally joined the talks in 1990. On August 4, 1998, Nisga'a, provincial, and federal negotiators initialled the final agreement. On December 2, 1998, the eve of the government's debate on the Nisga'a treaty, New Democratic Party premier Glen Clark invited Nisga'a chief Joseph Gosnell to address the B.C. legislature. Late on April 22, 1999, the legislature ratified the treaty, 39 votes to 32. After intense debate, the House of Commons approved the treaty the following December.

The treaty that the First Nation's members ratified by a 70 per cent vote recognized Nisga'a ownership of 1,992 square kilometres of land—about 8 per cent of the nation's traditional territory—and guaranteed $190 million in capital to be transferred over fifteen years. The Nisga'a also received forestry, fishery, and wildlife resources. Significantly, their treaty described the jurisdictions, authorities, and rights of the Nisga'a, provisions that effectively enshrined the nation's law-making powers in the Canadian constitution. In return, the Nisga'a gave up their claim to over 90 per cent of their ancestral homeland and their exemption as Indians from taxation. As the province's first modern treaty, Chief Gosnell told the B.C. legislature, the Nisga'a agreement was a triumph for all British Columbians:

> In 1887, my ancestors made an epic journey from the Nass River here to Victoria's Inner Harbour. Determined to settle the land question, they were met by a premier who barred them from the legislature. He was blunt. Premier Smithe rejected all our aspirations to settle the land question. Then he made this pronouncement: "When the white man first came among you, you were little better than wild beasts of the field…" Like many colonists of the day, Premier Smithe did not know, or care to know, that the Nisga'a is an old nation, as old as any in Europe… We governed ourselves according to Ayuukhl Nisga'a, the code of our own strict and ancient laws of property ownership, succession, and civil order…
>
> To us, a treaty is a sacred instrument. It represents an understanding between distinct cultures and shows respect for each other's way of life. We know we are here for a long time together. A treaty stands as a symbol of high idealism in a divided world. That is why we have fought so long, and so hard.[1]

Yet the battle had not yet been won at that point. Following the legislature's approval of the Nisga'a pact, B.C.'s Liberal Opposition mounted a determined campaign to undo the treaty, first in the law courts, then in the court of public opinion. Their campaign was fuelled by classic colonial resentment of any affirmation of Aboriginal title or self-government. As Thomas Berger wrote on April 15, 2002, in the *Vancouver Sun*, "For the B.C. Liberals, the most controversial feature of the treaty was the provision for Nisga'a self-government, for Nisga'a lawmaking power over Nisga'a land, Nisga'a language, Nisga'a assets and Nisga'a people. They persisted in condemning this aspect of the Nisga'a treaty as 'race-based.'"[2]

Throughout the Opposition campaign, Gordon Campbell, then the B.C. Liberal leader, now B.C.'s premier, repeated a refrain made familiar by Melvin Smith: "For us now to recognize your right of self-government would be contrary to our principles. We don't believe in race-based institutions."[3] Campbell and the Liberals were in denial of the obvious fact that treaties have always been deals between self-governing political communities, a principle established by American and British courts long before British Columbia became a province.

In October 1998, after the Nisga'a treaty had been initialled but not yet ratified, Campbell and his legislative colleagues Geoff Plant and Mike de Jong mounted a court challenge to the treaty's constitutionality.[4] The Liberals also published a pamphlet explaining their resistance: "The Nisga'a Template: Facts the Government Isn't sharing—An Alternative Guide to the Proposed Nisga'a Treaty." The pamphlet began with the dubious assertion that the Nisga'a were the first "third order" government in Canada. Arguably, Yukon First Nations could claim that honour. However, the Liberals were correct that the Nisga'a had the country's first constitutionally protected self-government agreement. The pamphlet warned, "Unlike any municipal government, the Nisga'a will have paramount lawmaking powers in at least 14 areas, meaning that some Nisga'a laws will be legally superior to federal and provincial laws in the event of inconsistency or conflict."

The treaty did indeed make Nisga'a laws on Nisga'a lands paramount in the following areas:

- Nisga'a citizenship;
- Structure, administration, management, and operations of Nisga'a government;
- Nisga'a lands and assets;
- Regulation, licensing, and prohibition of businesses, professions, and trades;
- Preservation, promotion, and development of Nisga'a language and culture;
- Direct taxation of Nisga'a citizens;
- Adoption;
- Child and family services;
- Pre-school to Grade 12 education;
- Advanced education;
- Organization and structure of health care delivery;
- Authorization/licensing of "Aboriginal healers";
- Annual plans for the harvest and sale of fish and aquatic plants; and
- Nisga'a wildlife and migratory birds entitlements.

"Under the proposed treaty, non-Nisga'a residents will not have the right to vote for their local government," the Liberal pamphlet complained. "We believe that that is not only fundamentally wrong, but also unconstitutional." Campbell and Plant's attack on the Nisga'a treaty repeatedly included the charge that non-Nisga'a residents of the area might become victims of Nisga'a taxation without representation. Chief Gosnell patiently responded to this charge by pointing out that existing property owners in the Nisga'a territory were outside Nisga'a jurisdiction. In fact, the treaty gives the Nisga'a government no legal power to tax anybody other than Nisga'a citizens on Nisga'a lands.

In Ottawa, Preston Manning, then national leader of the Reform Party, declared that the Nisga'a treaty was "based on socialist economics and collective ownership of land and resources."[5] From Vancouver, former B.C. Liberal leader Gordon Gibson added the charge that Nisga'a citizens might become victims of their own government:

> Because most cash and resources in the [local] economy will flow through the Nisga'a government by virtue of the terms of the Treaty, people will be uncommonly dependent upon and beholden to that government. This dependence will not be merely for municipal-type services—roads, garbage and so on—but also for matters of intense and immediate importance to the individuals concerned, such as housing, social assistance and employment.[6]

Manning and Gibson asked Indians to believe that the ideology that had stolen their lands and devastated their communities could provide the cure for ills it had created. Monoculture might be biologically perilous, but its economic equivalent was the only way forward.

Nor were Aboriginal critics silent. Gitksan leader Neil Sterritt complained that, through their treaty, the Nisga'a had taken their tribal neighbours' land. "Although the Nisga'a have based their treaty negotiations on a claim to 100 per cent of the Nass watershed, their territory actually extends only to the area near the mouth of the Kinskuch River. In the period from 1968 to the present, the Nisga'a have not presented any credible evidence to support their claim north of the Kinskuch River area."[7]

On July 24, 2000, the B.C. Supreme Court dismissed the *Campbell* action, ruling that "after the assertion of sovereignty by the British Crown, and continuing to and after the time of Confederation, although the right of Aboriginal people to govern themselves was diminished, it was not extinguished. Any aboriginal right to self-govern-ment could be extinguished after Confederation and before 1982 by federal legislation, which plainly expressed that intention, or it could be replaced or modified by the negotiation of a treaty. Post-1982, such rights cannot be extinguished, but they may be defined [given content] in a treaty. The Nisga'a Final Agreement does the latter expressly."[8]

Campbell and Plant, while in Opposition, had promised to fight the case all the way to the Supreme Court of Canada. However, as premier and cabinet minister respectively after the Liberals came to power, they reconsidered. Plant, now B.C.'s attorney general, announced that, while his party had not shifted its thinking about Aboriginal self-government, the provincial government could not sue itself. Ironically, the *Campbell* decision was now the affirming law on self-government.

With further court action out of the question, the Liberals changed their tactics. Some opponents of the northern treaties had advocated public referenda as the way to stop them. Smith's old ministerial boss in the Social Credit government, Rafe Mair, had been using his CKNW radio program to talk up a provincial referendum on the Nisga'a treaty. On December 14, 1998, Mair said in an on-air editorial: "The Nisga'a treaty is bad in principle, and the refusal of a province-wide referendum [by the NDP government] is morally wrong and flies in the face of Canadian tradition of putting matters of profound social and political change to the public."[9] Gordon Campbell had made a referendum on the treaty one of his election promises, vowing to "give all British Columbians a say on the principles that should guide B.C.'s approach to treaty negotiations, through a one-time, province-wide referendum, within a year." In 1998, reconciliation was not on Campbell's agenda.

Although a B.C. Treaty Commission spokesperson warned that treaties are about rights, not voter preferences, the B.C. Liberals pressed ahead. After the landslide Liberal victory in the 2001 provincial election, Plant crafted a set of referendum questions for the public.

On October 18, 2001, in a meeting of the Aboriginal Law Section of the Canadian Bar Association, he defended the referendum idea.[10] He agreed that treaty making could be a consensual process, but said that each party inevitably had its own objectives. The referendum would give the public a voice in setting a vision the provincial government could bring to the table, he argued, a necessary step as the government would be bound by the results. Plant intended the referendum to give the B.C. government negotiators mandates for what he called "workable, fair and affordable treaties."

The Liberals had made other treaty-related promises before the election, including their intentions to fast-track treaty talks; conclude fair treaty settlements; negotiate a delegated, municipal style of self-government with any First Nation that wanted to move beyond the failed *Indian Act*, and seek clear direction from the Supreme Court of Canada on constitutional questions regarding Aboriginal self-government. If the three parties at the treaty table continued to articulate diametrically opposed principles on self-government, Plant said, then the province could always refer the question to the Supreme Court. "But," the attorney general added, "in my opinion, the Nisga'a chapter 11 [on self-government] should not be in the treaty, and that will not happen in future. You cannot have self-government for 150 people, 50 per cent of whom are FAS or FAE."[11] (Plant was referring to Fetal Alcohol Syndrome [FAS] and the less visible, but still serious, health condition Fetal Alcohol Effect [FAE], both of which result from heavy alcohol consumption by the victim's mother while pregnant. Both FAS and FAE have plagued Aboriginal communities since colonial times.)

After public hearings by an all-Liberal legislative committee, Plant chose eight "treaty principles" for the public to endorse, or not, in the referendum:

1. Private property should not be expropriated for treaty settlements.

2. The terms and conditions of leases and licences should be respected; fair compensation for unavoidable disruption of commercial interests should be ensured.

3. Hunting, fishing, and recreational opportunities on Crown land should be ensured for all British Columbians.

4. Parks and protected areas should be maintained for the use and benefit of all British Columbians.

5. Province-wide standards of resource management and environmental protection should continue to apply.

6. Aboriginal self-government should have the characteristics of local government, with powers delegated from Canada and British Columbia.

7. Treaties should include mechanisms for harmonizing land-use planning between Aboriginal governments and neighbouring local governments.

8. The existing tax exemptions for Aboriginal people should be phased out.

Several of these eight principles were blatantly designed to elicit public support for Plant's own previously stated positions. Others reflected well-established public policy. For example, the previous New Democrat government's pamphlet on the Nisga'a treaty had included the following as negotiating principles:

· Tax exemptions for Aboriginal people will be phased out.
· Private land is not on the table.
· Treaties must be affordable to B.C. taxpayers.
· The Canadian constitution, Charter of Rights and Freedoms, and the Criminal Code will apply equally to all British Columbians— Aboriginal and non-Aboriginal alike.
· Public roads and access to treaty lands for recreational use will be guaranteed.

· Province-wide resource-management and environmental standards will apply.[12]

Given the apparent cross-party agreement on Questions 1, 5, 7, and 8, why did the Liberals raise them at all? For treaty negotiators, all these issues were far more complex and nuanced than the simplistic phrasing of the referendum questions allowed. Of the eight questions in Plant's list, the most significant concerned the self-government issue. This was perhaps the only question Plant really cared about, the one that would send a message to the Nisga'a and all other First Nations.

I offered my views about the wording of that question in an opinion piece for the *Vancouver Sun* on March 6, 2002.[13] To me, the way it was framed left the prospective voter in the dark about differing federal, Aboriginal, and provincial points of view. Without this crucial information, how could anyone be expected to participate knowledgeably in a public debate? The voter's only options were to answer yes or no to the referendum questions. Were a voter to "write in" some discussion of the complexities of an issue, his or her thoughts would count as a spoiled ballot. Many lawyers, columnists, and other experts on Aboriginal policy penned thoughtful pieces on the constitutional, legal, and political aspects of the referendum's self-government question. My perspective was based on my personal experience in the Yukon.

Looking around a Yukon Indian village decades ago, one might have observed log cabins, some outhouses, and a dirt road. There were no sewer systems, no stoplights, and no parking meters. One saw nothing resembling the usual southern municipal infrastructure. Clearly, the villagers did not live in their houses the way most Canadians do. In the boreal forest and on the lakes nearby, people hunted and fished. For centuries, their vital interests had resided in the lands and waters of their traditional territory—not in the dirt roads of their village.

Understanding this may help one understand why B.C.'s referendum question on Aboriginal government was a mistake.

In the land-claim and self-government agreements negotiated by Yukon Aboriginal communities, villagers retained title to a percentage of these traditional lands and gained mineral rights and significant governmental powers. Their treaty also guaranteed them co-management of fish and game resources and a voice in land-use planning decisions on public lands in their territory. We think of these areas as falling under provincial jurisdiction—and that's the problem. Plant had sworn that B.C. would never agree to another Nisga'a-type self-government agreement within a treaty. The province was not prepared to allow First Nations anything more than delegated local-government powers, and the Liberals planned to use the referendum to seek public affirmation of this "delegated municipal" bargaining position.

This had been the policy of conservative political forces in British Columbia since Melvin Smith invented the "Municipal Indian" in *Our Home or Native Land.* In Smith's vision for B.C., the Municipal Indian would have practically no land. She might dream of salmon nets, healing circles, and self-determination, but Smith wanted her kept busy with garbage collection and dog bylaws. For Smith, the Municipal Indian was the assimilationist solution to the problems of Indian demands for self-government, and he preferred not to use the term "First Nations."

The Liberal legislative committee that authored the first draft of the referendum questions heard submissions on the scope and source of First Nation government but chose to ignore them. First Nations are clearly not municipalities. They derive their powers from treaties and from federal and international law, not from provincial governments. Aboriginal leaders argue that they have an "inherent right" to self-government; Section 35 of the constitution acknowledges this right. Treaties are negotiated with Indian nations, not Indian municipalities. Indian governments are what U.S. Supreme Court chief justice John

Marshall called "domestic, dependent nations." But they have never been the creatures of provincial law.

Having failed to resolve the question in First Ministers Conferences from 1983 to 1987, Canadian premiers had spent most of 1992 wrestling with the question of Aboriginal self-government. At Charlottetown, Prince Edward Island, the First Ministers Conference eventually agreed on a proposal that resembled the Yukon model. The B.C. government's referendum proposal looked like a giant step backwards from the little progress that had been so painfully achieved. The complexities of the Aboriginal-governance question certainly warranted serious debate. Plant had almost conceded this point when he told Vancouver talk-show host Mair on October 29, 2001, that on self-government "there are differences of vision between us and First Nations and the federal government that may take a generation before they're resolved."[14]

Norman Spector, former advisor to provincial Social Credit and federal Conservative governments, published an opinion piece in the *Vancouver Sun* on April 22, 2002. "Campbell prefers to keep us ignorant about our history and the law," Spector wrote. "Had he been serious about the referendum, he would have crafted better questions. He would also have established 'yes' and 'no' committees, and provided funding to each. Most important, he'd have explained how the referendum would speed up, not retard, the treaty process."[15]

As if in response to Spector, the *National Post* published an opinion piece by Campbell in its April 27 edition. His government's referendum was intended only to ask if Aboriginal self-government should behave like municipal government, Campbell said.

> The model we propose is democratically accountable to the people under its jurisdiction—including non-aboriginals. It is equitable, in terms of ensuring all Canadians are treated equally, regardless of where they live. And it is the model for which we are seeking British Columbians' support... The determination

of public views is the very point of this initiative. By including the public, we can revitalize negotiations, and build a future that harmonizes the needs of all British Columbians: aboriginal and non-aboriginal alike.[16]

Earlier in April, also writing in the *Vancouver Sun,* Thomas Berger made what may be the most eloquent statement of his long career as an advocate for aboriginal rights.[17] "I won't be voting in Premier Campbell's referendum," Berger wrote. "Why? Because Campbell had already heard the answer to his self-government question. The July 2000 *Campbell* decision gave Campbell and Plant a clear answer: 'No.' Canada's First Nations do have an inherent right to self-government. That is the law. The *Campbell* case decided the issue. So why have the referendum?"[18]

Great statesmen know when to admit they are wrong, Berger argued. In 1969 Prime Minister Trudeau had rejected Aboriginal rights, but he rethought his position after the 1973 Nisga'a decision. By 1983 Trudeau was helping to construct the future of Aboriginal self-government. How contrary was the provincial premier's attitude towards the court, Berger remarked:

> What Mr. Campbell is, in effect, saying is: "We don't care what the Constitution says about your rights. We don't care that the courts have affirmed your rights. We are going to ask the people of the province to give us a mandate to treat your rights as non-existent. As far as we are concerned, you have no inherent right of self-government." This is a stance that should trouble us all.[19]

B.C.'s First Nations Summit decided, like Berger, to boycott the referendum, not least because they had not been consulted on the content of the questions. Some First Nations saw the referendum as a clear demonstration of bad faith and were ready to demand that the province withdraw from treaty negotiations. Others considered pressing this point by demanding that Ottawa return to purely bilateral negotiations with Aboriginal parties. A few nations considered litigating every provincially authorized incursion on lands or resources within their traditional territories.

In opposition, the B.C. Liberals had lost the legislative vote on the Nisga'a treaty, and then they lost the *Campbell* case. But as the incumbent provincial government, they won their 2002 referendum. By the May 15 deadline for the mail-in referendum, it transpired that a large majority of voters supported them. Of the 763,000 people who voted in the referendum, 87.25 per cent endorsed Plant's position on Question 6. Thirty-five per cent of the electorate had spoken. The rest remained mute.

Once the referendum was over, people wondered if there would be any more treaties in British Columbia. The courts could order the government to "consult and accommodate" and to negotiate interim measures and go to the treaty tables, but these steps alone would not automatically lead to treaty settlements. Without provincial government support, there would be no more treaties in British Columbia.

Of all the squabbles involved in the B.C. treaty process, none has drummed up more noise than the government's decision to conduct the 2002 referendum. The province justified its actions by arguing it had received wide public support for tough new mandates in treaty negotiations with First Nations. Those mandates were designed to lock provincial negotiators into fixed positions on certain critical issues. Although the B.C. government has since equivocated away from that hard posture, the polarization of opinion and bad feelings resulting from the referendum soured negotiations for months afterwards and strained consultations between the province and First Nations.

▼

CHAPTER 11

CONSULTATION

ALMOST TO THE END of the twentieth century, provincial consultation with Aboriginal communities remained a minimum-necessary exercise. Consultation sat at the bottom of a scale of interaction that extended upwards through interim measures—which provide for the management of lands and resources under claim during the treaty-negotiation process—to treaties themselves. Six years into modern treaty negotiations in British Columbia, the provincial government still had no coordinated approach to consultation. To a large extent, each department and agency had its own process. Some did a good job; some did not.

This situation prevailed despite the Supreme Court's 1990 *Sparrow* ruling, which provided a framework for government–First Nations consultation. The "*Sparrow* test" would supposedly allow an official to assess how a proposed action might infringe on an Aboriginal right and whether that infringement was justifiable. Specifically, the *Sparrow* test poses three questions:

1. Is there an existing Aboriginal right?

2. Does the proposed government activity interfere with the right because it:
   a. is unreasonable,
   b. imposes undue hardship, or
   c. prevents the holder of the right from the preferred means of exercising it?

3. If the right is interfered with, is the interference justified because there is a valid legislative objective, such as conservation?

These three questions suggested others. After meeting conservation needs, has government recognized a harvesting priority for First Nations? Also, in cases of expropriation, has the compensation been fair? Finally, did the government consult the First Nation concerned?

Even with the Supreme Court's guidance in this decision, consultation by the province of British Columbia remained a relatively undisciplined and uncoordinated affair until at least December 1997, when the court handed down its *Delgamuukw* decision. Then, on September 29, 1998, British Columbia released government-wide consultation guidelines that recognized the need to consult with First Nations on Aboriginal rights and title and gave detailed instructions for assessing title questions.

The *Delgamuukw* case began as an Aboriginal-title matter brought by the Gitksan and Wet'suwet'en people of northwest B.C. against the provincial government. The Supreme Court examined issues relating to the source of Aboriginal title but reached no conclusion on the specific claims. The court did state, however, that lands subject to Aboriginal title had an inescapable economic component, and that therefore governments must consult with First Nations when contemplating resource developments.

As the B.C. government's new consultation principles noted, *Delgamuukw* demanded more than "mere consultation"; in some cases First Nations' consent would be required. While the nature and scope of consultation might vary depending on specific circumstances, the fundamental principles of consultation remained the same for both Aboriginal-rights and Aboriginal-title issues. Consultation efforts must be made in good faith with the intention of substantially addressing a First Nation's concerns about the infringement.

The 1998 B.C. government guidelines included the following principles, which the guidelines stated should "apply to all consultation efforts, and should be followed throughout the entire process of consultation":[1]

- As the onus to prove Aboriginal title lies with First Nations, staff must not explicitly or implicitly confirm the existence of Aboriginal title when consulting with First Nations.
- The province must assess the likelihood of Aboriginal rights and title prior to land or resource decisions concerning Crown-land activities.
- Consultation should be carried out as early as possible in decision making.
- Consultation is the responsibility of the Crown.
- Statutory decision makers should take steps to ensure consultation activities contain proper representation from all potentially affected Aboriginal groups.

Not surprisingly, the guidelines caused some bureaucratic consternation. For example, provincial officials were now required to "assess the likelihood of Aboriginal rights and title prior to land or resource decisions," but under no circumstances were they to "explicitly or implicitly confirm the existence of Aboriginal title." Even for a senior manager, this could prove a tricky dance to perform with a straight face. Moreover, the guidelines did not address capacity building, interim measures, or linkages to treaty negotiations, all three of which lay along a continuum of reasonable expectations for effective consultation.

First Nations liked the *Delgamuukw* ruling on Aboriginal title, but not so much the requirement to "prove" Aboriginal title by demonstrating continuous and exclusive occupancy prior to 1846.[2] And governments could still, with justification, infringe on Aboriginal title; justification could include "compelling and substantial legislative objectives" such as land settlement, economic development, and environmental protection. However, governments now might have to compensate First Nations for any such infringements of their title.

While the 2002 debate about the forthcoming British Columbia referendum occupied legislators, opinion makers, and the media, another round in the Aboriginal-rights struggle wound up in the courts. In cases involving the Haida Nation and the Taku River Tlingit, the B.C. Court of Appeal handed down decisions that profoundly changed perceptions about the duty of both government and industry to consult with and accommodate First Nations about resource projects.

In the January 2002 *Taku River Tlingit First Nation v. Ringstad et al.* decision, the Court of Appeal ruled that the province must consult the Taku River Tlingit prior to issuing a project permit to Redfern Resources Limited to reopen the Tulsequah Chief Mine in northwestern British Columbia.[3] The Tlingit had sued initially because they believed a B.C. official had short-circuited the assessment process and obtained ministerial signatures on a certificate of approval.[4] The lower court set aside the Aboriginal-title issue for trial. At judicial review, the judge quashed the certificate and sent the matter back to the provincial administration. Redfern Resources and the province appealed, with the province arguing it had no obligation to consult a First Nation unless and until that nation had proved its Aboriginal rights or title. The Court of Appeal, in a majority decision, wrote only about the Indian-law issue, saying that the province had a duty to consult and accommodate the First Nation. The court said: "To say, as the Crown does here, that establishment of the aboriginal rights or title in court proceedings is required before consultation is required, would effectively end any prospect of meaningful negotiation or settlement of aboriginal land claims."[5]

In a later assessment, Art Pape, lawyer for the Tlingit, explained that this outcome was unexpected: "An environmental assessment clearly established that the Telsequah Chief mine access road would negatively impact the habitat of wildlife on which the Taku River Tlingit depend and, therefore, the sustainability of their community. It was early days for the treaty process, so no land-use planning process had gotten underway." The decision meant the Crown's fiduciary obligation to First Nations is both substantive and procedural, Pape said.[6]

Randal Kaardal, Redfern's lawyer, agreed that the judgment was a surprise, but for different reasons: "The appeal court did not make any finding of fault by Redfern or the province in respect to the environmental-assessment process. They found only that the matter must go to the minister, who has a fiduciary duty to consult the Taku River Tlingit." In Kaardal's view, what would be required in future was the same kind of "due diligence" as would be normal in the corporate world.[7]

In their February 2002 ruling on the *Haida* case, the B.C. Court of Appeal found that Victoria and the forestry giant Weyerhaeuser did not properly consult the Council of the Haida Nation when the government renewed a company tree-farm licence on Haida Gwaii (the Queen Charlotte Islands). The court stated that the defendants owed a legally enforceable duty to consult, at least until a treaty or a court had determined Haida title and rights.

This duty flowed from the Haida's claim to Aboriginal title in Haida Gwaii, the court said. Everybody knew the Haida Nation wanted to protect old-growth forests from clear-cutting, and the tree-farm licences in question covered an area with old-growth red cedar, a species that had cultural significance to the Haida Nation. In his ruling, Justice Douglas Lambert wrote:

> Consultation requirements ought to be calibrated according to
> the nature and extent of Aboriginal interests and the severity

of the proposed Crown action in order to provide incentives to the parties to reach negotiated agreements. In most cases, the duty requires the Crown to make good faith efforts to negotiate an agreement with the First Nation in question that translates Aboriginal interests adversely affected by the proposed Crown action into binding Aboriginal or treaty rights.[8]

Although the court did not invalidate the licence renewal, it did impose the obligation to consult and to accommodate the rights of the Haida Nation on both government and corporations, in this case, Weyerhaeuser.[9] The company's lawyer, John Hunter, later expressed his opinion that the *Haida* and *Taku* cases, by covering forestry and mining, represented the full range of issues involving resources and Aboriginal law.[10]

Globe and Mail columnist Jeffrey Simpson disliked the *Haida* and *Taku* decisions. Before, Simpson said, the law had been clear. Now governments and companies had to accommodate First Nations' interests. "If aboriginals don't have a veto over projects on land they claim but courts insist their interests must be 'accommodated,' just what rights do they have? A right that walks, talks and smells like a veto is probably a veto, even if the courts did not use that word."[11]

Simpson complained that the Taku River Tlingit had not only been consulted but also had agreed with elements of Redfern's plans. The only thing the Tlingit objected to was the road; with no road, there would be no mine. "The issue of consultation as discussion or consent amounting to a veto might be rendered passé if negotiated settlements were falling into place," Simpson wrote. "But negotiations in B.C. are stalled pending a referendum. Even before they stalled, they moved at a pace that made snails seem like Northern Dancer."[12] Regrettably, the whole matter would now end up in the Supreme Court, Simpson predicted—rightly, as it turned out.

Weyerhaeuser, for its part, hoped the Haida decision would revitalize stalled treaty negotiations. For the company, the Haida grievances represented a potentially costly problem that government alone could solve. In the meantime, Weyerhaeuser did what it could to mend relations, accommodating the Haida in interesting new ways. For example, the company sponsored "The Spirit of Haida Gwaii," a fund-raising concert for the Bill Reid Foundation. One of the performers was Haida Nation president Guujaaw singing a war song.

At a May 2002 conference organized by the Pacific Business and Law Institute, corporate and government officials gathered to consider the implications of the court's rulings in *Taku* and *Haida*.[13] Obviously, the decisions mandated new relationships among governments, corporations, and First Nations. Yet Weyerhaeuser lawyer Hunter noted that, according to the *Delgamuukw* ruling, an Aboriginal group must prove title, and governments can infringe with "justification."[14] Consultation was a necessary step towards such justification because Aboriginal title is interest in land and, hence, an encumbrance on Crown title.

Aboriginal advocate Louise Mandell cited the *St. Catherine's Milling* case, which held that the right of the province to a beneficial interest in the lands within its borders is available as a source of revenue whenever the burden of Aboriginal title has been removed by treaty or extinguishment. That means, Mandell said, that if Aboriginal title has not been "disencumbered" (which it has not in B.C. generally), such lands may not be available to the province as a source of revenue.[15] Perhaps, then, provincial Crown title is a burden on Aboriginal title, not the reverse.

The courts do not seem to understand that the B.C. claims process is not rights-based but political, Denis de Keruzec, a lawyer in the federal Treaty Negotiation Office, complained at the conference. In practical terms, there had not yet been much practical guidance from the courts on consultation or accommodation, so Canada's approach to accommodation was policy driven. De Keruzec reported that the federal government had been thinking about re-engineering the treaty process to include legislated consultation codes;

federal/provincial/First Nation accords; and co-management and resource-revenue sharing, both of which meant consultation and accommodation.[16]

In October 2002, after considering the implications of the *Haida* and *Taku* decisions, British Columbia published a new Provincial Policy on Consultation with First Nations.[17] The 1998 guidelines were substantially revised, but the new document reiterated the previous four-step approach to consultation:

· Considering Aboriginal interests;
· Considering the impact of decisions;
· Considering justification of likely infringements; and
· Reaching workable accommodations or negotiating a resolution.

Victoria's policy had two purposes: to ensure that decision makers both considered Aboriginal interests and accommodated their legitimate concerns. The policy also contained what must have sounded like a lawyerly warning to First Nations: "The Crown has an obligation to consider evidence of aboriginal interests that is available on reasonable enquiry, when assessing the soundness of those interests." In other words, show us your fish traps, traplines, and culturally modified trees, or else.

In the section called Operational Guidelines, the government implicitly acknowledged some of the problems with the 1998 policy: "It is essential that consultation activities are well defined and carried out efficiently, prior to approvals/authorizations being made."[18] As people were starting to understand it, the consultation obligation derived from the trust relationship between the provincial government and First Nations, particularly when the two parties are actively engaged in treaty negotiations to settle Aboriginal rights and title issues. The Haida decision required both consultation and accommodation. Short of a treaty, the most common form of accommodation would be the "interim measure."

Lawyers had much to say about the new policy—and with good reason. First Nations Summit leader Edward John, a lawyer himself, thought the new consultation policy was written in contemplation of litigation: "Basically, what the Attorney General has stated is that the government of British Columbia is tired of 'getting its head slammed against the wall.' Consequently, all negotiations will be 'with prejudice.' We can live with that but let's deal with it up front and not through the back doors."[19]

The *Sparrow* and *Delgamuukw* judgments clarified the nature and scope of consultation but did not provide the last word on the subject. *Delgamuukw* referred to the forms of consultation, which ranged from occasional or "mere consultation," the lowest form, to a "veto," the highest form. Aboriginal-law expert Thomas Isaac noted at the January 27, 2003, Cordilleran Roundup mining conference that most cases required something deeper than mere consultation. He argued that the *Delgamuukw* principles were "strikingly similar to administrative-law principles respecting the duty to be fair." Based on his readings of the court's rulings, Isaac saw two elements to successful consultation: the process and the decision. Nowadays, Crown agents are actively engaged with Aboriginal people all over the country, and this engagement likely includes a degree of accommodation and mitigation. Governments must take Aboriginal concerns seriously; that means consultation processes need to be fair, reasonable, and transparent. "Consultation is legally correct, but it is also good business," Isaac said. Business, he said, needed to understand that "incremental" certainty might be all that was possible.[20]

In its May 2004 report, "The British Columbia Treaty Process: A Road Map for Further Progress," the Business Council of British Columbia questioned whether consultation could increase certainty.[21] The courts had created more uncertainty, the report said, not less. Worse, there was no consensus on either the issues or the means to resolve them. The report also expressed the council's fear that the environment for consultation was in danger of becoming "a Catch-22 scenario." Among its grievances, it listed the following:

- The B.C. government requires business to meet the requirements of the provincial consultation policy.
- The federal government does not have a policy on First Nation consultation and accommodation.
- First Nations tend to believe that only the Crown can properly consult with them and will often advise private businesses attempting to engage in a dialogue that "this is not consultation."
- Line ministries have differing interpretations on the implementation of the B.C. consultation policy. Federal departments are usually unclear and inconsistent about roles and responsibilities.
- More than one First Nation sometimes claims the same territories. At times this means that if a proponent deals with one First Nation, another nation will refuse to talk to the company.[22]

The Business Council report suggested that the interested parties should establish an agreed-upon model for consultation and accommodation. It also called for a universally recognized, adequately funded body to oversee consultation and accommodation processes.[23]

When the Supreme Court of Canada ruled on both the *Haida* and the *Taku* cases in November 2004, the response of the business community was largely positive, not least because the nine judges removed the obligation on the part of industry to consult. The court gave favourable mention to British Columbia's consultation policy, but it flatly rejected the province's legal argument that it owed First Nations no duty to consult. Governments have "a duty to consult" Aboriginal peoples and accommodate their interests, the court said in *Haida*. Good-faith consultation was a two-way process, the decision observed. Government consultations must be meaningful, but Aboriginal peoples cannot obstruct the process, and Aboriginal claimants do not have a veto over development projects. The Crown is honour bound to balance societal and Aboriginal interests. "More hard bargaining will not offend an aboriginal people's right to be consulted," the judges found.

British Columbia's lawyers had repeated to the Supreme Court the line that First Nations should prove their claims before the province was required to accommodate their interests, but the court saw that this might leave Aboriginal peoples with only "denuded" lands and resources.[24] However, the obligation to consult did vary with the seriousness of the Aboriginal claim: "A dubious or peripheral claim may attract a mere duty of notice."[25] In the *Haida* case, the court found that Victoria had not adequately consulted the *Haida*. In the *Taku* case, the judges concluded the province's process was "adequate." As always, the court urged the parties to negotiate resolutions to their issues.

Somehow, the solution to one problem always seems to produce a fresh problem. Responding to the numerous new requests for consultations has proved onerous, particularly for small First Nations that don't have the capacity to respond to the many consultation documents spewing from the fax machine onto the floor of their band offices. One senior provincial negotiator has suggested the solution to this dilemma is to "go straight to accommodation."[26] And as often as not, accommodation means "interim measures."

CHAPTER 12

RENTED CERTAINTY

Interim Measures

ALTHOUGH THE B.C. Treaty Commission process has produced no treaties, it has generated hundreds of interim measures. Indeed, interim measures may be the most concrete product of the ongoing government negotiations with Aboriginal communities. This fact poses profound questions for the treaty-making process.

Interim measures agreements (IMAs) are supposed to provide for the management of lands and resources under claim by First Nations during the treaty-negotiation process, so that each party's interests are protected. In practice, an interim measure might be designed either to expedite the delivery of a service or program or to provide some defined economic benefit to the members of a First Nation, in exchange for allowing some forestry or other development to occur on their traditional territory. Some negotiators see IMAs as an opportunity to experiment with new accommodation or treaty-settlement models. Others see them as building blocks towards self-government. Some negotiators, however, view IMAs merely as distractions or diversions created by cynical governments who have no genuine interest in settling land or self-government questions.

Even though the 1991 B.C. Claims Task Force report imagined that treaties in the province might take only a few years to complete, it was clear that, during the start-up period of negotiations, the three parties would need to balance competing interests. The task force's preferred method for achieving this balance was the interim measure—"interim" referring to the duration of treaty negotiations. Fairness required that governments first give proper notice to First Nations about proposed developments in tribal territories. Following this "notice," negotiation of an interim measures agreement could begin. The task force observed that interim measures had the potential for wide land- and marine-resource-management impacts, and that IMAs might also be used to help solve difficult issues between the parties. Task force recommendation Number 16 urged that "the parties negotiate interim measures agreements before or during the treaty negotiations when an interest is being affected which could undermine the process." But the task force failed to anticipate that an interim measure might have negative consequences for the success of treaty negotiations.

Interim measures promised to work best as mutually beneficial agreements en route to a treaty, helping to facilitate negotiations by building good relations and trust between the parties. However, serious questions subsequently arose as to whether such measures ought to be used in cases where the treaty process was floundering or approached as an alternative to treaties themselves. Ideally, negotiators could design interim measures so that First Nations received some benefits of reconciliation well in advance of a final treaty. In exchange, the First Nation usually acceded to a particular development on the lands it claimed. However, if treaties were not imminent and interim measures became an end unto themselves, First Nations might have reason to be concerned. If, through an interim measure, the province obtained access to strategically important resource lands while the First Nation received inadequate compensation, this might fatally undermine the tribe's bargaining position at treaty tables.

In the early 1990s, several B.C. departments and agencies started negotiating interim measures. Often, these were "fire fighting" exercises in response to civil disobedience such as a First Nation road blockade. Rarely did the province approach these crisis-driven negotiations with a clear picture of what it was prepared to give or what it wanted to get. Worse, these interim measures tended to have little connection with the treaty process. Following several unhappy experiences with "all give and no get" deals, the province became reluctant to participate in such negotiations, particularly as its partner in the treaty process, the federal government, was not prepared to share either costs or associated risks.

John Walsh, B.C.'s deputy minister of Aboriginal affairs during the early days of treaty negotiations, described the situation's imperfections. During this period, both the Mike Harcourt and the Glen Clark New Democratic Party governments used interim measures to address long-standing issues between the province and First Nations that were outside the treaty process. Some of these were negotiated prior to the formal establishment of the treaty process or before a particular group elected to go into the process. In most cases, no provincial politician or bureaucrat even met with the groups involved. According to Walsh, "the problems festered and then became public issues that negatively affected the white man's economy, never mind the legitimate, now court-defined aboriginal interests."[1]

Following the 1997 *Delgamuukw* decision, First Nations in B.C. began to demand more interim measures, and the potential for land and resource conflict grew. The province became interested both in accelerating treaty settlements and in negotiating interim measures that were more focused. The federal government had irritated Victoria by joining the First Nation lobby for more interim measures, and provincial officials insisted that Ottawa should share costs and risks on the basis already agreed for treaty making. Several other factors had dampened the province's initial enthusiasm for interim measures: blank mandates, the blunt tools available to provincial negotiators, and inappropriate linkages to unrelated issues. For example, Victoria sometimes felt pressured to cover the costs of removing road block- ades set up to protest federal failures to address Aboriginal-title issues on lands slated for development, while Ottawa stood on the sidelines. Senior bureaucrats believed the province needed a new approach. In 1998 B.C. stated that its interest in interim measures would be based on four objectives: settling treaties, meeting legal obligations, facilitat- ing resource developments, and giving First Nations opportunities in land- and resource-management planning. Hereafter, the province proposed to negotiate two types of interim measure:

1. Social/economic benefit—or program—arrangements.
2. Treaty-related measures (TRMs).

The social/economic arrangements closely resembled the by-now- familiar interim agreements between Victoria and First Nations. These agreements could convey measurable benefits to First Nations to facilitate land and resource developments, major social programs, or strategic provincial initiatives. Such arrangements would be available to all First Nations in British Columbia, whether or not they were involved in the treaty process.

TRMs, a completely new instrument, were to be tripartite, federally cost-shared deals. Previously, First Nations had negotiated provincial interim measures and federal interim measures separately. TRMs would simultaneously commit all three parties at treaty tables.

On March 26, 1999, as chief negotiators for the federal and provincial governments, Jay Kaufman and I signed "Principles for Cost-Sharing Treaty-Related Measures." Within six months of our starting negotiations, both Ottawa and Victoria had endorsed the TRM accord. Under the new accord, matching funds for TRMs would come from the federal government, and First Nations would need to agree that any TRM be counted against the value of an eventual treaty settlement. TRMs might involve:

· Land set-asides or land banking;
· Protection measures on lands identified for settlement;
· Acquisition of fee-simple lands (from willing sellers) for inclusion in treaty settlement;
· First Nation participation in land, resource, park-planning and management regimes; or
· Cash and asset transfers to First Nations for treaty-settlement benefit sharing.

Although tied to potential treaties, TRMs would not challenge existing jurisdictional arrangements. Negotiators could make TRMs time-limited or link them to the completion of a final agreement. The hope was that TRMs would expedite treaty negotiations by creating advantageous economic, social, environmental, and governmental benefits for First Nations, guaranteed by both federal and provincial governments. The provisions of a TRM could be included in the final treaty-settlement package, form the basis of a substantive provision to be included in the final agreement, or facilitate the process of negotiating and concluding a treaty. To encourage progress, TRMs were to be implemented as negotiations proceeded. The more advanced the negotiations, the larger the TRM governments would consider.

Very reluctantly in the beginning, a few B.C. First Nations agreed that TRMs should form a component or "down payment" on their final treaty. By then, some nations had come to view interim measures as preferable to a land-selection treaty. One chief joked that he imagined his nation's settlement consisting of an infinite number of interim measures; for him, TRMs seemed to threaten "closure." Another chief attacked TRMs as "merely a manipulative public relations technique to paint Aboriginal Nations and peoples as greedy and unreasonable."[2] There was also trepidation among provincial negotiators, some of whom feared that a more disciplined approach to interim measures might further decrease the chances for treaty agreements.

The B.C. Treaty Commission had early on published calls for a more "incremental" approach to treaty making. TRMs appeared to be a good example of both the commission's concept of "incrementalism" and the kind of "accommodation" specified by the judges in the *Haida* and *Taku* court cases. Moreover, since the province's position on self-government made treaty making more difficult during and after the 2002 referendum, incrementalism became an art of the possible. However, incrementalism without end would be quite another thing. Without treaties, there would still be no final reconciliation of Crown and Aboriginal title.

The courts had not provided much direction for the negotiators of interim measures. However, the possibility remained that judges might one day identify existing interim measures, even TRMs, as guideposts for defining the meaning of "Aboriginal title" or "workable accommodations." Such judicial determination would be a high-risk alternative to treaty negotiations for First Nations. And if treaty negotiations maintained their plodding pace, interim measures might become the only practical product of the treaty process. In that event, First Nations needed to be especially careful not to undermine either their Aboriginal rights or their Aboriginal title in quickly negotiated interim agreements.

ONE ABORIGINAL ADVOCATE has argued that interim measures can accomplish only two things: preserving the honour of the Crown and satisfying the consultation requirement.[3] All interim measures agreements, this advocate suggests, should therefore explicitly acknowledge that the benefits they provide to First Nations constitute only partial compensation. Furthermore, the advocate proposes, interim measures should always leave unsettled the questions of whether or not the agreed-upon project is a valid legislative objective and whether or not the First Nation involved has Aboriginal title and Aboriginal rights.

Dozens of TRMs have been negotiated in British Columbia since 1999. Unfortunately, however, although the federal and provincial governments have been happy to fund planning TRMs, they have balked at signing land or resource TRMs, which means these tools have not been employed as originally intended.

Just prior to the 2001 election in British Columbia, the New Democrat government and a coalition of coastal First Nations known as Turning Point signed a General Protocol Agreement. Under the terms of the protocol, the province and the First Nations agreed, among other objectives, to identify certain geographical areas for permanent protection. The signatory coastal First Nations included the Haida Nation (Old Masset and Skidegate Councils), Gitga'at First Nation (Hartley Bay), Haisla Nation (Kitamaat Village), Heiltsuk Nation (Bella Bella), Kitasoo/Xaixais First Nation (Klemtu), Metlakatla First Nation, and Wuikinuxv First Nation (Rivers Inlet).

Turning Point First Nations were seeking sustainable economic opportunities in forestry, fisheries, and tourism. Previously, these groups had suffered from government policies and economic constraints that limited their access to business opportunities in the forestry sector. These missed opportunities included access to timber, tenure structures, capital, capacity building, and marketing strategies. The Turning Point coalition assists its partner First Nations in forestry sector negotiations. It also provides fish and aquatic resources through several separate initiatives. Turning Point does not negotiate treaties or manage social programs.

From the beginning, Turning Point advisor Garry Wouters agreed that interim measures should avoid definitions of Aboriginal title and rights, and this approach reflects current thinking among coastal First Nations. Since the appeal court's decision in *Haida*, First Nations' lawyers usually advise that interim measures be described as partial compensation or "accommodation" of the Aboriginal interest, rather than simply existing "without prejudice" to those interests, the phrase commonly used in pre-*Haida* interim measures. The new wording reflects the emerging reality of incrementally negotiating Aboriginal rights and title.

But could such "incremental certainty" with interim measures be a dead end? Could First Nations find themselves with their Aboriginal rights and title only partially recognized once the province has achieved all the "certainty" it needs to alienate their lands? And what might be the legal implications of this situation? First Nations are wrestling with exactly these questions.

At the "Treaty Negotiations: Key Questions" conference on April 16, 2003, at the Morris J. Wosk Centre for Dialogue in Vancouver, one of the four key questions was: "Can interim measures become 'permanent,' and should this change the way negotiators approach these agreements?"

Some negotiators see interim measures as important tools for building trust relationships and providing concrete benefits to the parties during years of treaty talks.[4] The Haida Nation's lawyer, Louise Mandell, told the conference that court rulings in consultation cases might serve as tools for the creation of new forms of interim measures. Others offered the view that interim measures are a distraction.

Turning Point's Garry Wouters told the assembled group that the term "interim measures" should be redefined. First Nation negotiators had formerly agreed to interim measures that were "without prejudice" as to final agreement language, and now that the courts had called on governments to consult and accommodate First Nations, Crown negotiators would surely demand that any payment under an interim measure amounted to a down payment on the final treaty.

Wouters went on to suggest that treaty making, as envisioned by the Royal Commission on Aboriginal Peoples, involves the creation of sustainable and healthy communities: in other words, the rebuilding of First Nations governments. If interim measures are used to establish appropriate building blocks, then such arrangements should allow both the Crown and First Nations to experiment with new strategic alliances. However, Wouters warned that negotiating an interim measure or a treaty with a single First Nation, especially a small one with limited capacity for governance, can be counterproductive. Interim measures should create strategic alliances, start strategic planning, and build intergovernmental relationships or legitimacy.

Lawyer Thomas Isaac told the Key Questions conference that he did not see a role for interim measures in the treaty process: "Although there is a reconciliation aspect to treaties, when you look at the interim measures that are actually working, they possess three key factors: accommodation, consultation and some form of capacity building." These factors form part of many agreements right across the country, both inside and outside the treaty process, Isaac said, and they should be standard in any government proposal to Aboriginal peoples, to signal respectful approaches to Aboriginal rights. Although treaties have been sold in British Columbia as the central means of achieving "certainty," Isaac continued, this could also be achieved through a more comprehensive approach to Aboriginal rights: "If treaties were the only tool at our disposal, then certainty would be an elusive goal for this province for a long time to come. I posit that, at present, certainty can be commenced and achieved without treaties, and the Supreme Court of Canada has been expressly clear on that point... There are numerous examples of governments taking a proactive stance to formulating practical approaches, which are not necessarily all about treaties. These examples represent real possibilities and optimism for the future." Across the country, Isaac said, governments are urging the mining and forest industries to consult with and accommodate First Nations, and Canada does not need a treaty process to facilitate this. "I conceive of interim measures as being part of an overall strategy incorporating accommodation, consultation, reasonableness, common sense and good business sense."

Lawyer Michael Hudson, who works with the federal Treaty Negotiation Office in British Columbia, was a member of the three-party working group that, prompted by the B.C. Treaty Commission, issued a report in May 2002 entitled "Improving the Treaty Process."

The report acknowledged that incremental approaches to treaties were liable to have varying significance for different parties. Nevertheless, the report proposed, treaties could be negotiated over time by means of a series of agreements, each of which was implemented as it was negotiated. Interim measures and other incremental approaches offered a "safe space" that could encourage innovative thinking and creative solutions, Hudson told the Key Questions conference, something impossible when crafting a "constitutional" document like a treaty. However, he warned that advocates of interim measures or other incremental approaches should not regard them as a panacea for the B.C. treaty process.

According to chief provincial negotiator Doug Caul, treaty making in B.C. has turned out to be far more complicated than the 1991 task force report imagined. One-third of B.C. First Nations have yet to join the process, Caul told conference participants. On the other hand, interim measures agreements had become more practical. British Columbia now knew what it was bringing to the table and what it wanted from it: namely, predictability and stability. Caul suggested that treaty making and interim measures should not be seen as an either-or proposition: "We need interim measures, and we need treaty negotiations, and they need to be linked. I see interim measures as an important part of the long-term vision. We would have a much better chance of success in a treaty negotiation where we have built capacity and built the relationships through interim measures."

The late Randy Brant, a Mohawk, was at the time of the Key Questions conference the senior negotiator for B.C. Hydro. Gary Yabsley is a constitutionalist and legal advisor to First Nations. Brant and Yabsley had sat on opposite sides of the table while negotiating economic measures between Hydro and First Nations, and both addressed the conference. Brant pointed to the practicalities of Hydro's relationships with Aboriginal communities; B.C. Hydro's work affected 500 of the 1,600 Indian reserves in British Columbia and 150 of the 197 bands. Could an interim measure take the place of a treaty? Brant thought not. He continued, "Does it enhance the treaty? I don't know the answer to that, but it certainly enhances our relationship with First Nations in order for us to do business."

Yabsley, however, observed that the jargon of both treaty making and interim measures tended to hinder business communications, since industry customarily uses different terms for the economic tools and legal instruments discussed in negotiations with Aboriginal groups. Businesses want to be economically viable, Yabsley said, and they have no idea what Aboriginal title is: "If we talk to them about royalties and jobs, then we are speaking the same language. If we start calling some deal an interim measure, they question what we are talking about." This language gap inevitably raises concerns about certainty. In addition, Yabsley pointed out, "interimism" in the treaty process makes it hard for First Nations to calculate whether, at the end of the day, they would be better off with or without a treaty. For many of them, treaties represent uncertainty, not certainty. By comparison, the business deal, even an interim measure, gives First Nations something real and definite.

Jack Weisgerber, former provincial minister of Aboriginal affairs and now the province's appointee to the B.C. Treaty Commission, distinguished between interim measures tied to the treaty process and those that are not. Although the treaty commission had limited experience with the proposal for "incremental treaty making," Weisgerber told the conference, he could imagine "that a nation or group of nations might want to negotiate only natural-resource matters and leave things like governance to a later time, or vice versa, and those could be incremental in nature, but then there is some question as to whether they could, in fact, be constitutionally protected in a treaty that only deals with a limited number of topics."

Michael Hudson agreed with Weisgerber that an incremental approach can be a step towards a final treaty; however, Hudson asserted that, whether it was a permanent framework in the form of a sectoral treaty or a rented certainty for a fixed period of time, governments would always want a quid pro quo.

Lydia Hwitsum of the Cowichan Nation had different thoughts about quid pro quos. Hwitsum explained that First Nations have real concerns when governments come to the table with a secret settlement formula but cannot—will not—evaluate Aboriginal title, even though cost-sharing arrangements based on land values drive the bilateral discussions between Canada and British Columbia. "First Nations are not in a position of knowing how Canada and B.C. are accounting for the agreement and how it is impacting the value of Aboriginal title," Hwitsum said. "At some point, from a treaty perspective, if it is focused around this formula-driven process, we could hit the wall in terms of what percentage or amount of our settlement being contemplated by governments has been utilized."

Kathryn Teneese, chief negotiator for the Ktunaxa/Kinbasket Treaty Council in the Kootenay region of B.C., reminded conference participants that interim measures agreements are symbols of good faith. Remember, Teneese said, that First Nations are the only party to treaty negotiations with nothing to put on the table. First Nations have no power. "If a small nation is attempting to negotiate a treaty and somebody comes up with one great idea, it results in a distraction and one which poorer First Nations will explore because they don't have the ability to do anything else except to find out what the benefits are for them… We need to be able to see some benefits without being seen as giving too much."

Jim Aldridge, for twenty years a negotiator for the Nisga'a Nation, argued at the Key Questions conference that the negotiation of interim measures could be a "distraction" for treaty negotiators. A problem that might lend itself to quick resolution could become a huge aggravation, Aldridge said. "When we started on interim measures, what we meant by that was 'measures to be in place to protect the lands and resources of the Nisga'a Nation during the negotiations process.'

In other words, here we are negotiating while we are watching the trucks continue to take the timber out of the territory."

For Haida litigator Louise Mandell, interim measures offer a chance to experiment. For corporate lawyer Thomas Isaac, they provide an alternative route to certainty. Others see interim measures as the ultimate bait-and-switch game, giving industry and the province everything they want without the cost and controversy of a treaty. Around the Key Questions roundtable, the discussion on interim measures created interesting partnerships. Federal, provincial, and First Nation negotiators Caul, Hudson, and Teneese collectively argued for interim measures as an adjunct to treaty negotiations. Corporate and Aboriginal-rights lawyers Isaac and Aldridge felt that interim measures should be disconnected from the treaty process. Others agreed that the term is still poorly defined and inadequately understood. One thing is clear, however: interim measures might be an increment to treaty making, but they simply cannot function as an alternative to treaties in settling the historic land or governance questions in British Columbia.

V

CHAPTER 13

MANIPULATIVE MANDATES

DESPITE THE FORMALITIES of federal behaviour in treaty negotiations, there is something organic about the way government mandates evolve. As in the case of the numbered treaties, government negotiators at northern treaty tables in the 1970s arrived with land- and money-settlement formulas in mind. In the Yukon, the federal government tried to import the "extinguishment" of Aboriginal-rights language from the James Bay agreement. The Nisga'a treaty built on the taxation provision of the Yukon treaty.

The mandates that governments write to give direction to their negotiators follow a particular theory of modern treaty making, academic Douglas McArthur argues.[1] The theory holds that settlements should involve a negotiated exchange of existing undefined Aboriginal rights for a new set of specific treaty rights, including governance rights. Accordingly, modern treaties should be settled on an equitable basis. To governments, this means constructing their mandates around a per capita cash calculation, with the total value based on the number of members in the particular First Nation. For argument's sake, McArthur says, "every First Nation, when the land and capital are added, is going to receive approximately $90,000 per capita in [their] treaty. If a First Nation has more land, then they will receive less cash or vice versa—the more cash, the less land... It is not likely that government will accept that one First Nation's settlement might be worth $200,000 per capita and another might be worth $75,000 per capita."[2]

First Nations have often complained that government mandates rule the treaty process, and that, rather than promoting reconciliation, these mandates are designed to manipulate the Aboriginal parties at the negotiating table. On four occasions in 2002, 2003, and 2004, senior negotiators from all three parties in the B.C. Treaty Commission process, along with some legal experts and political leaders, assembled at Simon Fraser University's Morris J. Wosk Centre for Dialogue to discuss, among other issues, the problem of mandates. As the following excerpts from these dialogues demonstrate, the mandates question is something of a never-ending discussion.

Former chief federal negotiator Robin Dodson agreed that Ottawa's concept of a modern treaty is based on precedent. "The idea of land selection, the idea of the concurrent jurisdictions of law-making authority and the idea of involvement in management of traditional territories, if looked at conceptually, that is a kind of model."[3] Governments might consider variations on these concepts, but they are not prepared to consider completely different models. Precedent ought not to stifle creativity, however, says Grand Chief Edward John. When governments come to the table with a pre-conceived formula, that then becomes the treaty. "That is the argument we hear in [British Columbia], constantly. We can't give you a better deal than Nisga'a or the Yukon or James Bay. No one is talking about a better deal. We are talking about different deals and different kinds of arrangements."[4]

The 1991 B.C. Claims Task Force report recommended against a standard treaty-making formula, arguing instead for compensation based on past land and resource uses and the individual circumstances of each First Nation. But the current British Columbia treaty process requires that participating First Nations buy into the broad terms on which governments will settle. The Nisga'a, for example, accepted the evolving model, that of the Yukon treaty, with some improvement and variations. Without that precedent, Nisga'a treaty negotiations might not have been successful.

Because the pre-determined formulas for land and money settlements have never been made public, the mandates that corral First Nations into the process can seem quite manipulative. Cowichan chief Lydia Hwitsum links "cookie-cutter" mandates to bureaucratic cultures and contrasts that mindset with the "give and take" needed for effective negotiations.[5] Not surprisingly, according to a B.C. Treaty Commission report published in February 2002, the First Nations Summit views government mandates as "the primary obstacle to making progress in treaty negotiations."[6]

Federal negotiator Jim Barkwell agrees, in part. "Prescriptive mandates and excessive rigidity are enemies of interest-based agreements, while vision and principled flexibility are their friends," says Barkwell.[7] Lawyer Thomas Isaac, a former provincial negotiator, blames the mandate problem on governments' lack of vision, he said at the round-table.[8] Nisga'a negotiator Jim Aldridge disagreed. Governments do have a vision, Aldridge said: "According to that vision, aboriginal title is a burden, and we have to get rid of it; we want to get certainty; we want to get investment, and we want to do it for the cheapest possible cost with the least possible disruption to the status quo."[9]

Mandates fit into two categories, financial and policy, Jim Barkwell says. The financial category includes lands, resources, and other quantitative issues that lend themselves to traditional forms of positional bargaining; policy, or qualitative, questions are better worked out in interest-based negotiations. Financial mandates are usually prescriptive, Barkwell points out, meaning that governments will dictate limits to their negotiators' authority, although there may still be opportunities for "tailoring settlements to the table context—the ratio of land to cash, allocations of different species of fish, the ratio of timber-rich lands to less valuable but larger land quantums, and so on." Interest-based negotiating techniques may work better with qualitative policy matters.[10]

Lorne Brownsey, long a senior negotiator at both the federal and the provincial levels, thinks First Nations share some responsibility for prescriptive mandates or templates. When government negotiates one arrangement with First Nation A and a different arrangement with First Nation B, sometimes A will have ratification problems as a result, Brownsey says. This pushes governments towards common approaches and away from local solutions. Brownsey thinks a partial solution may come from bringing more politicians closer to the table: "When senior negotiators get isolated from policy makers, they are more likely to be handed prescriptive mandates."[11] As a senior negotiator, Robin Dodson said he spent as much time negotiating within the federal government for his mandates as he did negotiating across the table with representatives of First Nations and the province. In one case, a third set of negotiations required that he deal with stakeholders who could be affected by the outcome of the negotiations and who might influence whether or not the negotiated result would be ratified.[12]

Jim Barkwell argues also that First Nations do not always under-stand federal negotiators must deal not only with the parties at the table but also with the separate departments of the federal government: "The chain of command in the Department of Indian Affairs and other departments, Finance, Justice and Fisheries or Transport or Health, has to approve any significant moves at the table."[13]

Nisga'a negotiator Aldridge believes that prescribed departmental mandates relating to forestry, fish, cash, and land complicate nego-tiations for First Nations, because the secrecy around the land and financial mandates makes it impossible for negotiators to trade federal fish for provincial trees, or vice versa. Governments always have hidden mandates, Aldridge says: "I remember this comic strip when I was a kid. The husband comes home and asks, 'What's for supper?' and his wife says, 'You name it, and you can have it.' Husband says, 'Great, steak.' Wife: 'No.' Husband says, 'Turkey.' Wife, 'No.' Husband says, 'Wait a minute, you said if I name it I can have it.' Wife: 'You haven't named it yet.' That's what it felt like at the Nisga'a table."[14]

Barry Stuart remembers an occasion when he and Dave Joe were, respectively, the chief negotiators for the Yukon government and Yukon First Nations. Both men knew that Yukon elders would never sign an agreement that extinguished Aboriginal title on treaty lands, but federal negotiators had never before entered into a treaty without a blanket extinguishment clause. To outflank the federal team, the Yukoners had hired top constitutional experts, who so successfully blunted Ottawa's arguments that the emperor was left without any legal clothing. When Stuart asked if the federal government had a single reason for insisting on the extinguishment of Aboriginal title on lands in the treaty, an awkward silence was broken by a federal lawyer who suggested that, one day, the Supreme Court of Canada might find that Aboriginal title exempts the First Nation from the application of criminal law. To this preposterous statement, Dave Joe, a thoroughly respectable lawyer, replied: "That's a good thought, since most of my people are in jail, and the few of us here in this room are all out on day parole." When the laughter died down, the negotiations moved on.[15]

Maintaining positive interpersonal relationships is extremely valuable in a long-term negotiation process; difficult compromises are often influenced by the trust levels among the parties. In the Nisga'a talks, the interest-based technique Jim Barkwell valued most was a "hard on issues, soft on people" approach.[16] Barkwell feels that the complexities involved in treaty making can always be tempered by getting the right people in the right room: "Agreements are reached on behalf of larger political entities, but they are made by and between individuals, and succeed or fail primarily on that basis." The "right room" includes table factors, techniques, negotiation modes, and process principles. It is important to note that, at any one time in British Columbia, there might be no more than six tables at which the "right room" exists, because of a shortage of really skilled negotiators, or "closers."

NO TREATY HAS been concluded in Canada in the last thirty years until the "closers" and senior politicians have come to the table. Government structures can retard negotiations, but strong negotiations and attentive ministers can speed things up by tweaking and refreshing mandates. According to provincial negotiator Doug Caul, very senior negotiators always know how to creatively "read" their mandates; they see the possibilities of solutions, and they have a commitment to settling, as opposed to simply negotiating.[17]

Government ministries will need far more creativity in their mandates if they are to successfully address all the issues currently on the tables. Consider, for example, the critical issue of taxation. Section 87 of the *Indian Act* exempts Indians from taxation for money earned on-reserve. Generally, Canada does not charge first citizens income tax or sales, utility, gasoline, or tobacco tax for income earned or goods and services purchased on-reserve. This tax exemption stirs strong feelings. Some Aboriginal people see it as a right, but non-Aboriginal Canadians generally find it unfair. At the time this book was written, the Supreme Court had still not passed judgment on the question. The exemption will continue to be a hot political issue, especially as First Nations and the federal government contemplate the creation of new urban reserves.

The northern treaties and the Nisga'a treaty removed the tax exemption with a negotiated eight-year transition period for transaction taxes and a twelve-year phase-in for income tax. Ottawa bought out the tax exemption in the Yukon treaty but refused to do the same for the Nisga'a. Despite that precedent, First Nations entering negotiations may well decide to assess the monetary value of their current exemption and bargain hard to have Ottawa purchase it for a fair price.

Ottawa would also like First Nation governments to start collecting taxes or "own source" revenues. First Nations complain that federal

Finance will want commensurate "claw backs" of capital transfers in treaty settlements to offset the funds Aboriginal governments raise to pay for services to their members, and this is something federal treaty negotiators know will hamper the prospect for treaty settlements. A less "penny wise but pound foolish" policy might allow a First Nation to retain all its own source revenues until its community has achieved a Canadian standard of living. Mandate writers say they want to see Aboriginal people "get off welfare," but they seem reluctant to do what it takes to make that happen.

Manny Jules, former chief of the Kamloops Indian Band, has long supported the kind of financial independence that local taxation provides. The reserve at Kamloops is 13,355 hectares, but the Shuswap Nation recently bought an 18,000-hectare ranch that it plans to add to the Kamloops reserve. "This is what we have accomplished by buying the land using our own revenues," Jules says. "We effectively bypassed the 20-years-or-so land-claim process and resolved the matter between ourselves."[18]

In Douglas McArthur's view, Aboriginal self-government will never be credible until Aboriginal leaders take responsibility for not just property taxation but wealth and income taxes.[19] However, First Nations cannot exercise such responsibilities under current federal policy. Nor can they negotiate them at B.C. treaty tables, even though First Nations who signed the Yukon treaty can already collect income tax there.[20]

First Nations in Canada have good reasons for wanting to administer their own monies. In the United States, Indians have had to sue to collect over billions in trust funds held by the Department of the Interior.[21] Although Indians in the U.S. owned 1887 *Dawes Act* allotments, the U.S. government "retained title and generated income for the Indians from use of the land."[22] No complaint of this magnitude has so far reached the Canadian public's attention, although Alberta's Samson Cree First Nation is suing Ottawa for hundreds of millions of dollars in lost resource revenues. Some Alberta First Nations enjoy financial windfalls from oil wells on their reserve lands, but they are a minority. The Yukon treaty provides a measure of oil and gas-revenue sharing; it pools and shares those monies among the territory's First Nations. At B.C. treaty tables, First Nations will want to negotiate revenue-sharing agreements, and some will view these monies as "compensation" for historic grievances.

The question of compensation is another hot-button issue. The Yukon treaty openly describes the cash component of that settlement as "compensation," and the federal government seemed to have no objection to this language during negotiations.[23] It appears to have had second thoughts, however, and in the Nisga'a treaty compensation is called a "capital transfer."[24]

Fearful of both the complications and the expense involved in negotiating "compensation" for historic grievances, the British Columbia Treaty Commission process deliberately does not use the word. As chief federal negotiator Robin Dodson explained at the 2002 roundtable, the B.C. process differs from the one that produced the northern treaties in that it requires no proof of claim to title or rights: "We both come to the table, at least in the federal view, with our hands over our eyes and our hands over ears and our fist in our mouth."[25] Compensation arises only out of damages, Dodson said, and damages arise only out of an infringement of rights. Government will not negotiate compensation unless and until it acknowledges that rights exist.

Dodson's explanation astonished Chief Edward John: "We have been involved since the 1990s, and I have never heard anyone say this before. We always came to the table based on the fact that we are negotiating rights. Now you are telling me, after twelve years, we were fundamentally wrong in our approach."[26] John believes that Canadian courts have found that compensation is still an issue to be negotiated in any accommodation with First Nations.

In 2004 the Tsawwassen First Nation in B.C.'s Lower Mainland negotiated a $47-million deal with the Vancouver Port Authority. The

deal compensates the First Nation for decades of negative environmental and resource effects from the port development at Roberts
Bank, near their community. It also includes job and business opportunities for Tsawwassen members, as the port authority expands
its container-terminal operations in the area. Since the Tsawwassen
Nation is currently in treaty negotiations with the federal and provincial governments, this could set an important precedent in which a
First Nation gets both a treaty and a compensation package. Building
upon this precedent might be necessary to achieve reconciliation with
the Hul'qumi'num Treaty Group on Vancouver Island, which was
never compensated for the lands it lost to farms, forest companies,
and rail lines in the colonial period, and for whom there is now little
public land available for a treaty settlement.

In 2004 the B.C. Treaty Commission published a report stating
that treaty settlements would have "large net positive financial and
economic benefit for British Columbia."[27] According to the report,
the net financial benefit to British Columbia from treaties should be
nearly $5 billion. But such promises invite cynicism and encourage
opportunism, some commentators feel. Of the United States, historian
Felipe Fernández-Armesto writes, "Indian rights today usually means
the right to exploit gambling casinos, golf courses, and shopping
malls."[28] A May 6, 2004, story in the *New York Times* fed exactly this
kind of sneering: "The Congressional Committee on Government
Reform is concerned that financial giants like Trump are bankrolling suspect tribal groups in order to snare a piece of Indian gaming
industry."[29]

In contrast to American stories about the riches of tribal casinos,
Canadians are more used to hearing reports about Aboriginal poverty.[30] Assuming there are First Nations in British Columbia prepared
to accept the government's land-and-cash formula and other fairly
standard elements of recent treaties covering wildlife-management
agreements, taxation, and the application of the Charter of Rights and
Freedoms, how long would it take to get such a treaty? Robin Dodson

suggested the process could be completed in five years.[31] With the combined political will of the parties, determined negotiators could do it even faster.

SOME INSIDERS SUGGEST that the B.C. process may be more about building relationships than settling treaties. If so, it is surely an extraordinarily expensive way to do that, for all parties, and not a very successful one. The 1991 B.C. Claims Task Force report insisted that First Nations could negotiate with governments "on an equal footing" only if they had "adequate resources available to them." Yet 80 per cent of the funding the B.C. Treaty Commission provides to First Nations for negotiations comes as loans, repayable once a final agreement is reached. These loans now amount to hundreds of millions of dollars. Observers worry that some First Nations may have already borrowed more than they are likely to receive in their settlements. Moreover, if a First Nation drops out of the treaty process because it cannot accept the limitations of government mandates, it is supposed to immediately begin repaying the negotiating loans. Stó:lô Nation chief negotiator Dave Joe says this requirement creates an unequal relationship at the negotiating table: "Canada can use the process and begin to apply some not-too-subtle pressures upon First Nation clients."[32] In the current situation, high hopes about "equal footing" have become low-grade anxieties about the difficulties caused by uneven tables. Unless governments change their policy, negotiation loans might have to be repaid before treaties are signed.

Are government mandates really designed to get settlements? A federal Finance official once told me that treaties take so long because it is cheaper to negotiate than settle. A short-sighted view, to say the least. One retired mandarin complains that the processes set up to negotiate these agreements have "entrained a whole bunch of rent-seeking people, organizations and behaviours... We have capped the costs of the claims, but not of the negotiations."[33]

A September 2001 B.C. Treaty Commission review discussed the delays in treaty making. "The Treaty Commission does not negotiate treaties," explains the report.[34] Unfortunately, nor does anyone else. One way to examine the effectiveness of the current B.C. process is to do a product analysis. What exactly, by way of measurable benefits, has BCTC machinery produced for each of the parties?

· The federal government has admitted to using the treaty commission to diminish the frequency of road blockades and office occupations; in that sense, the treaty process has been a tool for managing the "Indian issue" in British Columbia.
· Without suffering the financial expense of settling any treaties or the time-consuming challenges of communicating the contents to the public, the provincial government might have achieved exactly what it wanted: hundreds of interim measures and accommodation agreements that reflect the government's primary interest in fostering economic development and improving the investment climate.
· First Nations have used government funding, it is often suggested, to build a "land-claims industry" that employs hundreds of consultants, lawyers, and negotiators. This industrial effect caused one First Nation lawyer to liken the treaty process to a fish farm. "We're all penned up and fed our little pellets," she complained. "We can look at the sky and dream our small-fry dreams, but most of us are going nowhere. Someday, someone may escape towards a treaty, but most can only dream."

Everybody gets something, but nobody gets treaties. If the people of Canada want treaties in British Columbia, then the treaty process needs an overhaul.

Every senior negotiator has experienced sitting in a community hall and listening to outpourings of anger, only to receive at the end of a long evening the heartfelt thanks of his audience for hearing them out.

Listening is the start of a relationship. Because negotiating is more about listening than talking, it is often a profound mutual learning experience. There is no better way to get to know organizations or their leaders than by facing them across a negotiating table.

In theory, interest-based bargaining seeks "win-win" outcomes through the discovery of shared interests, such as a common desire for the parties to establish a productive relationship. Practitioners see the technique as an improvement on traditional positional bargaining, in which two chief negotiators creep towards each other's positions, alternating moves in carefully choreographed steps. Interest-based bargaining involves cooperation; position-based bargaining is competitive, often achieving deals while ignoring underlying problems, according to critics. However, interest-based approaches run the danger of settling the easy issues while piling up "too hard to solve now" problems.

At the beginning of Yukon's interest-based treaty negotiations, the "too hard to solve" pile included the three key questions: land, money, and self-government. Despite five years of negotiations, those three "big ones" were still in the pile. Nevertheless, former Yukon government chief negotiator Barry Stuart insists that interest-based techniques enabled major breakthroughs in the Yukon negotiations. In a 2004 draft of a paper prepared for the federal justice department, he sketched out an ideal interest-based negotiation. First of all, "be prepared," Stuart argues. The preparation stages should bring all parties together to do what government mandates do not: namely, articulate a shared vision that will focus and drive negotiations. At this stage, parties should park their mandates, he says, because "fixed mandates entrench positions and expectations." Rather, the negotiators should try to design a process that leads to the desired product.

Engage a facilitator, Stuart goes on to suggest. Explore alternative negotiation processes, and appoint a panel of mediators at the outset. He affirms the necessity of strong negotiators, "free of pressures from the hierarchy and from consequences of actions they take that may jeopardize their future within a bureaucracy." These negotiators should also have ready access to key decision makers in departments and to political leaders. Inform the public of your activities from the beginning, Stuart says, and keep doing so throughout the negotiations.[35]

At the 2002 What Works conference, Chief Edward John stressed the negative impact of secret or hidden government mandates. "Be honest with First Nations and state what is being offered," said John. "For example, if it is $70,000 then state that and allow First Nations to take it or leave it or to negotiate."[36]

What might the public say about a general per capita treaty formula of $70,000 in land and cash value? Would the average citizen think $100,000 a fairer number? There has never been public discussion of a fixed per capita amount, nor of what First Nations believe might be just. "$100,000: Yes or No?" Now that would have been an interesting referendum question.

Government mandates satisfy the need to lure First Nations to the treaty tables, but they do not seem sufficient to forge expeditious settlements. Fixed mandates come from an appropriate desire to finalize agreements that are broadly equitable among First Nation signatories, but defensiveness and inflexibility smother the creativity needed to craft treaties that truly reconcile Canada, British Columbia, and individual Aboriginal communities. That First Nations must choose between the alternatives of accepting government treaty offers or continuing to exercise their Aboriginal rights as defined by the courts raises questions about whether federal and provincial administrations have as their objective fair settlements or just negotiations.

CHAPTER 14

MORE BROKEN PROMISES?

Implementation Issues

P**OLITICIANS ARE NOTORIOUS** for announcing
programs, passing bills, and signing agreements—
then losing interest. Assuming you could find a cabinet minister with
a long enough career, keeping him or her interested in a twenty-year-
long treaty process would be extraordinarily difficult. Getting the
minister to pay attention to a thirty-year implementation time frame
would be even harder. Yet implementation of treaties is a critical
issue. The northern treaties negotiated over the last three decades of
the twentieth century represent remarkable nation-building achieve-
ments for Canada. But if these agreements are not implemented as
negotiated, they risk becoming another sorry knot in a historic string
of broken treaty promises.

On February 14, 1995, the Yukon treaty and the final agreements
for the Champagne and Aishihik First Nations, the Teslin Tlingit
Council, the Vuntut Gwitchin First Nation, and the First Nation
of Nacho Nyak Dun took effect. All of these agreements included
implementation plans that identified the parties' obligations and the
time frames for meeting them. Among the obligations was a review at
the five-year period "to determine the adequacy of both the provisions
of the Final Agreement Implementation Plans and of the funding

provided under those Plans." For bureaucratic reasons, the five-year review of the self-government agreements was delayed, but the three parties did form a five-year Implementation Review Working Group (IRWG) in 1998, and that group began to review the dozens of specific obligations in the body of the treaty.

The IRWG's report covers the period from February 1995 to February 2000. The group observed enormous changes in Yukon during that time; many of these were very positive, particularly the emerging intergovernmental partnerships: "Although the Self-Government Agreements were not within the scope of the five-year review, the IRWG nevertheless believes it is important to note the very significant progress by First Nations in the transition from *Indian Act* bands to self-governing First Nations. This includes the establishment of new governance and administrative structures, development of enhanced financial management and accountability regimes, the enactment of critical legislation, and the successful negotiation of programs and services transfers and tax sharing agreements."[1]

First Nations have finite sums with which to operate. Especially in their structures of self-government, they can realize economies of scale by getting together, through either formal affiliations like tribal councils or informal associations with neighbouring First Nations, to share resources or the appointment of personnel such as coroners, judges, and so on.

The review group commented favourably on new administrative facilities constructed by the Champagne and Aishihik and the Vuntut Gwitchin First Nations, "which incorporate up-to-date technologies, through the careful management of program operations funding." Also found praiseworthy were the ongoing negotiation of tax collection, tax-sharing agreements, programs and services transfer agreements (PSTAs), and protocols to improve working relationships. Noting that Aboriginal employment in the Yukon government had reached 12 per cent, the group credited Yukon's First Nation Training Corps program, among others. At Indian and Northern Affairs Canada's regional office, 22 per cent of the workforce was Aboriginal by the time the report was published. The review also praised the management plans for the Nisutlin Delta National Wildlife Area and the Fishing Branch Ecological Reserve, the Vuntut National Park regime and territorial government, and First Nation cooperation in local renewable-resource councils.

Barry Stuart, Yukon's chief negotiator from 1985 to 1990, once likened the Yukon land-claim and self-government agreements for First Nations to "getting a brand-new Cadillac with no gas in the tank."[2] The review group acknowledged the continuing debate about the extent to which First Nations were responsible for their own implementation costs. Funding remained the major contentious issue. Lesley McCullough, a senior official with the Yukon government's Land Claims Secretariat, thinks that none of the three parties' negotiators had any idea of the true costs of implementing the agreements: "First Nations and the Yukon government negotiated their implementation agreements with Canada thinking it's not enough, but not realizing how much it wasn't enough." Like other Yukoners, McCullough is puzzled that Canada is willing to spend so much money negotiating agreements, but so little on implementing them. "First Nations are hampered by the lack of money and the corollary of lack of capacity, and that just colours everything."[3]

Since 1987, Tim Koepke has been the chief federal negotiator under contract to the Government of Canada for Yukon land-claim negotiations. Koepke agrees that funding disputes have been a problem: "One of the general recurring themes is 'The feds didn't give us enough money,' and I think every land claim settlement in Canada has heard that complaint."[4] Whether that is the reality or the perception is probably immaterial, Koepke says. "The formula financing, or the fiscal transfer agreements, provide for a five-year renewal and renegotiation and, needless to say, as five years comes up... First Nations are driving a much harder bargain based on the five-year experience as opposed to a five-year projection."

In his keynote address on November 12, 2003, at the Redefining Relationships conference in Ottawa on the implementation of northern land claims, Ed Schultz, grand chief of the Council of Yukon First Nations, argued that the problem is more than simply a matter of money. When Yukon First Nations look at challenges in areas like land, resources, self-government, and funding, they view these as a single community. Canada does not do that, Schultz said: "The problem today, as a community, and as a people, is that we see the whole picture. We see some of the shortcomings, some of the failures, some of the areas where we may need to put some more attention and work, based on the fact that we see the two agreements [on land claims and self-government] meshed together and implemented as one in the community. Canada's position, to be quite blunt about it, is that, 'No, we're not going to review the self-government components or any measure of the self-government agreement. We're only going to review the land-claims side of this agreement.'"[5] (Although the IRWG's report made much of the negotiations on programs and service transfer agreements, even by 2006 almost no substantial PSTA had been successfully negotiated.)

Schultz's concerns resemble those of Inuit leaders in Nunavut. The Inuit were among the first to the negotiating table, settling regional claims at Nunavik in 1975 and the Beaufort Sea in 1984. Inuit in the largest area, Nunavut, ratified an agreement in 1992. The Nunavut agreement made the Inuit, already proud Canadians, even prouder. However, serious issues have since arisen about implementing the settlement. These are well described in the unpublished 2003 paper "Inuit Self-Determination: Implementing the Nunavut Land Claims Agreement" by Terry Fenge, long-time advisor to Inuit leaders.[6] As Fenge points out, northerners might have been warned by the experience of the Alaska land-claims settlement, whose implementation was mired in years of costly litigation.

Responsibility for implementing the Inuit agreement belongs to the governments of Canada and Nunavut and to the Inuit, Fenge explains. The Inuit must maintain enrolment lists, invest compensation funds, and establish structures for managing land and resources, and they play important roles in public government "while, generally, pressing the national and territorial governments to live up to their responsibilities."

Article 37 of the Nunavut agreement creates a representative four-person panel to "oversee and provide direction on the implementation of the Agreement" and sets up a $4-million fund to help establish Inuit institutions. Article 37 states:

The plan shall:
- Provide those institutions with a degree of flexibility to allocate, re-allocate and manage funds within their budgets no less than that generally accorded to comparable agencies of Government, (and)
- Provide those institutions with sufficient financial and human resources to plan for and carry out the duties and responsibilities assigned to them in the Agreement in a professional manner with appropriate public involvement.

Article 37 obliges the federal and territorial governments and the Inuit to jointly implement the agreement. Even before the signing of the final agreement, the Inuit had started detailed planning. As Fenge points out, the eventual implementation plan, which specifies who does what and when, is almost as lengthy as the agreement itself.

At a general level, Fenge says in his paper, the Nunavut agreement was an obvious success. The new territorial government was at work by the time the agreement was signed, and Inuit values began to inform decision making at every level. The Nunavut government and Nunavut Tunngavik Incorporated (NTI), the Inuit political body responsible for implementing the treaty, are committed to healthy intergovernmental relations with Canada, the provinces, and the other two territories that "balance, and build upon, both the status of the Inuit of Nunavut as an aboriginal people of Canada and the jurisdictional competence and administrative capacity of the Government of Nunavut."

As with the Yukon treaty, the three parties in the Nunavut agreement appointed a panel to report on progress in implementation. In March 2000, the Nunavut Implementation Panel published an independent consultant's review of implementation over the first five years of the treaty. The consultants identified a number of concerns, among them:

· Lack of promised legislation by Ottawa to give further definition to the institutions of public government (Article 10);
· Lack of effort by the Government of Canada to achieve Inuit employment objectives within government (Article 23);
· Lack of progress in negotiating government-wide contracting procedures with the federal Treasury Board (Article 24);
· The expense to the Inuit, and the lack of preparedness by the Government of Canada, to negotiate Inuit impact and benefit agreements for national parks (Article 8); and
· Inequitable distribution of quotas for turbot in Hudson Bay and Davis Strait (Article 15).[7]

The review team found "a pattern of missed deadlines and slow starts, a lot of unproductive and extended discussions, backsliding on obligations, loss of corporate memory and capacity, and the consumption of resources without a full result."[8]

As Fenge observes, many of these problems still exist. Efforts begun in 2001 to improve the Nunavut Agreement Implementation Contract, including refinancing for public government institutions for the coming decade, from 2003 to 2013, have gone nowhere. "The Government of Canada, represented by a relatively junior civil servant from DIAND who failed to bring representatives of any other federal agencies to negotiations, approached the process with very modest intent, reflecting his narrow mandate," Fenge writes. "Renewing funding for the institutions of public government seemed the only issue of real interest, although complaints about the contractual status and legal enforceability of the implementation plan were often voiced."[9]

Although, as Fenge explains, the Nunavut agreement is alone among northern land-claims settlements in ensuring that the agreed plan to implement is legally enforceable, Ottawa has seemed uninterested in dealing with the principal proposals of either NTI or the Nunavut Territory. Every one of the agreement's problems could have been solved if the treaty's dispute-resolution process had worked; in general, both parties had agreed to be bound by the decision of an arbitration panel. But, in the face of conflicts, the federal government said it would "not be bound by decisions of the arbitration panel on financial matters and funding levels." As a result, not a single case has gone to the arbitration panels in the years since the settlement.

Finally, the Inuit asked the auditor general of Canada, Sheila Fraser, to look into the situation. Fraser examined the implementation of two northern treaties, the Gwich'in and the Nunavut, and in her annual report to Parliament in 2003, she devoted a whole chapter to northern issues. In it, she says:

> Our review of the work of the arbitration panels found that no cases had come before them since the claims were settled over 10 years ago. Yet disputes continue to remain unresolved. Therefore any belief that arbitration is there to resolve money-related disputes, and make the land claims work effectively, is an illusion.[10]

Fraser also found that, with the Gwich'in and the Nunavut treaties, "INAC's [Indian and Northern Affairs Canada] performance on both counts has left considerable room for improvement."[11]

THE AUDITOR GENERAL'S 2004 report addressed common concerns among northern treaty groups. Two kinds of implementation took longer than all others, she observed: money and dispute resolution. In fact, the two are connected. At the Redefining Relationships conference held in Ottawa in 2003, Nisga'a Nation representatives wondered aloud if the fiscal arrangements underpinning treaties were meant to enable sustainable tribal governments or simply minimize costs for the federal government.[12]

One example of unanticipated costs, the Nisga'a described, was the expense of drafting legislation and regulations. The Nisga'a First Nation was managing the enormous challenges of working with new jurisdictional and fiscal situations, the leaders reported, but people had not yet completed the transition from *Indian Act* thinking to recognizing the new Nisga'a authorities and responsibilities. The Nisga'a were learning how to be a self-governing community once more, and financial constraints were making the transition more difficult.

In a plenary session at the Redefining Relationships conference, Aboriginal-policy expert Andrew Gamble summed up the discussions on funding and fiscal relations. To nobody's surprise, inadequate funding was identified as the Number 1 issue plaguing northern treaty implementation. A "disconnect" in the negotiation of jurisdiction often frustrated the parties, because Indian and Northern Affairs was negotiating with a Finance ministry mandate, and the latter agency had little interest in, and no sympathy for, Aboriginal objectives. Also, those who negotiated agreements had no responsibility for their implementation. For example, some federal departments acted as if the Nisga'a treaty was a contract with Indian and Northern Affairs, not a covenant with Canada.

Every one of the northern treaty groups at the conference complained that Canada has not invested enough to meet its obligations under the agreements. Compounding this problem is Ottawa's reluctance to agree to a thorough review of the funding arrangements

Given that Canada has made "constitutional" commitments in these treaties, the government's hesitation about allowing either an independent review of implementation funding or an arbitration of funding disputes is deeply worrisome.

Gamble tabled his group's recommendations for Aboriginal groups trying to make treaties work:

· An adequate funding base at the outset is in everybody's interest.
· Meaningful periodic reviews should be scheduled, because groups may not know at the outset what is adequate.
· Clear, focused responsibilities for implementation on the federal, provincial, and territorial government sides should be set out.
· There should be better coordination and partnerships between governments, aimed at improving results within the parameters of available resources, including in-kind contributions, cost sharing, and joint initiatives.
· Greater access to own-source revenues—taxes and resource revenues— would help reduce Aboriginal dependence. This should include fiscal incentives, breaks on own-source revenue, and offsets in financing arrangements. A greater investment commitment by government in the transition period is needed, to build both the relationship and the capacity to make the agreement work. Government needs to be more flexible.
· There is an advantage in networking and in more collaboration among Aboriginal governments and claimant groups, because there are many common issues and a common cause.[13]

Lawyer Ron Doering, who chaired the Redefining Relationships conference's Legal Perspectives Working Group, presented some recommendations from his group at conference end. First, he suggested First Nations remind everybody in government that treaty settlements are with Canada, not a government department: "We don't sign treaties with INAC, we sign them with the Crown. That brings in the fiduciary duty; it brings in a much broader approach. It means that we can't get caught between departments, and parts of departments that don't get along. Our deals are with the Crown." Next, Doering called for new mediation or dispute-resolution procedures. Finally, he said his group felt a fundamental review of federal land-claims policy was long overdue.[14]

At the close of the Redefining Relationships conference, northern treaty groups resolved to form a coalition. All Aboriginal signatories had uncovered common problems of indifferent negotiations, poor federal coordination, dysfunctional dispute resolution, and inadequate funding. On March 24, 2004, northern leaders wrote to then prime minister Paul Martin:

> There is growing frustration with the Federal government's approach to implementation, and unmistakable signs that the original good will and hope generated with the signing of these agreements is being undermined. A coherent Federal policy on implementation of land claims agreements is required, and should be developed co-operatively with Aboriginal peoples. Federal agencies, particularly Indian and Northern Affairs Canada, take the view that agreements are successfully implemented if federal contractual commitments have been discharged in a way that withstands legal challenge. This is a minimalist view that prevents agreements from delivering to us the full range of rights and benefits we negotiated. Federal agencies have lost sight of the objectives of these agreements.[15]

The Department of Indian Affairs negotiated the Yukon, Inuit, and other northern treaties, and Parliament entrenched these agreements as appendices to the Canadian constitution. The Department of Finance, however, has chosen to take a nickel-and-dime approach in relation to implementation funding. In this, we experience an echo of the ancient misunderstanding between Indian Nations that saw historic treaties as sacred covenants and colonizers who viewed treaties as convenient short-term contracts. In order to reduce misunderstandings by implementing agencies, the objectives of treaty makers need to be clearly stated in the agreements. Dispute-resolution procedures should be tested during negotiation, so that when implementation issues arise there are well-understood mechanisms for resolving them. Most importantly, corporate responsibility for properly implementing treaties should be relocated to a central agency or a new minister of state. Better yet, the entire treaty-making operation, beginning with mandate setting, should move there. A central agency can better represent the government as the whole and reflect the political will of the prime minister of the day. Without that kind of commitment, the broken promises will continue to accumulate, and a generation of hard work by Aboriginal and government negotiators could unravel before our eyes.

REBUILDING NATIONS

Self-Government

ABORIGINAL SELF-GOVERNMENT has always been the fraternal twin to the collective ownership of tribal lands, and modern ideas about self-government are slowly replacing colonial-era thinking and the "wardship" notions of Canada's *Indian Act*. Aboriginal people see self-government as a constitutional right to a "third order" of government, alongside the federal and provincial orders. However, Canada's "inherent right" policy still treats that right as negotiable and, therefore, contingent. In 1992 Yukon First Nations became the first to negotiate "third order" self-government agreements. The self-government provisions of the Nisga'a treaty were the first to receive constitutional protection. Despite these developments, there remains a colonial element to public policies on Aboriginal government.

By 1995 the Canadian government's official position was that it supported the "inherent right to self-government" and recognized it as an existing Aboriginal right under Section 35 of the *Constitution Act, 1982*. A new federal policy announced, "The Aboriginal peoples of Canada have the right to govern themselves in relation to matters that are internal to their communities, integral to their unique cultures, identities, traditions, language and institutions, and with respect to their special relationship to lands and resources."[1]

In 1996 the Royal Commission on Aboriginal Peoples recommended financial support for the rebuilding of indigenous nations. The commission's report asserted that Aboriginal peoples maintained a right to govern themselves after colonization and that self-government had since evolved into a common law protected under Section 35.[2] Two years later, Ottawa released "Gathering Strength,"[3] a plan to carry out the commission's recommendations. The Canadian government wished to "reach practical arrangements on self government and to achieve harmonious and clear relationships among Aboriginal, federal and provincial jurisdictions,"[4] the plan said. The scope of self-government negotiations, Gathering Strength proposed, might include some or all of the following:

· Governing structures, internal constitutions, elections; and leadership-selection processes;
· Membership;
· Marriage;
· Adoption and child welfare;
· Aboriginal language, culture, and religion;
· Education;
· Health;
· Social services;
· Administration and enforcement of Aboriginal laws, and the creation of Aboriginal courts;
· Policing;
· Property rights, including succession and estates;
· Land management, including zoning; service fees;
· Land tenure and access; expropriation of Aboriginal land by Aboriginal governments;
· Natural-resources management;

- Agriculture;
- Hunting, fishing, and trapping on Aboriginal lands;
- Taxation: direct taxes and property taxes of members;
- Transfer and management of monies and group assets;
- Management of public works and infrastructure;
- Housing;
- Local transportation; and
- Licensing, regulation, and operation of businesses located on Aboriginal lands.

In negotiating these items, Ottawa anticipated the need to harmonize Aboriginal, provincial, and federal laws and established that "primary law-making authority" would remain with the federal and provincial governments. Areas where federal and provincial laws would remain paramount included:

- Divorce;
- Labour;
- Criminal law;
- Penitentiaries and parole;
- Environmental protection, assessment, and pollution prevention;
- Fisheries and migratory birds co-management; and
- Gaming and emergency preparedness.

Canadian sovereignty, defence, foreign affairs and Criminal Code matters were also off limits to First Nations.

Federal policy allows for self-government agreements to be protected in treaties, except that "the Government believes that the primary criterion for determining whether or not a matter should receive constitutional protection is whether it is a fundamental element of self-government that should bind future generations." Accordingly, a treaty might contain:

- A list of authorities or jurisdictions;
- A description of the relationships between Aboriginal, provincial, and federal laws;
- The geographic area covered by the Aboriginal laws; and
- Provisions establishing the legitimacy of the Aboriginal government and its accountability to its citizens.

At present, the right of Aboriginal people to govern themselves in matters "internal to their communities and integral to their unique cultures" operates under a concurrent-law framework, in which all federal, provincial, and Aboriginal laws apply unless and until a conflict between them arises.

British Columbia's New Democrat government in 1992 recognized the inherent right to self-government, while acknowledging that more detailed definitions of the concept would emerge during treaty negotiations. The original goal of its successor government, the B.C Liberal administration, was to prevent the creation of dozens of new governments with quasi-provincial powers. The source of self-government power is at the heart of the debate. For Aboriginal people, their power comes from the continued governance of their communities from the time before European colonization. Victoria initially took the view that federal or provincial governments should "delegate" any powers enjoyed by Aboriginal communities.

Aboriginal self-government agreements negotiated in treaties have constitutional protection under Section 35 of the constitution. However, according to the federal government, such protection is not automatic but depends on acceptance by the provincial government. Several court rulings have addressed the scope of Section 35 rights but so far have provided little guidance on intergovernmental relationships. The *Sparrow* and *Delgamuukw* decisions emphasized negotiation as the path to solving these complex questions, and the *Campbell* decision accepted that a limited right to self-government could be protected constitutionally. The Government of British Columbia has accepted only the limited rights of First Nations to manage their own affairs, including the right to tax, to pass laws on negotiated topics, to manage lands and natural resources, and to administer education, health, and welfare services.

Adding to the complexity of the debate is the fact that no two First Nations seek perfectly identical forms of self-government. Each First Nation approaches governance negotiations with a view to meeting the specific needs of its community. Therefore, the governance model proposed by the Tsawwassen might be quite different from that proposed by the Ktunaxa or the Maa-nulth. However, First Nations usually agree to be bound by laws of general application. Under this regime, Aboriginal governments might have significant powers limited only by paramount federal or provincial powers set out in the treaty.

On July 2, 2003, a group of B.C.-based experts assembled at Simon Fraser University's Wosk Centre for Dialogue for a roundtable discussion on the self-government issue entitled "Brainstorming Governance: Visions, Values and Structures." Senior government officials attending included Philip Steenkamp, then B.C. deputy minister for the Treaty Negotiations Office, and John Watson, at the time regional director general of Indian and Northern Affairs Canada. First Nation participants included Gerald Amos (Haisla), Kim Baird (Tsawwassen), Debra Hanuse ('Namgis), Sophie Pierre (Ktunaxa), Miles Richardson (Haida, and head of the B.C. Treaty Commission), and Neil Sterritt (Gitksan), who co-chaired the meeting with me. Rounding out the table were Jim Aldridge, lawyer and negotiator for the Nisga'a; Chris Kelly of the federal Treaty Negotiation Office; Murray Rankin, lawyer and former negotiator for the B.C. government; Lloyd Roberts of the B.C. Treaty Commission; Barry Stuart, former Yukon government negotiator and retired judge; former federal associate deputy minister Garry Wouters,[5] and special guest Stephen Cornell, director of the Udall Center for Studies in Public Policy at the University of Arizona and co-founder in 1987 of the Harvard Project on American Indian Economic Development, a highly influential long-term research project based at the John F. Kennedy School of Government.[6] The day-long discussion touched on five areas: jurisdiction or powers; institutions; size; finance; and intergovernmental relations.

Listening to a discussion of the jurisdiction issue is a bit like trying to watch the pea in a shell game. First Nations want powers that Victoria considers to be within provincial jurisdiction; Victoria wants First Nations limited to local-government powers. Ottawa considers First Nations a federal responsibility but will not let them have any powers opposed by Victoria. The roundtable group discussed several types of self-government, ranging from the nation-building model favoured by Aboriginal groups to the delegated municipal models promoted by the province. The 1986 *Sechelt Indian Band Self-Government Act*, which delegates municipal-type powers from both the federal and the provincial governments to the Sechelt, represents the best example of Victoria's preferred option. Most First Nations in Canada have firmly rejected the Sechelt model, however.

Of the forty-some tribal groups involved in the B.C. process, the Tsawwassen First Nation may be the closest to the final stages of negotiating a treaty, even though they have yet to settle the governance issue. "What I find frustrating with the current provincial position," Tsawwassen chief Kim Baird said, "is that the current model of government is permitted to expand its jurisdiction over First Nations issues and is not willing to recognize First Nations jurisdiction." First Nations naturally want at least what the Nisga'a have achieved, namely, the inclusion of their governmental powers in the text of the treaty. However, British Columbia still prefers that self-governance be covered in a separate accord.

"With all due respect, I don't think it is any of the province's business," said lawyer Aldridge, who insists only federal jurisdiction is involved. "As a matter of law, the province should have nothing to say about it at all." Indeed, Section 91 (24) of the old *British North America Act* had assigned constitutional responsibility for Indians to the federal government and, under that authority, Canada adopted the "inherent right" policy on Aboriginal self-government. A 1995 cabinet directive, however, required that negotiation and recognition of any "inherent" right depended on both federal and provincial approval.

Provincial deputy minister Steenkamp explained that the government wanted to balance its objective of certainty after treaty with flexible governance arrangements. Jurisdiction was one thing, political accountability another. John Watson added that federal policy supporting the inherent right to self-government had some caveats. Both the Charter of Rights and Freedoms and the Criminal Code would apply to self-governing First Nations, and the province had to be involved in any discussion of provincial powers such as health and education, Watson said.

Chief treaty commissioner Richardson asked the strategic question about exactly what threshold of power a First Nation needed for good government: "That is a crucial question for us, especially in B.C., where we have this seemingly intractable difference over source of authority. Is it totally delegated, is it totally stand-alone, and what is the threshold in between those that would enable good governance? Is it the Yukon example, is it Sechelt, is it Nisga'a or is it something else?" Remarkably, ten years into negotiations, even the head of the treaty commission had not found closure on this central question.

The other four issues examined by the roundtable—institutions, size, finance, and intergovernmental relations—proved easier to grasp, but all were connected in some way to the jurisdiction question.

Garry Wouters, who was partly responsible for Gathering Strength, the federal response to the *Report of the Royal Commission on Aboriginal Peoples*, has developed firm ideas about the "toolbox" needed to build First Nation institutions of good government. Wouters posed a series of questions a First Nation might ask itself in planning for self-government:

- Do we have the tools, in public policy and in First Nations policy, to allow for law making that will build institutional structures for separation of powers, checks and balances, dispute resolution and citizen engagement?
- Do we have the legitimacy and the ways and means to garner support from the community and make sure that what we design, within the community, has a cultural match?
- Do we have community support and cultural identity as part of our toolbox prior to working towards building good governance?
- Does the First Nation have both the capacity and the political will?
- Do we have appropriate size where size is required to make good programs?
- Can we build a professional public service?
- Can we undertake strategic planning in a way that builds cooperation among the three levels of government?

Former Gitksan-Wet'suwet'en Tribal Council president Neil Sterritt, who penned the 2002 *First Nations Governance Handbook*,[7] commented that treaty negotiations often involve idealizing structures based on former traditional systems. Miles Richardson added that it is hard to create a new government based on a half-remembered or poorly envisioned design. For this reason, Sterritt said, "Experience suggests that the government system used to negotiate a treaty may also be the system that most contributes to successful implementation." Rather than invoking idealized traditional structures, negotiations should aim to produce workable institutions, especially if First Nations want to create modern versions of ancient models.

Having endured many bad experiences with the federal government and with education and judicial institutions, Yukon First Nations had determined they would not use the dominant society's models for their tribal governments. According to Barry Stuart, however, the fourteen First Nations in the Yukon did not fully appreciate how fundamental the changes would need to be to make the transition out of Western-based systems. Now, in the aftermath of land-claims settlements, Yukon First Nations are having difficult conversations internally about what to do. "If you take one structure out and don't do any work on developing the capacity and skills to institute a new structure, the changes sadly fall far short of expectations," Stuart said.

"Governance capacity affects the treaty process at two stages: the negotiation stage and during implementation," Sterritt commented. "Many of us on the Aboriginal side of the treaty table blame the governments for blocking progress. However, if we genuinely want a treaty, we have a shared responsibility to examine our strengths and, more importantly, our weaknesses. But we hide our weaknesses, and keep them hidden and unexamined behind the 'buckskin curtain'."

American expert Stephen Cornell offered two observations about institutions. "When we talk about rules and how decisions are made," he said, "we're into designing governing institutions. Two questions seem to me to be crucial here: Who is the 'self' in self-governance? What form should self-governance take?"

These are two very different questions, Cornell continued. The first addresses issues of legitimacy and allegiance: Do people feel loyalty to their First Nation, to the tribal council, or to the larger Aboriginal society? Of these three, which government ought to have authority, and over what? How should power be distributed between a village and a regional authority? Only the Aboriginal members of these political units can legitimately decide these questions. Cornell's second question addresses the issue of effectiveness—that is, of who can best deliver particular services to the community. For example, "tribal communities need to decide whether the band, the tribal council, or a larger regional authority would best provide a public school system," he said. The authors of any constitution face these kinds of questions. For example, Canada is the only country in the Western world to have no national minister of education. Long ago,

B.C. made parking a municipal matter and hunting a provincial one. Likewise, a First Nation village might want to regulate hunting in its territory but contract out parking services. The community has to decide the best way to do things for itself.

Cornell went on to illustrate the difference between the "delegated municipal powers" model and the "nation-building" approach he advocates. For him, nation building involves reconstructing Aboriginal communities from the bottom up, according to their own agendas for reassuming substantive decision making over their lives. But in Canada, as in the United States, the federal government has tended to approach Aboriginal self-government with a focus on administrative activities. "It's a form of administrative subcontracting," Cornell argued, "in which bureaucrats in provincial or federal capitals allow indigenous nations to run the administrative show at the local level, while the big decisions still get made elsewhere."

The bottom-up approach to nation building can work even with the drafting of legislation. Barry Stuart pointed to his work with the Carcross-Tagish First Nation to incorporate that community's stories into the law-making process. "Most of our laws tell you what you can't do, without providing any reason… why you can't do it. They just say, "Thou shall not do X, and if you do X, you will be punished." The intention of Carcross-Tagish First Nation is to select stories that illustrate the consequences of various actions. In their vision of legislation, anyone should be able to pick up a law and see it exemplified in a story. In family law, for example, a person could read a story relevant to their specific responsibility as a mother, a sister, an uncle, or a father. Following the story itself, the legislation will define the moral and provide a description of the primary principles and values that can be read into the story. In this way, the legislation sets out processes that are compatible with underlying community principles and values. Sophie Pierre said this was how the Ktunaxa Nation developed its child-and-family-services agreement.

The group moved next to discuss size. Was there any necessary connection between the right to self-government or jurisdiction and the size of the Aboriginal community? The Royal Commission on Aboriginal Peoples considered size to be a critical feature, arguing that any self-governing First Nation should have a population of at least 10,000. The Nisga'a treaty enabled self-government for slightly less than 6,000 people, and for Jim Aldridge, that number had the necessary critical mass.

Neil Sterritt offered a "small is beautiful" perspective on the question. For space-exploration purposes, researchers have determined that the smallest viable social unit is about 175 people. "A lot of our communities are in the 150 to 200 range," he said, "and some may have 100 members but only 40 in the community." Stephen Cornell said this situation was not uncommon: "I look at some of the pueblos we work with in New Mexico, with populations of fewer than 1,000 people, who are doing exemplary work in self-governance."

Lawyer Debra Hanuse is a former treaty commissioner and a member of the 'Namgis Nation. Hanuse felt that size should not be a factor in jurisdictional discussions but would definitely affect financial and administrative-capacity negotiations. If First Nations have the inherent right to self-government, then that constitutional entitlement ought not to depend on population size, she said. It took 150 years or so to dismantle those First Nations, and it is going to take a minimum of 150 years to reconstitute them. "If you jump over to the administrative side of the equation, it comes down to the... practical reality of who is paying for it, and that is the only time that size matters."

Any discussion about the self-government capacities of small First Nations inevitably touches on aggregation—a much-discussed topic inside the federal government, said Chris Kelly. As funding agents, federal and provincial governments have an appropriate interest in fostering economies of scale. The problem is how to negotiate from such positions without being oppressively paternalistic.

Paternalism or top-down aggregation clearly does not work, and Gary Wouters reported that an expensive experiment in self-government at the provincial level in Manitoba had failed because local chiefs did not support it. Another such initiative struggled in Saskatchewan because political organizations such as the Federation of Saskatchewan Indian Nations had a difficult time converting themselves into governments. Simply put, they lacked the administrative capacity and democratic legitimacy. Cornell praised the Ktunaxa's approach, in which five communities had resolved to establish a government under one tribal authority, the Ktunaxa Nation.

Recalling Canada's failed constitutional rounds of discussion in 1992, John Watson said it had briefly appeared that Aboriginal people were making great progress in promoting jurisdiction at the community level, with upward delegation permitted at the discretion of the First Nation. Because he didn't see how some jurisdiction or powers could be exercised in a practical manner at the Indian-band level in the province, Watson thought questions of jurisdiction and administration should be separated.

Cornell had problems with Watson's statement: "These things cannot be—or should not be—pulled apart. To me, to talk about governance or capacity or administration without talking about jurisdiction is to have a pointless discussion. If government doesn't have jurisdictional power, what is the point of it, and why should we invest in it? Toothless governments are what indigenous nations have generally had during the colonial period, and they turn out to be extremely poor mechanisms for getting anything done."

"Part of the secret of the Nisga'a success is the fact that they had their own school authority, they had their own health authority, but many other communities do not," Watson countered. The Nisga'a had the advantage of testing governance structures before completing their treaty, he said, but locking the structures of an Aboriginal government into the text of a treaty might be counterproductive if the First Nation has had no opportunity to experiment over time with culturally appropriate arrangements.

Other Aboriginal communities have only non-Aboriginal neighbours, but that may not be a problem. "[Does] the unit that has the right of self-government necessarily have to carry out all the tasks of government? The answer is no," Cornell said. "A First Nation might have the right to self-government, but what that really means is that they have the right to set up the rules, to say, 'This is how we're going to do that.'" Even if the First Nation joined a consortium of communities to deliver health services or contracted out garbage collection, that would not mean they had given up their right to self-government. "On the contrary, they're exercising that right," said Cornell.

Everybody at the table agreed that, to have any chance of success, Aboriginal governments must have the same financial foundations as other governments. Tribal authorities need the authority to levy taxes, receive transfer payments, and borrow money on capital markets. All these matters can be addressed in self-government agreements.[8] Ottawa and Yukon First Nations signed a bilateral financial-transfer agreement as part of the Yukon treaty settlement. The principles of the agreement reflect the equalization principles contained in the Canadian constitution and are similar to the Yukon Territorial Government's formula financing agreement with Canada.

Economist Thomas Courchene, who advised Yukon treaty negotiators, explained that the formula sets the expenditure base needed to deliver services at a level comparable with those received by other Canadians. From this base, Canada subtracts First Nation revenues and other federal transfers to arrive at the financial transfer. "As is the case with equalization in Canada and Australia, the revenues that are subtracted are not actual revenues, but rather standardized revenues: the revenues that would exist if comparable tax rates were levied. The First Nations need not levy taxes, but the financial transfer will be calculated on the assumption that taxes at rates comparable to those elsewhere are being levied. Moreover, the offset rate for tax revenues against the gross expenditure base is less than dollar for dollar. Both these provisions encourage the First Nations to engage in taxation. But again, this will be their decision."[9]

Current government funding for education, health, and other services tends to make chiefs and councils financially accountable to the agents of Indian Affairs. When a self-governing community agrees instead to levy taxes to finance services, it makes its elected leaders accountable to the taxpayers, not to outside agencies, an essential aspect of autonomous regimes. As Garry Wouters remarked, most First Nations do not come to the negotiating table with detailed mandates for financing "good governance." To negotiate financing agreements, Aboriginal parties need expert advisors. Federal policies on transfer payments, resource-revenue sharing, and own-source tax revenues need careful examination as to their effectiveness by negotiators on all sides.

Good government requires a flow of revenue, and most First Nations rely on transfers from the federal and, sometimes, provincial governments. The continuity of these transfers largely depends on healthy intergovernmental relationships. If a First Nation cannot establish positive and effective working relationships with the federal and provincial governments, Wouters said, it will find the day-to-day exercise of its jurisdiction very difficult. However, a treaty or legislative base for the funding would be even better.

Neil Sterritt made a case for First Nations developing a wide variety of strategic partnerships with other governments, business, labour, and universities. Many communities do not have the opportunities available to First Nations in the Northwest Territories, who have oil and diamonds on their land. Because of their size, many First Nations lack viable economies and social systems. Partnerships might help to mitigate this problem. Leaders in the Northwest Territories, too, have found new partnerships a key to their success. There, the federal and territorial governments have helped create the environment for the diamond industry and pipeline companies to engage in training and capacity building with First Nations.

Summing up the day's discussion, Miles Richardson thought the whole debate came down to one proposition: "If a First Nation is not willing to jettison enough of their governance powers to please British Columbia, they are not going to be able to negotiate a treaty." First Nations might be able to achieve good governance through incremental treaty making prior to resolving jurisdictional matters, but that remains to be seen. This was a critical moment, Richardson cautioned. Exciting things were happening at treaty tables, but "on the governance side, we are so far apart on the major issues that it is not possible to assert inherent rights."

Stephen Cornell had the last word. Institutional dependency constitutes one of the biggest problems for American Indian nations, he said. "A lot of tribal governments were not designed by tribes, but were imposed upon them. They do not feel a sense of ownership in regard to those governments. Such governments are prone to abuse, just as other things are that people use but are not ultimately responsible for. I think *Indian Act* governments here have the same problem. Getting away from this institutional dependency seems to me to be the heart of the governance challenge."

Governing capacity has three components, according to Cornell: jurisdiction or authority; rules or institutions; and efficacy or implementation. Jurisdiction means the tribal group has the capacity to do what it wants. Good governmental institutions rely on the consistent application of sound rules. Successful implementation depends on having the right people with the right tools to get the job done. Too much discussion, Cornell said, focuses only on the third component: "You may train a good accountant to keep the books, but the big decisions are still going to be made somewhere else. That's not building governing capacity; it's building administrative capacity." In other words, self-administration does not equal self-government.

REFLECTING ON THESE expert views in the days following the roundtable, I realized that, although solving the self-government riddle remains the key mandate question at B.C. treaty tables, we should not see it as one insuperable problem. Rather, it is a question of negotiating the steps towards reconciliation.

While I am attracted to Stephen Cornell's view that self-government is necessary to Aboriginal economic development, I doubt that self-government is sufficient unto itself. The proliferation of reserve-based casinos in the United States may be a product of tribal autonomy. While gambling brings dollars to the tribal homelands, it brings more than its share of problems, too. Also, I feel cautioned by Neil Sterritt's observations on the absence of economic opportunities for many of B.C.'s small Aboriginal communities.

In the North, Canada's Indian agents moved some Aboriginal communities from their traditional locations to spots that were administratively more convenient. As White River, Yukon, elder Nelnah Bessie Johns used to say, "When the white men built roads, the Indians stopped travelling." Unfortunately, the new locations also undermined subsistence economies. In the Yukon villages I know well, beyond the subsistence economy—which remained important although not quantified in national economic accounts—many a community depended on government transfers. Self-government may well drive further change, and its impact will be significant, but it alone will not bring prosperity. Location, assets, and access to markets stand as indisputably more significant factors. Self-government is not solely a cultural and economic question, either, since the social health of First Nations also depends on community members taking control of their lives.[10] Ironically, this may be easier to accomplish in northern, rural, and remote communities than in southern cities.

Even sympathetic scholars like J.R. Miller, author of *Lethal Legacy: Current Native Controversies in Canada*, believe that the kind of self-government powers enjoyed by the Nisga'a and Yukon First Nations may not be realistic in or near B.C.'s urban centres. "Perhaps similar solutions might be fashioned in northern British Columbia, the Far North, northern Quebec, and Labrador," Miller writes. "However, in more southerly, more densely settled parts of the country such as the heavily-populated and agriculturally well-developed Lower Fraser Valley in B.C., a separate First Nations territory with self-governing institutions is impossible to achieve. However, there are other ways of maximizing the ability of First Nations to exercise control over those areas that most matter to them without disrupting existing political boundaries."[11] Indeed, Aboriginal leaders are already experimenting with Aboriginal school, health, and social-service agencies in urban settings.

Debra Hanuse made an excellent point at the roundtable about the "right" to self-government belonging even to Aboriginal communities whose populations have been decimated by colonization. But how do the majority of First Nations, which are villages or collections of villages, exercise that right? Jurisdiction should trump administration but, because most First Nations in Canada have the population of villages, size does matter. Might and right should both figure in negotiations about funding and institutions.

If Canada, with its international trade and development initiatives, can promote effective, ethical, and democratic governance abroad, then there can be nothing wrong with it investing in Aboriginal institutions that reflect the same values. Having recognized a First Nation's legitimate jurisdiction, for example, the funding agencies would be perfectly entitled to say that they would finance a school for a community of two hundred people but not a school board. However, if that First Nation pooled its resources with members of a tribal council or some other regional group, the federal and provincial governments should be prepared to invest in incentives for that kind of aggregation, because the public interest in good government requires it.

Canada's founding fathers drafted a constitution that divided all powers between the federal and the provincial governments. They did not consult First Nations or leave them any constitutional "room" to recover and to grow. Fairness, then, requires that both Ottawa and the provinces become less possessive about their jurisdiction. First Nations need certain tools to heal their communities and rebuild their governments, and the federal and provincial governments have a legitimate interest in spending economically, efficiently, and effectively. In treaty negotiations, Ottawa and Victoria should provide financial incentives for First Nations to create financially sustainable, economically efficient, and politically effective institutions. Furthermore, the formula for financing self-government should be built right into a treaty, married to a fair and effective dispute-resolution system that has been road-tested during negotiations. Self-government will be pointless if it merely leaves First Nations managing their own misery.

The British Columbia government has said bluntly that no self-government agreement will work without its support. Members of most B.C. First Nations insist they will never ratify a treaty with anything less than the Nisga'a self-government provisions. By the spring of 2005, however, optimists in the ranks of government negotiators thought First Nations might be prepared to accept self-government agreements outside treaties, provided those agreements do not speak to the source of First Nations authority to make them: that is, their inherent right to self-government. One official told me:

> The negotiations would then focus more on the placement of specific authorities between the treaty and the self-government agreement. They would also seek, and the Crown is prepared to concede, that whatever aboriginal rights may be embedded in a self-government agreement, would not be released, but would not be asserted for the life of the self-government agreement.[12]

The device he is describing may be artful, but is it really necessary? I have often wondered if bureaucrats and lawyers don't unnecessarily complicate the self-government issue. At my first interdepartmental meeting of provincial deputy ministers at Saskatchewan in 1995, I listened with alarm to a long discussion about possible provincial self-government programs for Aboriginal communities. Finally, a colleague asked me, the newcomer, what I thought. "Well, I think either First Nations can have self-government or the province can have programs," I said. A provincial self-government program would be an oxymoron, it seemed to me. Yet if treaties signed in the twenty-first century acknowledge tribal ownership of large land holdings, then First Nations signatories will surely need "provincial" powers to manage those lands and the resources on them. Ottawa and Victoria must ensure that Aboriginal peoples have the legislative and financial tools they need to reconstruct their home communities according to local designs and national standards.

CHAPTER 16

HAIDA FORESTS

A New Model

HAIDA GWAII, THE Queen Charlotte Islands off the northwest coast of British Columbia, nurtures the culture of its permanent residents, the Haida. An economy based on cedar and salmon has fed, housed, and transported the Haida for centuries. The Haida also fished the seas for crabs, clams, mussels, and kelp. They harvested deer, mushrooms, and berries from the land. Ethnobotanist Nancy Turner's book *Plants of Haida Gwaii* documents Haida uses of more than 150 local plant species.[1] To construct their homes, Haida carpenters, like those of other West Coast First Nations, developed their own specialized woodworking tools.[2] By both Haida law and European conventions, the Haida "owned" the lands and trees.

With abundant sources of food from the sea and the forest, the Haida had the time for a rich cultural life and the creation of art works that French anthropologist Claude Lévi-Strauss considered as important as those from Greek and Roman civilizations. Haida society is matrilineal; hereditary titles, names, crests, masks, songs, and property are passed down through the mother's side of the family. Archaeologists have recorded hundreds of Haida village sites around the islands. Forty family lines survive in Old Masset and Skidegate, the two major Haida communities on the islands today.

When the Haida welcomed Spanish explorer Juan Perez in 1774, the population of their fifty villages numbered 30,000 people. By 1915 a series of smallpox epidemics had reduced their number to less than 600. Until the Europeans arrived, the "islands of the people" were called Haida Gwaii. The British claimed sovereignty in 1846 and renamed the place Queen Charlotte Islands after George III's wife. Neither the British nor their successors, Canada and British Columbia, ever made a treaty with the Haida, and the Haida have never sold their land.

In the twentieth century, forest industry giants like MacMillan Bloedel and Weyerhaeuser began to load the Haida's heritage onto barges and ship it south. Guujaaw, president of the Council of the Haida Nation, observes that "logging companies are taking the best timber as fast as they can."[3]

Renowned Haida artist Robert Davidson links the legendary Raven to the current crisis on Haida Gwaii in his sculpture *Ravenous*. In a Haida story, Raven steals and then eats one eye from each sleeping human. "Raven creates an imbalance with his voraciousness, because if you take away one eye, you take away depth of vision," Davidson says. "Right now on Haida Gwaii, there is logging in very sensitive areas where the marbled murrelets live. We are so ravenous, so voracious. There is no thinking of the next generation—even then, we're not fulfilled."[4]

Over the past few decades, the Haida have been regaining their numbers and their political strength. In 1980 the communities of Old Masset and Skidegate formed the Council of the Haida Nation, and in 1993 the council entered the British Columbia treaty process. Indian and Northern Affairs Canada reports approximately 3,700 Haida on its band lists of registered Indians. At the B.C. Treaty Commission, the Haida Nation claimed 7,000 members. "All people of Haida ancestry are Haida citizens," the council said.[5]

In Haida Gwaii's forests, the logging rate has long been the subject of hot debate. Local residents believed that logging had been far too rapid and the annual allowable cut—the volume of wood, measured in cubic metres, that the government permits a tenure holder to harvest—too high. The old-growth forests were vanishing, the majority having been logged over the last thirty years. Because trees need at least eighty years to grow large enough to produce marketable timber, island people worried that, once the remaining old growth was gone, the jobs provided by the forest would also disappear.

Non-Aboriginal residents shared the Haida's concern. During the summer of 2002, even Weyerhaeuser's loggers went over to the Haida. This loggers' revolt made front-page news in Vancouver. Newspaper stories described a company vice-president, Tom Holmes, negotiating with protesting workers while pesky insects buzzed around his head. In his hand, Holmes held a piece of paper. On the paper, he had drafted an outline of an agreement with the Haida. That agreement amounted to a radical plan that could reform forest practices on Haida Gwaii and perhaps the whole West Coast. To ensure peace in the woods, Weyerhaeuser offered to reduce its harvest by half. By then, however, that was too little, too late.

Earlier that year, Weyerhaeuser had been surprised to lose a judicial contest with the Haida Nation. When the B.C. government transferred a forest licence from the previous operator, MacMillan Bloedel, to Weyerhaeuser in 2000, the Haida challenged it in court. The province and Weyerhaeuser, for their part, said they had no obligation to consult the Haida about logging on the Queen Charlotte Islands until a court had recognized Haida Aboriginal title over Haida Gwaii.

On February 27, 2002, the B.C. Court of Appeal concluded that both the Crown and Weyerhaeuser did have a duty to consult with the Haida. Justice Lambert wrote:

In my opinion, there is a reasonable probability that the Haida
will be able to establish Aboriginal title to at least some parts of
the coastal and inland areas of Haida Gwaii.[6]

Many observers considered it remarkable that, in a consultation
case, the B.C. Court of Appeal had commented on the strength of
the Haida claim to Aboriginal title. A few weeks later, on March 6,
2002, the Haida took the cue and filed a lawsuit in B.C. Supreme
Court asserting title over the "land, inland waters, seabed and sea" of
Haida Gwaii. The Haida statement of claim sought compensation, the
quashing of forest tenures and licences, and the recovery of land.[7]

The Haida title action greatly increased media and public interest
in their nation's cause. A Canadian Broadcasting Corporation (CBC)
story noted that the Haida claim included Hecate Strait between the
islands and the mainland, and that this area might contain billions
of dollars worth of oil and gas. For environmental reasons, the federal government had imposed a moratorium on offshore oil and gas
drilling in B.C. thirty years earlier, but the provincial government
had recently questioned the moratorium. Guujaaw told the *Vancouver
Sun* on March 16, 2002, that court recognition of Haida Aboriginal
title would give the Haida "overlapping jurisdiction on crown land
and veto power over things they don't want, such as unrestrained
logging, environmentally-unfriendly development, development
of oil and gas properties, and fishing lodges that impact local
salmon stocks."[8]

Following the decision, Weyerhaeuser expressed support for the
Haida's Aboriginal rights and for treaty settlements. However, the
company still faced demands for increased community control of
forest management, objections to raw-log exports, and grievances
about sawmill closures.

Of all the potential Aboriginal-title cases to be built upon the
1997 *Delgamuukw* decision, the B.C. government had most wanted

to avoid this Haida action. For a start, Haida lands are not covered by any "overlapping claims" from other First Nations. Second, the Haida have benefited from having a series of articulate and forceful political leaders. Third, thanks to artists like Bill Reid, whose *Spirit of Haida Gwaii* sculpture has recently been reproduced on Canada's $20 bill, the Haida have enjoyed widespread respect for their traditional culture and public sympathy for their efforts to preserve it.

Still, the Haida title case will not be a "slam dunk." In his book *Aboriginal Title*,[9] Thomas Isaac, a lawyer for third-party interests in the consultation case, argues that the Supreme Court of Canada has set a high standard for proving Aboriginal title, even on land, and that the remedy for infringement will likely amount only to financial compensation. Under the best of circumstances, the case might not yield a decision before 2010. Regardless, the Haida Nation's lawyer, Louise Mandell, believes that, because the appeal court's decision in the *Haida* consultation case created the potential for a "cheap, affordable remedy," lawyers can now mount an Aboriginal-title case without incurring huge costs. "[We] just have to figure out how to do that and still get people a remedy that the governments are going to be obliged to implement. Because these guys—the governments—have been ignoring title for so long they're like repeat offenders; they don't seem to know how to stop."[10]

Guujaaw concedes that there is one other big issue: water. The Haida are claiming offshore areas with oil potential, and Victoria and Ottawa will certainly oppose this. The courts have not recognized the Aboriginal title of any First Nation in B.C., so there are serious risks associated with the Haida title case. Nevertheless, Guujaaw insisted at the time the claim was filed that the Haida would not sit and wait for the court's decision. Life would go on, he said, as would business.[11]

Faced with consumer boycotts in Europe, Weyerhaeuser and four other companies (Canadian Forest Products, International Forest Products Limited, Norske Canada, and Western Forest Products) participated with four environmental groups (Forest Ethics, Greenpeace, Rainforest Action Network, and the Sierra Club of B.C.) to create the Joint Solutions Project in 2001. The project's purpose is to develop a conservation plan for forests on the central and north B.C. coast that will be credible both locally and globally. The David Suzuki Foundation has also worked with central- and north-coast First Nations, including the Haida, to develop ecologically sustainable alternatives to industrial logging and fishing practices that First Nations and the foundation feel have caused ecological damage and economic instability for those who live in the region. The Turning Point alliance, formed in 2001, allows various First Nations to work together, although individual First Nations still negotiate their own deals.[12] According to Turning Point advisor Garry Wouters, the alliance has several purposes: "Number one, we have an agreement to undertake government-to-government negotiations on land-use planning. Two, we have commitments to negotiate our land-use plans through an ecosystem-based management arrangement. And, third, we have set up the political and technical processes within Turning Point to provide us with the capacity and power to negotiate fair and just agreements on land-use with the Province."[13]

As pressure grew from European markets for more environmentally friendly logging and from American competitors for market-based pricing for timber from public lands, forest policy reform climbed to the top of the provincial cabinet's agenda. In an April 18, 2002, column, "The Liberals' Bottom Line on Forests Reform," *Vancouver Sun* political columnist Vaughn Palmer described a "market reforms" package that the B.C. government had tabled at softwood-lumber negotiations with the Americans.[14] The province proposed to ditch its policy of tying timber sales to bidders' commitments to local processing. Henceforth, timber would be sold to the highest bidder at public auctions, rather than through long-term deals with a few large operators, and stumpage charges would be based on market prices. The winners of the tenure bids would manage their own harvest levels, and they would no longer be forced to process their wood within the region of its harvest. In turn, the B.C. Liberals would expropriate from all tenure holders up to 20 per cent of tenures. Some of that 20 per cent would be reserved as a supply of timber for First Nation and community tenures.

Vancouver Sun columnist Stephen Hume demanded a public debate on the issues: "Do we want the vast majority of our old-growth forests, the inventory of high-value wood they contain and the complex ecosystems they sustain simply liquidated to make way for fast-rotation, genetically engineered tree plantations that produce inferior-quality wood and ultimately won't be able to compete with the cost structures for similar plantations farther south?"[15]

Ken Drushka of *Business in Vancouver* weighed in on the other side: "The fundamentals of U.S. forest policy were shaped during the American Revolution when Crown authority was overthrown and state ownership of land rejected. U.S. forests ended up predominantly in private hands and market factors of supply and demand determine, to a large degree, how the U.S. forest economy functions." Drushka said nineteenth-century policy had liquidated forests to make way for agriculture, and continued public ownership of forestlands effectively "subsidized" B.C. mills.[16]

Other commentators called for more diverse ownership of tenures and licences. As far back as 1997, the provincial government had begun thinking about new kinds of community-forest tenures and pilot projects. By increasing the direct involvement of communities and First Nations in local forest management, the government hoped to maintain forestry jobs, economic stability, and provincial revenues. The idea attracted many B.C. communities, not just First Nations.

Serious differences of opinion about forest policy had complicated treaty negotiations with the Haida from the beginning. In 1993, the Council of the Haida Nation had entered Stage 1 of the B.C. Treaty

Commission process with a statement of intent. However, they made little progress and so began to pursue other strategies, including litigation. Chiefs around the province who worried that Attorney General Geoff Plant was pursuing his own aggressive "litigation" strategies, rather than the good-faith negotiation of treaties, had their worst fears confirmed in September 2003, when Plant suddenly offered the Haida a land settlement far in excess of his offers to other First Nations: control over 20 per cent of Haida Gwaii. "[W]e have been looking for a way to kick-start the [treaty] process," Plant said at the time. "The offer of 200,000 hectares of provincial Crown land includes lands previously identified by the Haida Nation for their cultural significance and economic value. British Columbia is committed to settling land claims through negotiations, and this land offer is contingent on the Haida Nation re-engaging in treaty negotiations. The offer is designed to encourage the Haida Nation to return to the treaty table with British Columbia and Canada. It does not include cash and is open to the Haida Nation until March 3, 2004."[17]

Guujaaw commented on the offer in a CBC Radio interview: "What they're talking about is not giving us 20 per cent of the Crown land on the Queen Charlotte Islands. They're talking about asking us to surrender 80 per cent of Haida land."[18] That the Haida did not immediately bite at Plant's bait probably did not surprise the B.C. government. In fact, Haida reluctance may have been exactly the reaction the government expected and wanted. As explained, in the B.C. treaty process the federal and provincial governments are fifty-fifty partners and jointly present offers to First Nations. In simple terms, Ottawa puts up money, and Victoria provides land. Their joint offers are usually based on a negotiated land-and-money formula. So, without Ottawa signing on, could this Victoria "offer" really be considered a treaty offer at all? In addition, the treaty process had begun in the province with then premier Mike Harcourt inviting First Nations to select up to 5 per cent of their traditional lands. The

Nisga'a had settled for 8 per cent of their traditional territory. B.C.'s unilateral offer of 20 per cent upped the ante so dramatically as to suggest that the judiciary, not the Haida Nation, was its intended audience. Under pressure from the forest industry, the province no doubt hoped to weaken the Haida title case.

BECAUSE THEY BELIEVE so strongly in their continued ownership of Haida Gwaii, the Haida have never been much interested in the province's land-selection process. Instead, they have consistently sought to negotiate arrangements that would see them jointly manage the Charlottes, especially in the area of natural resources, with government. They have pursued such arrangements in land-use planning, forest management, and fisheries. Guujaaw has a vision of one day assembling all these agreements into a formal treaty based on Aboriginal title.

Certain First Nations assert that they remain sovereign in their territory until Canada has purchased their land through treaty. Others take a different approach. For all their determined drive to settle the land question, the Nisga'a have never challenged Canadian sovereignty.[19] Indeed, they explain their treaty as the ticket to full partnership in Canadian society. The Haida come down somewhere in the middle. Guujaaw might be reluctant to see a Haida-owned forest company operating under a provincial licence, but, he joked, that doesn't mean he would refuse to use the provincial highway system because it requires a provincial driver's licence.[20]

After the Haida legal victory on consultation, Guujaaw observed that it would be smart for the province to issue forestry tenders to First Nations. Under a new Forestry Revitalization Plan, the B.C. government started doing exactly that. The plan was announced by B.C.'s Ministry of Forests in March 2003. It contemplated the province signing agreements with First Nations in areas where an undercut of the current allowable harvest or part of the 20 per cent take-back sales could be reallocated. Under such agreements,

Aboriginal communities would gain access to timber and revenue sharing. In exchange, the First Nation would concede that, during the term of agreement, all economic consultation issues had been addressed. Consultation would continue, however, on non-operating decisions and cultural accommodation questions. The *Forest (First Nations Development) Amendment Act, 2002* (Bill 41) allows First Nations to access forest tenures by direct ministry award and without competition, through "agreement with a First Nation and the Province respecting treaty-related measures, interim measures or economic measures."[21]

The Forestry Revitalization Plan promoted forestry interim measures as opportunities for First Nation involvement in forestry businesses, including: "Joint ventures with existing forest licensees and contractors; Forest tenures, which may include Community Forest Pilot Agreements; the development of a forest management workforce, including silviculture crews; involvement in contracting for forest management services; and other forest related opportunities."[22] Economic measures would be financed by a $40-million fund managed by B.C.'s Ministry of Forests.

By 2005 Aboriginal groups had signed fifty Forest and Range revenue-sharing agreements. Each agreement requires the First Nation to acknowledge that the economic benefits amount to a workable interim accommodation of Aboriginal interests in the forests covered by the agreement. No doubt, the First Nation signatures hinged on that word "interim." One such agreement gave the Gitga'at a $1.57-million share in forestry revenues over five years, a direct ministry invitation to apply for a forest licence in the North Coast Timber Supply Area of 125,000 cubic metres, and a second invitation for up to 165,000 cubic metres. The B.C. Business Council expressed annoyance that negotiation of the Gitga'at agreement had involved no consultation with the forest industry and no talks with the area's tenure holders.[23] Nonetheless, the province and First Nations continue to sign similar agreements.

True to form, the government has a formula for these schemes: approximately $500 per First Nation member for revenue sharing, and 30 to 50 hectares per person of forest lands to harvest, depending on quality of stand, with stumpage continuing to be paid to the province. Under these new forestry economic arrangements, the modest "revenue-sharing" formula bears no relationship to timber volumes or timber revenues, and some First Nations hate this "take it or leave it" approach.

On May 29, 2003, Minister of Forests Mike de Jong offered the Haida $1.8 million in annual forest revenues and forest tenure of "125,000 m³ in annual allowable cut."[24] Guujaaw, for one, was not impressed. In his reply of June 4, 2003, he restated the Haida position: "You have made an 'offer' whereby you would give us a few of our own trees and a few dollars, which are generated through the exploitation of our forests. In exchange, you suggest that we accept your authority on all counts, including dominion over and management of our culture. You propose that we forfeit our constitutional and legal rights, leave your government to its devices, and allow the forest industry to have its way with our homelands. What you are proposing is that we sit quietly by and place the fate of the land and our people in the hands of your government."[25]

When the Supreme Court of Canada finally ruled on the Haida consultation case in November 2004, the business community reacted positively to the news that government, not industry, would be responsible for consulting and accommodating Aboriginal interests. Weyerhaeuser lawyer Anne Giardini thought the decision would clarify the process. "We're delighted," she said.[26]

The B.C. Treaty Commission declared that the decision reinforced the need for treaties. "The Supreme Court's ruling is helpful to the treaty process," said Acting Chief Commissioner Mike Harcourt. "This court decision is one more strongly worded encouragement to negotiate. It lays out an obligation on the part of the Crown to negotiate."[27]

The Supreme Court seemed to have come down in the middle.[28] It rejected the B.C. government's argument that it owed no duty to consult. Government must carry out meaningful consultations with First Nations, the court ruled, but First Nations had to participate constructively in such process. Absent treaty settlements, government could still manage the lands under negotiation. However, "the Crown is bound by its honour to balance society and aboriginal interests." The province had again argued that Aboriginal claimants should prove their title before the government had to accommodate their interests, and the judges' response probably cheered the Haida: "When the distant goal of proof is finally reached, the aboriginal peoples may find their land and resources changed and denuded. That is not reconciliation. Nor is it honourable." The province had failed to properly engage the Haida, the court decided. But although the Haida had wanted a veto, they did not get it.

A few days after the ruling, on November 26, Premier Gordon Campbell's office issued a news release announcing the appointment to a "pilot position" of Allen Edzerza, a Tahltan and former negotiator for the Kaska Nation, "to undertake policy work of importance to both the First Nations Summit and government." Edward John was among the many chiefs who cheered Edzerza's appointment.

On March 22, 2005, however, the Haida set up a road blockade to protest the sudden sale of Weyerhaeuser's licences to a Toronto-based multinational corporation, Brascan[29] —without consultation with the Haida. Supported by many non-Haida residents, the Haida shut down logging on Graham Island, as well as forest-ministry offices. The blockade ended weeks later when the B.C. government agreed to protect large areas from logging and to provide the Haida with 120,000 cubic metres of harvestable timber a year and an initial $5-million payment for resource revenues.[30] The Haida and the province also committed themselves to reaching a series of agreements on land, revenue sharing, fisheries, economic development, and shared decision making.

Guujaaw has continued to complain about the province issuing new logging permits, but by 2006 the Haida have managed to get approximately 50 per cent of their lands protected through a combination of political action and participation in joint government and Haida land-use planning processes. All in all, this is a remarkable achievement, and treaty negotiators everywhere wonder if these arrangements might be the early prototype of a new model treaty.

Since 2004, Victoria has involved itself with a number of First Nations in land-use planning, interim measures, and forestry agreements. These cover the whole of a First Nation's traditional territory, not just the limited amount of settlement land provided by recent treaties. For many First Nations, these recent agreements constitute the building blocks of new institutional arrangements. In time, the province may realize that the agreements also add up to governance arrangements incompatible with its anti-self-government ideology. Without having thought through the consequences, the province has apparently been drifting surprisingly close to making co-jurisdictional arrangements. This is something that no Canadian government has ever publicly countenanced.

At the moment, the B.C. treaty process does not encourage negotiations for anything other than the federal/provincial land-and-money formulas. Yet co-jurisdiction arrangements might be the best possible model for a true accommodation of Aboriginal ideas about land tenure and governance. Co-jurisdiction could mean the crafting of nation-to-nation protocols and institutions founded on government recognition of Aboriginal title, rather than its extinguishment. For example, co-jurisdictional bodies with at least 50 per cent First Nations representation could determine land-use allocations in a nation's territory, although tenure holders might still manage the harvest. Funding for such arrangements would come from resource revenues shared between the government partners.

Some steps have been taken in the area of co-management, but co-jurisdiction also means sharing policy-making powers. "At worst,"

Jessica Clogg, a lawyer for West Coast Environmental Law, has written, "co-management bodies have merely an advisory function. Some co-management bodies, such as the Clayoquot Sound Central Region Board, established through the Clayoquot Sound Interim Measures Agreement, and involving 50% representation from the Nuu-Chah-Nulth First Nations and 50% from the Province, have come close to the co-jurisdictional approach at some point in their history, and provide worthwhile models to build on."[31]

Many First Nations, frustrated by the existing treaty process, find the co-jurisdiction alternative very appealing. For this reason alone, the B.C. Treaty Commission should create a co-jurisdiction policy table and invite senior thinkers from each of the three parties to engage in an open dialogue about the concept. Were governments to send entrepreneurial or thoughtful bureaucrats rather than unimaginative careerists to the table, some contentious issues might be worked through. For public policy makers, this would be time well spent.

MEDIATION WORKS

T HERE CAN BE little argument that First Nations' high expectations of the 1991 B.C. Claims Task Force report have not been met. Politicians have also conveniently forgotten their optimistic statements that all B.C. First Nation claims might be settled by the turn of the century. The response from critics and the public has ranged from frustration to boredom and from trashing the parties' mandates to decrying the shortage of skilled negotiators. However, one significant and often overlooked factor is the absence of any established mediation or other dispute-resolution process for the treaty process. Mediation and alternative dispute-resolution techniques are widely employed in business, labour relations, and personal disputes, and there are very good arguments for bringing the mediator's skills to treaty tables as well.

All of the recent northern treaties, including the Nisga'a treaty, contain dispute-resolution chapters. True, evidence is emerging that some of the procedures laid out in these chapters are not working well.[1] But these failures should not be seen as an argument against the proper use of dispute-resolution tools. Rather, the workability of the proposed procedures should have been thoroughly tested during negotiations, instead of waiting until the treaty's implementation stage.

After the Inuit sued the federal government over implementation issues, for example, the parties appointed Thomas Berger as conciliator
in the dispute. In his interim report, Berger criticized negotiators on
both sides for the vague language in the treaty and for punting some
difficult issues to the implementation stage. The parties might have
avoided this conflict if they had test-driven their dispute-resolution
chapter before embedding it in a constitutional document or sought
the assistance of trained mediators from the start.

As former B.C. Labour Relations Board chair Stan Lanyon and
I pointed out in a paper presented at the national Key Questions
conference at Simon Fraser University's Wosk Centre for Dialogue
in 2003, a growing body of court decisions has urged governments
and First Nations to get serious about negotiations. However, as
mentioned, government policy has forced First Nations to choose
how to have their rights recognized: through negotiation or through
litigation, but not both.

In practice, governments, First Nations, resource companies,
and others are busy negotiating a variety of interim measures, treaty-
related measures, and other agreements. These initiatives generally
provide financial, economic, and other benefits to First Nations for
allowing developments to proceed, without prejudice, while treaties
are pending. But when negotiations break down, the parties sometimes find themselves before the courts. There are currently dozens
of Aboriginal-rights cases in litigation.

The Supreme Court decisions on *Haida* and *Taku* changed negotiating realities by asserting that governments have the duty not only
to consult First Nations whose claims may be affected by industrial
developments, but also to accommodate First Nations interests in
the processes of issuing permits and allocating resources, particularly
when government and industry are contemplating the extraction of
resources from lands subject to Aboriginal-title claims. The field
of labour relations offers a good example of this approach. The
basic legal framework in collective bargaining assumes a long-term

negotiating relationship between the union and the employer. For good reasons, the parties have almost always favoured the kind of framework where they maintain the most control. They, not a third party, are the experts about their own interests. The parties also have devised a wide variety of processes to break the impasses that inevitably occur from time to time.

The dispute-resolution processes in labour relations proceed through a hierarchy of steps, involving progressively more senior people on both sides and moving from low-cost to higher-cost methods. The first—and least costly—step is for an individual worker to file a grievance under the terms of the collective agreement between the company and the union. If the union's shop steward and the worker's supervisor cannot resolve the issue, the union files a written grievance. At this stage, a more senior manager tries to settle the complaint with the union's staff representative or business agent. Eventually, the two sides may refer the dispute to an arbitrator, who will normally receive submissions from both sides before rendering a final and binding decision.

As union researcher John Calvert has pointed out, the labour-relations approach to dispute resolution also incorporates a "duty to consult" and a step-by-step approach to finding solutions. This means that only those issues the parties have failed to resolve at lower levels end up at the highest level of dispute resolution, namely, binding arbitration. In practice, most disputes are resolved before reaching the highest stage. "In labour relations," Calvert writes, "dispute resolution processes are used not only to reach agreements, but also to deal with the interpretation of agreements. Collective agreements are complex documents whose language is often subject to a variety of interpretations. However, clarification is required so that each side knows precisely what its rights are and how they will be interpreted in practice."[2] As the grievance procedure illustrates, much of the focus of labour-relations dispute resolution is on finding ways to clarify the precise meaning of a previously negotiated contract between the parties. The system has arrangements to facilitate both the reaching of agreements and the interpretation of those agreements.

The 1991 report of the B.C. Claims Task Force recommended that "the [B.C. Treaty] Commission provide advice and assistance in dispute resolution as agreed by the parties." The report said that the commission, where requested by First Nations, should make dispute-resolution services available for overlapping territorial claims issues between neighbouring nations, and stated also that, at Stage 3 of the negotiations—the framework agreement—the parties should "adopt a dispute resolution procedure." The report unfortunately did not spare much thought for the dispute-resolution challenge itself. Its recommendation was brief and insubstantial: "The Parties should also develop a dispute resolution mechanism to resolve disputes about matters of interpretation and implementation." So far, however, none of this has happened, because the treaty commission has not seen fit to bring mediation professionals to treaty tables.

The task force report further stated that "interim agreements," which could be "raised at anytime," should be considered prior to concluding Stage 3. Interim measures were intended to balance "conflicting interests until these negotiations are concluded." The report noted that interim measures "may facilitate the access to and development of resources" and may often provide "a useful means of dealing in a preliminary or experimental way with a contentious issue, or provide transition to implementation of the treaty."[3]

As set out in the task force report, the B.C. Treaty Commission's role is "to facilitate the negotiation of treaties and, where the Parties agree, other related agreements in British Columbia." The compact edition of the *Oxford English Dictionary*, 1984, defines "facilitate" as "to render easier the performance of (an action), the attainment of (a result); to afford facilities for, promote, help forward (an action or process)." As the word is commonly understood in the labour-relations field, "facilitation" encompasses a range of activities, including everything from arranging meetings all the way to conciliation or mediation and, sometimes, arbitration. Negotiations in many other fields—commercial, labour, and matrimonial—often require facilitators, mediators, and adjudicators.[4]

Article 7.1 (h) of the agreement setting up the B.C. Treaty Commission details the duties of the commission, stating that it shall "assist Parties to obtain dispute resolution services at the request of all the Parties." Article 13 directs the commission to "refer to the Report of the Task Force, dated June 28, 1991, to provide the context for this Agreement and as an aid to its interpretation." The task force report plainly speaks in terms of "dispute resolution" and "interim agreements."

Clearly, the treaty commission has the authority to provide dispute-resolution services for treaty negotiations and other related agreements. The Supreme Court of Canada has said many times that a negotiated settlement, by treaty or some other agreement, is better than a judgment rendered after litigation. Parties to the treaty process normally prefer negotiation to litigation, too, because it gives them more control over the outcome. With regard to treaty negotiations, the politically constructed wall between negotiation and litigation should come down, especially because it looks like a throwback to the time when the law did not allow Indians to hire land-claims lawyers. When required, mediators—either court-appointed or appointees of the parties—could be assigned to assist in negotiations. In situations of impasse, one or more of the parties could refer issues to the courts, in order to get a decision on a particular point. Regardless of the court's involvement, all decisions would remain connected to the negotiations; instead of court actions being seen as a failure of the treaty process, they could constructively be incorporated into the overall design of "facilitation and dispute resolution," in which negotiation is the primary public-policy goal. All this could be done under the auspices of the treaty commission.

Interim measures obviously include economic arrangements, but they could involve other matters as well. The parties in treaty negotiations might also wish to distinguish between treaty-related measures, bilateral interim measures, and economic measures unrelated to the treaty process. Economic arrangements negotiated by parties outside the treaty process could access a wide variety of dispute-resolution options under the federal and provincial commercial-interest arbitration acts. These peacemaking options would permit, as suggested in the 1991 task force report, the development of resources in "preliminary or experimental ways" and might provide a transition to the negotiation of treaties at a later date.

In labour relations and other fields, British Columbia enjoys an abundance of mediation talent. To be sure, not all professional mediators demonstrate the sensitivity required to work in a cross-cultural setting. However, nothing prevents the treaty commission from developing a list of appropriate mediators. The commission could encourage the use of these mediators by recommending them to tables that are experiencing difficulties. Over time, the commission and the parties to the treaty process might acquire the experience and expertise to enable them, confidently, to use mediation as a tool to expedite negotiations and improve the negotiating environment in British Columbia.

The parties to the treaty process are fairly sophisticated negotiators. In addition to their own expertise, all parties have lawyers on their teams who could advise negotiators about mediation and dispute-resolution techniques as these operate in other fields. In labour relations, for example, mediators try to translate the hardest bargaining positions of even the most powerful of the parties into neutral statements of the parties' interests. The mediator tries to locate the middle ground between the power of the parties and the power of their positions. A skilled mediator can also help parties design a dispute-resolution procedure that feeds directly back into the negotiating process. Having all parties contribute to the design of the dispute-resolution process helps as well to balance inequalities in power relations.

In British Columbia, labour-relations procedures are structured so that, in a dispute, the parties may make their case before an arbitration board, a mediation/arbitration professional, or the Labour Relations Board. By law, the government chooses the board's vice-chairs equally from the ranks of management and labour. If they wish, an employer and its union can create a tribunal by contract, which does not require legislation; from the start, the parties can retain a facilitator and design a dispute-resolution procedure that never loses its connection with the negotiating table. The use of a mediator, facilitator, or tribunal merely expedites the negotiations. Since the Second World War, Canadian labour-relations systems at provincial and federal levels have experimented with a great variety of such techniques. Whether it is collective bargaining, environmental mediation, or treaty negotiations, the context may be different but the tools are the same.

The same flexible arrangements could be applied to treaty negotiations. The parties could design their dispute-resolution system to fit their expertise and cultural perspectives. The design would be aimed at enhancing, not reducing, the parties' control of the negotiation process. For example, the treaty commission could appoint a representative panel of culturally sensitive and experienced mediators. An individual treaty table could contract with a professional facilitator. The three parties might even arrange an alternative dispute-resolution process with the courts to provide timely and less costly determinations. Treaties are constitutional documents, but their funding agreements are short-term contracts. The B.C. parties do need to nail down the key financial elements of any treaty, but workable treaties require not only a firm financing formula but also effective dispute-resolution processes.

To illustrate the wide array of alternatives, it is helpful to examine some of the standard dispute-resolution tools. These offer possibilities for both rights-based and interest-based negotiations. The overall dispute-resolution design may address treaty negotiations, interim measures, and/or economic development. Any hybrid process adapted for treaty tables might include the following elements:

· In the investigation or fact-finding process, a neutral expert is engaged to gather all relevant information and then to provide a factual determination. The parties could also choose a neutral expert to provide a professional opinion or determination within the area of his or her specific expertise. This process is called early neutral evaluation.
· An ombudsperson is a neutral person who, at the parties' request, conducts an investigation, mediates, and makes binding or non-binding recommendations.
· In a mediation/arbitration process, a neutral person attempts to mediate a solution. Failing that, he or she renders a binding award.
· In an arbitration/mediation process, a neutral person conducts a hearing. Before ruling on the question, he or she tries to mediate a solution.
· A mini or summary trial is a trial conducted without the calling of evidence; the parties introduce evidence through affidavits or submissions.
· A single-issue referral describes a situation in which a single point of law is referred to a neutral person, possibly a retired judge.
· In a process called final-offer selection, two positions are presented, and a neutral person is required to choose one. He or she is not at liberty to choose a third position or suggest a compromise solution.

Facilitation, mediation, and other non-binding processes do not require a legislative framework and can be structured solely by contract. Procedures like these allow the parties to:

· Design—and, if necessary, redesign—the systems themselves;
· Choose their own arbitrators, experts, facilitators, mediators, neutral persons, and judges;
· Set their own schedule;
· Decide the rules of the chosen process;
· Avoid the high cost of litigation;
· Create more accessible forums;
· Meet public expectations that agreement is the goal;

- Achieve resolutions tailored to the parties' needs, rather than court judgments that may please nobody; and
- Focus on long-term relationships rather than on the short-term problems of the past.

As things are at present structured, it would probably be unwise for treaty commissioners, who are mostly appointed by one party or another, to personally take on mediation or alternative dispute-resolution duties. However, if the commissioners wished to take a more active role in negotiations, they might look to the labour-board model, bearing in mind that the composition of any such administrative-law body should reflect the specific kinds of expertise required by the treaty-negotiations process and be perfectly balanced in its composition. Under the wide umbrella of the treaty process, it might also be possible to establish agencies ranging from mediation/arbitration panels to administrative tribunals.

Despite government resistance, mediation is not an eccentric idea. Witness the 2004 B.C. Business Council report on the treaty process: "The Business Council would like to see a mediation body established for the treaty process to which the negotiating parties can refer questions on which they have failed to reach agreement."[5] In a recent statement on treaty negotiations, the Assembly of First Nations also supported mediation: "It is absolutely necessary for the parties to have access to efficient, competent and trustworthy facilitation, mediation and/or arbitration to benefit the process generally and, especially, in situations of impasse."[6] Former Yukon judge and negotiator Barry Stuart goes further than this: he argues that mediators should be an integral part of the process from the outset. Consistent with the aims of "certainty" and "finality," the tripartite agreement that created the B.C. Treaty Commission calls for the commission to fold its tent when the treaties have all been signed. As I shall suggest later, it may make sense to consider the possibility of an ongoing role for the commission in the implementation stage of treaties.

All of the mediation and dispute-resolution processes described in this chapter are well within the mandate of the B.C. Treaty Commission. Six principles might guide treaty-related dispute-resolution processes:

1. That treaty making not exclude legal processes (an anomaly in public policy)
2. That negotiation, mediation, and adjudication be combined as needed
3. That the parties design the process to fit the issues in dispute
4. That mediation aims to break impasses while maintaining the negotiating relationship
5. That all processes to break impasses feed back into negotiations
6. That all dispute-resolution procedures designed for inclusion in the text of a treaty be tested during negotiations

It is in everybody's interest that both treaty negotiations and treaties themselves include two critical components: a clear statement ranking the priority of shared objectives and an effective dispute-settlement mechanism. Unfortunately, at the moment, Canada's treaty processes have neither. If treaty talks do not soon show more progress, and if implementation problems continue to plague the northern treaties, governments may decide to enact new legislation to deal specifically with the adjudication of treaty disputes throughout Canada. Such legislation would not be necessary were the parties themselves to develop alternative dispute-resolution processes. With the astute use of these tools, the parties could get past issue resolution and beyond mere settlements to sustainable relationships. The great advantage of such an initiative might be some real progress in building treaties that are cohesive rather than divisive—and that are completed in the twenty-first century.

∇

CHAPTER 18

FAST-TRACK TREATIES

THE NORTHERN TREATIES negotiated with Arctic and sub-Arctic Aboriginal groups over the last thirty years have typically run to between two hundred and four hundred pages. These comprehensive settlements include far more than the meagre provisions of the nineteenth-century treaties for reserve lands, annual annuities, and farm implements. They cover subjects as varied as eligibility and enrolment, lands, access, forest resources, fisheries, wildlife, taxation, dispute resolution, and implementation. Being the work of dozens of lawyers, these treaties do not make light reading.

In an ideal world, both the beneficiaries of a treaty settlement and the average taxpayer would be able to read and understand the treaty document. Had they had the courage, the parties to the Yukon treaty might have tried to distill the twenty-nine chapters and 200,000 words down to a readable précis; at the time, nobody wanted to face the months of editorial wrangling and legal interpretation this might entail. The 1984 Inuvialuit settlement for the NWT's Mackenzie River Delta area, which had notably only two principal negotiators as draftsmen, stands as the most readable of modern treaties.

"Brief and to the point" describes the writing style of the numbered treaties signed in Western Canada in the nineteenth century. Drafted by the government's treaty commissioners before negotiations started, these documents contained no language that was surplus to obtaining the surrender of the Indian land. Ottawa and Washington frequently violated the early Indian treaties, however, and indigenous peoples have had good reason to distrust settler governments. In recent times, governments have become obsessed with "certainty" in treaties. The need to dot every "i" and cross every "t" has created treaties that are inaccessible to the average reader.

The United States wrote a constitution that ran to less than a dozen pages. The Nisga'a self-government chapter alone runs to twenty-four pages. The Nisga'a ratified their final agreement on November 7, 1998, and by 2003, the Nisga'a government already faced financial difficulties in paying lawyers to draft the legislation necessary to implement such a complex accord. Perhaps it is unfair to compare an eighteenth-century constitution with one from the twentieth century. But compare the new European constitution, a two-year project of 333 pages for a population of 450 million, with the Nisga'a treaty, a twenty-year exercise of 252 pages for a community of six thousand. The authors of existing treaties may protest, like Voltaire, that the documents would have been shorter if only they had had more time. The elegant and beautiful U.S. constitution is the product of bright people framing an accord based on high principle. Attention to detail may be a virtue of modern Canadian treaty making, but inattention to principle has surely amounted to a fault.

At the time of the 1997 *Delgamuukw* decision, I was serving as B.C.'s chief negotiator in negotiations with public sector employers and unions. Although my hands were full, the government named me to chair a new committee of deputy ministers formed to deal with post-*Delgamuukw* issues. The committee included deputies from the key central agencies, the Attorney General and Finance, as well as from Aboriginal Affairs and the "dirt" ministries: Forests, Highways, Fisheries, et cetera. Concurrently, the province appointed me its chief negotiator for talks with the First Nations Summit and the federal government about expediting treaty negotiations. To work with me on this task, I was given a small, high-powered negotiation-project team consisting of officials seconded from the cabinet office, Attorney General, Forestry, and Aboriginal Affairs.

In accepting this last assignment, I asked permission to test ideas I had developed through participating in Aboriginal negotiation in both Yukon and Saskatchewan. Over the next few months, our team met with summit and federal officials in a series of negotiations. Equally important, we worked inside the system by consulting with officials throughout the government. The provincial team's efforts produced new consultation guidelines and a new approach to interim measures, including the treaty-related measures. The team also worked on a proposal for a fast-track treaty process—potentially the most important, and also the most quickly forgotten, product of our labours.

In the main, B.C. civil servants believed the *Delgamuukw* decision had increased economic uncertainty. Some had the opposite view, however. Internal debates about the meaning of the Supreme Court decision meant that the government took its time in responding to the new reality. Some steps seemed obvious. Canada, the First Nations Summit, and the province agreed to jointly review the treaty process and recommend changes to improve it. All three parties agreed that B.C.'s treaty making had become a painfully slow and costly process. First Nations expressed deep concerns about the continued alienation of resources in their territories, from which they received little or no benefit. The province's crying need for economic certainty made urgent its desire for treaty settlements.

In the course of discussions among the parties, our project team members wondered if there might be a faster route to a Nisga'a-model treaty, with which the people of British Columbia were now becoming familiar. Based on my northern experience, I questioned whether it was necessary to load up modern treaties with all the verbiage one found in the James Bay, Inuvialuit, Yukon, Nunavut, and Nisga'a treaties. Since 1982, the government had appended modern treaties to the constitution under the provisions of Section 35. But if treaties were constitutional documents, why were they not written in constitutional language? In other words, why didn't the treaties themselves document the principles agreed to by the parties? Why didn't negotiators write a treaty in plain language, so that someone with a high-school education could read it? And if certain elements of modern treaties—taxation, wildlife management, the application of the Charter of Rights—were becoming standard, if not template, why did lawyers need to reinvent the wheel every time they drafted a new treaty?

Other tough questions consumed us. After *Delgamuukw*, the federal Finance official's mantra—that it was cheaper to negotiate than to settle—became a little white lie. Had the negotiating culture become dysfunctional? Were too many risk-averse career civil servants delivering fixed messages at the table? Did the contract consultants, negotiators, and lawyers have a pecuniary interest in dragging out negotiations? Why, among all of the negotiators for all the parties at the fifty tables around the province, could senior negotiators privately identify only five, possibly six, "closers"? If Canada cared about treaty making, why didn't it hire the best negotiators available?

In thinking over the years about how to speed up negotiations, I have long wondered if it might be possible to write a treaty that focuses on land, resources, and financial elements and leaves the critical, but controversial, self-government dimension to a second stage. Everybody involved in treaty negotiations knows that the federal and provincial governments have jointly worked out land and money mandates to take to negotiating tables. Nobody will admit publicly exactly what that formula is, although most observers have a pretty good idea about the magic number. The two governments do not normally make a land-and-money offer to the First Nation negotiators until the latter stages of the treaty process. If governments truly want to expedite the process, however, why wait? Why not *open* negotiations with such an offer? And why stop there? Instead of waiting years for the rolling draft of a treaty to emerge from lawyers' offices, why not start negotiations with governments tabling a draft treaty that plainly describes the principles underlying their proposals and includes a specific land-and-money offer? First Nations could then respond with their own version of the treaty in question.

Land selection is another area where negotiations could be expedited. For most First Nations, the land-selection process, which requires that the selections be representative of the general character of lands in the area, takes some time. This seems to be the case even when selections prove uncontroversial. But, strictly speaking, completing land selections might not be necessary to the signing of a treaty. Certainly these comprise one essential ingredient of final agreements. But in theory at least, land selections could await the implementation stage. In Alaska, land selections followed Congress's passage of the *Alaska Native Claims Settlement Act*. Like Alaska, British Columbia has lots of Crown or public lands, and some of these could be made available for post-treaty selections under the fast-track model. If a First Nation's land selection can be completed in time to be included as an appendix to the treaty before signing, all well and good. If not, the treaty could be signed without this component.

What might such a fast-track treaty look like? At a minimum, our project team concluded it should list among its contents the following headings:

- Certainty and General Provisions—legal and financial certainty, conflict of laws, overlap, dispute resolution;
- Lands—ownership of settlement lands, acquisition of additional lands, certainty of access, ownership of rights of way and easements, provincial acquisition of settlement lands;
- Resources—wildlife harvest, allocation, and management; owner-

ship and management of forest, subsurface and cultural resources; environmental standards;
· Cash—amount of cash transfer, terms of negotiation of loan repayment, set-up and operation of settlement trust, taxation; and
· Self-government—principles of governance and fiscal framework, commitment to negotiate elements within five years of treaty, land-management arrangements in the interim, transition measures.

Could all these elements be captured in something less than three hundred plus pages? This would be possible if the drafters of treaties punted administrative details like the quorum rule for the surface-rights dispute-resolution process, or when and where the local wildlife-management committee was to meet, to the treaty's appendices, where they properly belong. As lawyer and constitutionalist Gary Yabsley pointed out to me in a private conversation, there is also real danger of incorporating in treaties details that may become stale-dated or "frozen in present time." Relegating administrative details to a treaty's appendix would make these particulars easier to amend as the thinking of the signatories evolves. The signatories might in fact avoid many of the difficulties around amendments if they drafted treaties, like constitutional documents, to embody in readable English the main principles of the agreement. Parliaments write statutes this way. Legislators debate the act, then officials draft; cabinet approves, amends, and appends the act's regulations.

Modern treaties like the Yukon and Nisga'a settlements define new relationships. The 1991 B.C. Claims Task Force report recognized this, stating that, as the relationships among them grow and change, the three signatories should be able to amend a treaty if necessary: "The possibility of amendment to treaties must receive careful attention during the negotiations."[1] Modern, book-length treaties, however, are written in such infinite detail that they are extremely tricky to amend.

Treaty negotiators suffer great stress in concluding the "so long as the sun shines" constitutional deal. First Nations face considerable risk in trading ancient rights for a fat binder full of lawyerly words open to interpretation and litigation. As one retired Indian Affairs deputy minister confided to me, those at the treaty table face enormous pressure to get everything right the first time; as a result, risk-averse behaviour dominates, and all molehills become mountains. Tim Koepke, as chief federal negotiator for the Yukon claim, experienced precisely this frustration: "Probably ninety per cent of the negotiating time was spent arguing over clauses that had about a one-per-cent likelihood of ever being needed."[2]

With all of this in mind, the B.C. project team experimented in 1998 and 1999 with successive drafts of a fast-track treaty. Elizabeth Argall, the attorney general's lawyer on the team, drafted most of the document. Lindsay Staples, a former provincial negotiator, worked on the resources section. Others worried over the language in the lands, cash, and self-government sections. Argall consolidated our work into a single treaty, and the final draft came to thirty pages.

In subsequent submissions to government departments, I argued that, even if negotiations caused us a treaty double the projected length of the fast-track treaty, we would still be further ahead. Moreover, by tabling a substantive offer early and focusing from Day 1 on a draft treaty, it ought to be possible to complete negotiations on a treaty in two years. Of course, like every forecast about expedited treaty negotiations, this one looked optimistic. But no one blinked.

Initially, the project team asked for no more than an opportunity to consult internally and with the federal government on the fast-track model. If the province believed that the legal and economic certainty it sought could be achieved by quickly settling outstanding Aboriginal land claims, then it should act accordingly. Accelerating the process by offering a new-model fast-track treaty would dramatically demonstrate to investors and to industry that the province was responding decisively to the challenge. Further, a new-model treaty would show a renewed political will to settle treaties and thus effectively revitalize the whole treaty process. Indeed, on the heels of *Delgamuukw*, governments faced an increasing likelihood that frustrated First Nations would walk away from treaty negotiations to pursue their interests in the courts.

As we evaluated the responses we received from provincial officials, the project team began to reflect on one serious problem with our proposal: namely, the delayed self-government negotiations. Concluding a treaty without setting out how treaty lands and resources would be governed could leave a big hole in the agreement, since what we today call Aboriginal self-government is wide-ranging enough to include program management, delegated law-making authority, and recognition of an inherent right to legislate in areas internal to the community and integral to the culture.

Given the Nisga'a experience, provincial ministries expressed concern about exactly how long self-government negotiations might take, even in an accelerated process. Governments were aware of the large debts that First Nations were running up in treaty negotiations. If it were possible to make rapid progress on the core elements of a fast-track treaty, First Nations might agree to negotiate self-government on a parallel but slower track. Might any apprehensions they felt about this separation be mollified if the fast-track treaty contained a commitment to finalize a self-government agreement within five years of the signing of a treaty—as we had proposed with the fast-track idea? The Yukon land-claim agreement had contained such a provision, essentially a constitutional commitment to timely negotiations of a self-government agreement.

Since 1995, Canada has officially recognized the inherent right to Aboriginal self-government under Section 35 of the 1982 *Constitution Act*. Yet almost every aspect of this "right" must be negotiated. First Nations are frustrated with Ottawa's "now you see it, now you don't" approach, and there remained in 2004 a significant gap in perceptions about self-government, even between the time of the British

Columbia Supreme Court's *Campbell* decision and the Supreme Court of Canada's ruling in *Pamajewon*. The *Delgamuukw* decision seemed to muddy the water, since the Supreme Court did not rule on the precise question of whether a right to self-government exists. Instead, the justices referred the matter back to the lower courts. The B.C. government knew that, elsewhere in Canada, self-government negotiations had proved to be costly, complex, and time-consuming. Public debates about the Nisga'a treaty had also shown the self-government chapter to be the most controversial aspect of the agreement.

The Nisga'a final agreement describes a central government, Nisga'a Lisims, and four village governments that resemble municipal administrations. The Nisga'a constitution defines the structure, functions, and duties of the central government and requires that it be open, democratic, and accountable to its Nisga'a constituents. Nisga'a law-making powers are concurrent with those of British Columbia and Canada. Their laws apply only to Nisga'a lands and peoples. Law making in the areas of marriage, adoption, and social services apply, with their consent, to Nisga'a citizens wherever they may live in the province. That many institutions in the areas of education and health existed prior to the treaty proved a great advantage to the Nisga'a in self-government negotiations. However, the enormous legal bills owing from implementing self-government structures, especially those surplus to Nisga'a needs, have proved a definite disadvantage.

There are two other parties that might have good reason to slow down the pace of self-government negotiations, even in a fast-track process. The federal government sees the development of Aboriginal self-government in British Columbia as an evolutionary process. First Nations, on the other hand, are not so sure how to translate their governmental traditions into modern institutions. Tools such as treaty-related measures and incremental treaty agreements should allow the parties to experiment with a variety of structures and institutions.

After many internal discussions, in 1999 the B.C. cabinet authorized our project team to air the fast-track treaty model with the First

Nations Summit, the federal government, and other private sector stakeholders, particularly those who had participated in the Treaty Negotiations Advisory Committee. The B.C. Liberals had cut the advisory committee's funding, but under the New Democrat government it had functioned as a major, multiparty consultative forum for the province's private interest groups.

Many of the advisory committee's stakeholders declared themselves interested in the fast-track idea. Small-business groups appeared skeptical, but then they often spoke dismissively of Aboriginal claims. The larger companies, especially those in the resource industries, well knew the price the province paid in lost investment because of uncertainty over the title to its lands and resources. Labour and environmental groups also gave their support. After some early criticism, some summit First Nations began to make inquiries about the possibilities of moving to the fast-track option. But not everybody in the provincial government was keen on the idea. Although we were suggesting the fast-track option as an addition to the current negotiating structure, some officials were wedded to the existing process. In January 1999, the Tripartite Review of the B.C. Treaty Process—Report of the Working Group eventually released an outline of the "fast-track treaty" idea:

> British Columbia proposes a fast-track treaty process which would deal with acceleration of land, resource and cash agreements and a commitment to negotiate the details of governance later, recognizing that certain governance powers would be required to deal with land and resources in the interim. B.C. suggests that the issues of consultation, interim measures, and treaty form part of a continuum... [3]
>
> British Columbia believes it is possible to set aside much of the governance negotiations from an accelerated land, resource and cash agreement and conclude the governance agreement at a later date. Some self-government provisions would be required in an

accelerated land, resource and cash agreement. These might include land management powers, a fiscal framework, a commitment to conclude self-government with a set time frame, and a list of powers that would be negotiated in a full self-government agreement. The list of powers might set out authorities to be exercised by the First Nation's government. In order to provide a sense of what might be included in the governance agreement, principles to be negotiated could be set out in the land, resource and cash agreement.[4]

Shortly thereafter, a new premier took office in British Columbia. Government priorities changed, and project team members returned to their departments. The current B.C. government may no longer subscribe to all the above statements, and the fast-track model would not suit every First Nation. Some lack the necessary clarity about what they want from the treaty process. Others, as did the Nisga'a, want to integrate governance with the other elements of their treaty. Some nations, though, may still be attracted to the possibilities of a fast-track process.

Sooner or later, ordinary citizens are going to start asking if their country is well served by a slow-moving treaty factory, staffed with bureaucrats, consultants, and lawyers, that produces massive, unreadable agreements difficult to interpret and impossible to adjudicate affordably. We would all be better served by treaties that are relatively brief, visionary statements of principle. If there are First Nations genuinely interested in following this path, governments should not stand in their way. Bureaucracies, federal and provincial, need to understand that younger, better-educated chiefs will not be willing to spend ten to twenty years at a negotiating table to get a settlement, the broad outlines of which are clear on the day negotiations start.

Nineteenth-century treaties, which typically took only a few days to negotiate, had a text that was too short. The norm for the twentieth-century treaty was a text that was too long and took twenty years to negotiate. In the twenty-first century, let's hope negotiators get it right.

CHAPTER 19

UNITED NATIONS

MANY CANADIANS SEE treaty issues like consultation policies and interim measures as purely local matters, but these issues are often international in scope. Even a casual scan of the news reveals a world of stories about indigenous peoples. As ever, the mass media focuses on the negative stories, such as the fact that half the world's languages are doomed, but some good stories are heard, too. And behind every story there is history.

Around 800 AD, the Maya in the Peten region of Guatemala faced an ecological disaster. Their community had reached the population density of modern China. To feed themselves, the people cleared the mountain slopes of trees and planted every centimetre of ground with crops. Soon, erosion silted up waterways and reservoirs. Then drought came. Within a century, 90 per cent of the Maya had died. In a paper he presented at the 2003 World Archaeological Congress in Washington, D.C., NASA archaeologist Thomas L. Sever concluded: "The Mayan collapse may well be the greatest demographic disaster in human history."[1] Not a few environmentalists fear the same kind of precipitous collapse for Western society.

Nowadays, Guatemala is one of two Latin American countries with an indigenous majority. But thanks to a conquistador-inspired hierarchy, the Mayan majority remains poor and powerless. When Guatemalans elected a land-reforming liberal president, Jacobo Arbenz Guzman, in 1954, the U.S. Central Intelligence Agency deposed him, an act that triggered a long civil war. On December 6, 1982, the day after United States president Ronald Reagan visited Guatemala's rightist president, Efrain Rios Montt, an elite unit of the Guatemalan army invaded the Mayan village of Las Dos Erres and slaughtered 162 inhabitants, including 67 children.[2] Reagan later said that human-rights activists had handed Montt a "bum rap" in blaming him for military atrocities during the country's civil war. That war took hundreds of thousands of Mayan lives. The country now has a shaky peace treaty, and Spain, for one, has contributed generously to Guatemala's reconstruction. When the Guatemalan judiciary proved unequal to the task of prosecuting military officers for murdering civilians, the United Nations stepped in with special prosecutors. Unfortunately, Oscar Berger, Guatemala's president, seemed afraid to sanction their work.

By contrast, Venezuelan president Hugo Chavez has angered the Bush administration in Washington by increasing taxes on oil companies and redistributing his country's wealth. Chavez has turned over unused land to the landless and promoted a new constitution that would enshrine indigenous peoples' rights. The president undertakes these reforms as part of his policy of "Bolivarism."

Bolivia's Aboriginal majority is the poorest population in South America.[3] In 1781 Tupak Katari led thousands of Aymara in a two-hundred-day siege of La Paz, Bolivia's capital, protesting cruel exploitation by Spanish colonists. In the more than two hundred years since, the Aymara have never stopped denouncing their oppression by the colonists' descendants.

In the course of the last decade, Argentina, Bolivia, Brazil, Chile, the Dominican Republic, Uruguay, and Venezuela elected leftist governments committed to shifting the currents of Latin American history and reconciling human rights with economic development.[4] Throughout the Americas, indigenous peoples' movements seek to reclaim Aboriginal autonomy and enough land for their communities to prosper. Movement leaders protest that global economic forces continue to undermine tribal cultures and new trade agreements ally nascent democracies to the machinery grinding away at tribal peoples. For them, globalization began with the conquistadors.

Canada is implicated in at least one serious conflict with indigenous peoples beyond its borders. A few months after signing the Yukon land-claim agreements in May 1993, Canada ratified the North American Free Trade Agreement (NAFTA). The two treaties are founded on quite different principles. Negotiators wrote the Yukon treaty to protect the Aboriginal subsistence economy. The trilateral trade agreement with Mexico and the United States outlawed exactly this kind of "protectionism." Given the long history of government failures to carry out treaty promises, many worry that Canada will betray Yukon Indians and the "protection" guaranteed them in the Yukon treaty if that protection ever offends NAFTA's "free trade" principles.

In Mexico, the NAFTA deal provoked the Zapatista uprising by hundreds of poorly armed Mayan peasants in 1994. The uprising began in Chiapas, Bartolomé de Las Casas's old Episcopal province, on January 1. The Zapatistas took over highland villages and towns and communicated their demands over the Internet. The world media called it a peasant rebellion; the Zapatistas described it as a movement for indigenous rights. They demanded that Mexico renegotiate NAFTA, especially a provision that undermined what the Indians called their "constitutional" rights to subsistence farming.

When, as a Yukon legislator, I wrote to then prime minister Jean Chrétien about the apparent contradiction in federal government policy through signing both the trade deal and the Yukon treaty, I received the following reply:

> In no way does NAFTA require Mexico to amend its constitution to remove protection for the communal lands of indigenous peoples in Mexico. Indeed, by mutual agreement, discussions

between the Mexican government and the Chiapas rebels have been exclusively on domestic political and social concerns.[5]

Despite every attempt to eradicate them, Aztec, Maya, and other indigenous cultures never completely died. Americans remember César Chávez as a founder of the United Farm Workers movement but forget his Aboriginal roots. According to journalists Roberto Rodriguez and Patricia Gonzales, the origins of most farm workers in the southwestern United States are in the Maya, Nahuatl, Otomiw, and Zapotec communities of Central America: "Like most campesinos [agricultural workers], César Chávez was the color of the earth. There's little doubt that history will one day look back on the United Farm Worker movement as an indigenous insurrection—a struggle for dignity and human rights for a people who have been here forever."[6]

When U.S. president George W. Bush arrived at the November 5, 2005, Summit of the Americas in Argentina with a plan for a Free Trade Area of the Americas treaty, he encountered several newly mandated regional leaders who refused to discuss it. Change continues in the region. On January 15, 2006, Chile elected its first woman president, the socialist and pediatrician Michelle Bachelet. On January 22, 2006, Evo Morales, an Aymara Indian and former leader of the coca growers' union, was sworn in as president of Bolivia and declared an end to the colonial and neoliberal model of development. The day before, Morales had told a crowd of tens of thousands of Aymara and Quechua Indians, "We are not alone. The world is with us. We are in a time of triumph, a time of change."[7] Indigenous people hope to make more gains with forthcoming elections in Costa Rica, Peru, Mexico, Ecuador, and Nicaragua. For historian Niall Ferguson this is troubling: "The new populists are coming to power in large measure because of the successful mobilization of indigenous peoples against the Hispanic or Ladino elites who have dominated Latin American politics since the era of conquest and colonization."[8]

Everywhere in Latin America, citizens want not just fair trade but also healing from centuries of economic exploitation and colonial trauma. They want balance and reconciliation. Aboriginal political agitation in Canada is part of an international movement of indigenous consciousness, giving treaty making a new urgency and relevance.

In 1999 United Nations special rapporteur Miguel Alfonso Martinez completed "a study on treaties, agreements and other constructive arrangements between States and indigenous populations."[9] The special rapporteur surveyed the historical arc, geographic reach, and legal complexities of treaties. Treaties are honourable instruments with a long history, Martinez wrote in 1992, but we ought to avoid "ethnocentric" interpretations of them. Treaty making has always been manipulated to facilitate settlement.

> For at least in theory, treaty-making requires some sort of recognition of equality. The proof is that European Powers (or their successors) started to dispense with treaties when they felt superior, notably in military terms, unless it was judged expeditive or necessary to enter into a form of accord with extra-European peoples, in particular to establish "rights" and priorities over competing European Powers.[10]

Ethnocentric writings intentionally diminish the international status of indigenous nations, Martinez said. This thinking affected the creation of the League of Nations and the United Nations itself. Efforts by Aboriginal peoples to assert their international standing at the league or the International Court of Justice have failed.

Martinez believes that Canada differs from the United States mainly because "settler pressure" was long delayed and legislation like the 1887 *Dawes Act* avoided. But Canada's current approach is still paternalistic, he said. Ottawa signed treaties with Indian nations, then made them dependent children with the *Indian Act*.

Martinez identified numerous historical examples of the law being used as an instrument of colonialism, including:

· The doctrine of *terra nullius*, the encomienda and the repartimiento systems instituted in Latin America by the Spanish Crown in the sixteenth century;
· The so-called removal treaties imposed on the indigenous nations of the southeastern United States under President Jackson in the 1830s;
· Various types of state legislation encroaching on (or ignoring) previously recognized indigenous jurisdiction, such as the *Seven Major Crimes Act* and the *Dawes Severalty Act* passed by the United States Congress in the 1880s;
· The federal *Indian Act* in Canada; and
· Post-*Mabo v. Queensland* legislation in Australia, and many pieces of legislation throughout Latin America.[11]

By drawing lines on maps, colonial powers consistently sought to deprive Aboriginal nations of their lands, sovereignty, and status in international law. For this reason, Martinez strongly supported the recommendation of the final report of Canada's Royal Commission on Aboriginal Peoples that First Nations' oral histories of treaty negotiations be considered alongside the written text of the agreements. This remains a controversial idea. In the post-land-claims period, northern biologists have become more comfortable with including "traditional Aboriginal knowledge" in their wildlife-population estimates. But Canadian courts are still skeptical about the evidentiary value of oral history, despite the Supreme Court's stated openness to it in *Delgamuukw*. Martinez affirmed that, everywhere, the principle of reciprocity "represents a cross-cultural feature of treaty-making." This view, he said, was supported by the Aboriginal interpretations of historic treaties: "A case in point—but not the only one—is the indigenous understanding of some of the numbered treaties in present-day Canada, which has become easily accessible thanks to recently published research."[12]

Martinez found that Eurocentric attitudes inevitably have led to indifferent efforts towards full implementation of treaties, and this is the biggest issue for treaty making today. For this reason, he was not prepared to give blanket endorsement to the modern Canadian treaty process: "In general it remains to be seen in what manner the enforcement and implementation of the provisions of possible constructive arrangements of this type can be ensured, especially for the indigenous parties to such agreements."[13]

This is a troubling observation. The northern treaties of the late twentieth century are demonstrably superior to the numbered treaties railroaded through the western tribes in the century before. The modern agreements are richer, fairer, and more comprehensive. Yet Martinez is correct. There remain serious issues with implementation. To deal with the problem, he advocates funding new structures to facilitate and adjudicate such treaty issues: "States with significant indigenous populations should establish a special jurisdiction to deal exclusively with indigenous issues." This structure, he says, must be an independent, publicly funded body that will eventually replace existing structures. It should have four separate branches:

- A conflict-resolution agency to facilitate resolution of treaty-implementation issues;
- A body to draft legislation based on agreements negotiated with indigenous peoples;
- A judicial body to arbitrate disputes between government and indigenous peoples; and
- An administrative branch to manage logistical and intergovernmental relations.

If this body sounds a bit like a treaty commission, nobody should be surprised. The difference is in the adjective "independent."

Martinez did not underestimate the difficulties of creating such new structures. He said only strong political determination, particularly on the part of non-indigenous leadership, could make this approach viable. Another element was also clear. The effective participation of indigenous peoples in all four of the recommended branches—on a basis of equality with non-indigenous people—is absolutely central to the "philosophy" of overall approach.[14]

Controversial Canadian legal scholar Bruce Clark has made a not-dissimilar argument. Witness this extract from the *Law Society of Upper Canada v. Bruce Clark*:

> Mr. Clark's argument... is based upon the proposition that certain native lands (or "hunting grounds") have never been properly surrendered to the Crown. It follows, he contends, that the Canadian courts have no jurisdiction over indigenous peoples who reside on the unsurrendered lands. Mr. Clark argues that the statutes of Canada and the provinces do not apply to indigenous people who live on unsurrendered lands, and that the affected indigenous people have the right of access to an independent and impartial third party court—to adjudicate the law.[15]

For his manner of expressing this view of the Canadian courts, Bruce Clark was disbarred. Martinez, by contrast, was honoured for his diplomacy as the United Nations representative and his proposal for independent tribunals on treaty issues.[16]

The only Canadian incidence of an Aboriginal and a non-Aboriginal jurist jointly adjudicating an issue occurred in the 1980s, when the Government of Manitoba appointed Justice Murray Sinclair and Justice A.C. Hamilton to conduct Manitoba's Aboriginal Justice Inquiry, which, in part, investigated the police killing of First Nation leader J.J. Harper.[17] A better example is found in the tribunal New Zealand established in 1975[18] to address issues arising from the 1840 Treaty of Waitangi, which Britain signed with the Maori. That this bipartite, bilingual tribunal is unique hints at how significant a reform the UN representative has proposed.

To do all that Martinez advocates in Canada would involve the wholesale replacement of the Department of Indian Affairs, the federal and provincial treaty negotiations offices, and, ironically—because it has only delegated powers—the B.C. Treaty Commission. If substantial reform of the latter body proves impossible, then there might be much to recommend the Martinez proposal.

About five thousand indigenous cultures remain in the world, most under relentless threat from globalization, land developers, and Western "civilization." Most, like the Saami, who live in northern Finland, Norway, Sweden, and Russia, suffer enormous pressure to assimilate. The Saami have hunted reindeer since the ninth century and herded them since the sixteenth. At the Norwegian Supreme Court in 1968, Saami reindeer herders from Sweden won compensation for pastures lost in Norway when a hydroelectric project at Alta Lake damaged their traditional herding range. Of greater import, the court concluded that Saami Aboriginal rights pre-dated the Lapp Codicil of 1751,[19] an appendix to a treaty defining the border between Norway and Sweden; the codicil was previously thought to be the source of those rights. Norway has recently debated new legislation, the "Finnmark Bill," aimed at resolving this insecurity and the dispute concerning Saami and other indigenous rights to land and water in Norway's northern Finnmark region. In April 2004, a group of MPs from the Norwegian parliamentary justice committee visited Ottawa and Vancouver before going on to B.C.'s Nass Valley to study implementation of the Nisga'a treaty.

On September 21, 2004, thousands of tribal representatives from hundreds of Aboriginal communities across the Americas assembled on Washington's National Mall to celebrate the opening of the National Museum of the American Indian. A multimillion-dollar act of atonement by the United States government, the museum's original design was the work of Canadian Blackfoot architect Douglas Cardinal.

However, a powerful New York firm, the Polshek Partnership, known for its steel-and-glass towers, took over Cardinal's plans. Cardinal refused to attend the opening, but many important Aboriginal leaders could not stay away. Among the throng was Alejandro Toledo, president of Peru. Toledo, that nation's first democratically elected Indian head of state, had been inaugurated at Machu Picchu, the mystical Inca ruins. Colorado's Senator Ben Nighthorse Campbell, a northern Cheyenne chief, called the museum a "monument to the millions of native people who died of sickness, slavery, starvation and war."[20]

Whenever people imagine that the crimes of colonialism are ancient history, something happens to remind us that imperialism is not quite dead. To make room for an American air base in the 1970s, the British government forcibly removed the inhabitants of Diego Garcia, islands in the middle of the Indian Ocean. The islanders thought their eviction illegal; they sued the British government and began to negotiate a settlement. Sadly, in 2004, at the behest of its American allies, the government of British prime minister Tony Blair passed a secret order-in-council denying the islanders their right of return.[21]

The indigenous peoples of Africa have also suffered greatly at the hands of imperialism. As recently as the 1950s, the Mau Mau movement grew in resistance to the forty thousand British settlers who had pushed Kikuyu tribesmen onto "native reserves" and detention camps in Kenya. Certain Kikuyu cash crops undercut the colonizers' prices, so colonial authorities prohibited the Kikuyu from growing them. Before the British quit Kenya, they had killed tens of thousands of Kikuyu.[22]

In his book *Dreams from My Father*, United States senator Barack Obama wrote of a visit to Kenya, his father's homeland: "I hadn't met many Masai in Nairobi, although I'd read quite a bit about them. I knew that their pastoral ways and fierceness in war had earned them a grudging respect from the British, so that even as treaties had been broken and the Masai had been restricted to reservations, the tribe had become mythologized in its defeat, like the Cherokee or Apache, the noble savage of picture postcards and coffee table books. I also knew that this Western infatuation with the Masai infuriated other Kenyans, who thought their ways something of an embarrassment, and who hankered after Masai land."[23]

Nothing better illustrates the marginal position of Indians in the New World even today than the fact that no Aboriginal American people are recognized as a nation state; therefore, none is a member of the United Nations. The International Labour Organization (ILO) adopted the Indigenous and Tribal Populations Convention (Number 107) and the corresponding Recommendation (Number 104) in 1957. Although Convention 107 recognized collective indigenous rights to land ownership and compensation for government appropriation of lands, some indigenous commentators thought the document promoted "assimilation." In 1989 the ILO produced Convention 169 concerning Indigenous and Tribal Peoples in Independent Countries. Few nation states have ratified it, and many Aboriginal groups believe the convention falls short of present Canadian standards.[24] Nevertheless, it is cited internationally as a benchmark and brought regularly into the debate on the draft declaration on indigenous rights. The Saami Council is a major supporter.

As indigenous peoples in Central and South America are finding their voices again, Aboriginal peoples in the Far North have been stepping onto the international stage. The Arctic Council, a Canadian conservative initiative, represents an important innovation. The inclusion for the first time of representative Aboriginal bodies from seven of the eight Arctic states as non-voting "permanent participants" in a major international forum counts as a special event. The Arctic Council's founding documents affirm the commitment:

The representatives of the Governments of Canada, Denmark, Finland, Iceland, Norway, the Russian Federation, Sweden and the United States of America (hereinafter referred as the Arctic States) meeting in Ottawa... Hereby declare:

1. The Arctic Council is established as a high level forum to:
   a. provide a means for promoting cooperation, coordination and interaction among the Arctic States, with the involvement of the Arctic indigenous communities and other Arctic inhabitants on common arctic issues, in particular issues of sustainable development and environmental protection in the Arctic.[25]

Supreme Court chief justice Beverley McLachlin has presented a positive view of Canada's efforts to respond to the pressing nature of Aboriginal rights:

> The task of reconciling aboriginal interests with the interests of the descendants of colonial settlers is a complex and difficult one. Yet, as the universal experience of virtually every country faced with that task attests, sooner or later it must be faced, if countries wish to ensure a stable and prosperous future. In Canada, we are tackling these issues. Governments are addressing them, and courts, when called on, continue to discharge their task of resolving disputes where conflicts arise and of determining entitlements under treaties and at common law. The goal is simply stated: respectful accommodation and reconciliation of interests in the context of our unique history and the legal framework that it has produced. The task is not easy, but I for one, take comfort in the knowledge that our country is not alone in facing it.[26]

Special Rapporteur Martinez sees good things and bad in existing Canadian policy. The international significance of developments in Canada cannot be overstressed, he says, if only because these developments highlight the importance and potential utility of establishing sound, equitable "ground rules" for the negotiations required for "constructive arrangements." These rules are important also as mechanisms for the practical implementation of accommodation agreements, constructive arrangements, or treaties, not only in Canada but in all multinational countries with similar problems.[27]

Nisga'a chief Joseph Gosnell told the B.C. legislature in 1998 that the Nisga'a settlement and other treaties could be "a beacon of hope for aboriginal people around the world."[28] As the global economy gobbles up forests and buries arable lands, and Indians across the Americas assert themselves politically, Canada may have things to teach the world about intersocietal conflict resolution, although we also have many lessons to learn from our continental neighbours.

CHAPTER 20

POLITICAL WILL

B.C. **TREATY COMMISSIONER** Mike Harcourt said in 2004 that the next three to five years in the province would see fifteen treaties completed: "We want to create a new relationship based on mutual respect. What flows from that is mutual certainty, decreasing the risk for investment and the creation of probably $100 billion to $150 billion of economic activity in the next 20 years. It's going to be the biggest economic megaproject in this province's history."[1] But British Columbians well remember that, fifteen years ago, experts gave the public pretty much the same time frame. Now, as then, Harcourt remains an optimist.

Public-policy professor John Richards calls himself a pessimist. He rejects the "optimistic anthropology" of the 1996 Royal Commission on Aboriginal Peoples that sought to restore to Aboriginal governments the authority they exercised before colonization. Over the years, Aboriginal lobbyists have succeeded in increasing Ottawa's annual expenditures on Indians, Inuit, and Métis from millions to billions—a percentage of which now goes directly to Aboriginal communities—and, by 2005, Richards thought public opinion would swing back towards assimilation agendas.

One reason for forecasting such a swing may be the transparent failures of the B.C. treaty process. "If treaty making is to be a genuine component of aboriginal policy and be more than an 'industry' providing jobs for lawyers and their academic hangers on in anthropology and law faculties," Richards says, "then it must come to a conclusion in a reasonable time." He thinks the process in B.C. "is verging into irrelevance given its inability to generate actual treaties."[2]

This "irrelevance," combined with a rightward shift in public opinion, could conceivably send Canada back to the "assimilation games" of another time. On January 23, 2006, Canada elected a minority Conservative Party government and a new prime minister, Stephen Harper, who comes from the right wing of the party. Harper appointed Jim Prentice, a moderate MP, as minister of Indian Affairs, and so far his government has proceeded cautiously on the Aboriginal file. Still, fears remain about what a majority Conservative government might do. Judging from previous statements by Conservative MPs, the possibilities include Aboriginal leaders' worst nightmares:

· Deeply cutting financial transfers for education, health, and housing programs;
· Using the constitution's notwithstanding clause to limit Canada's obligations to Aboriginal peoples;
· Ending the separate Aboriginal fishery;
· Adopting Harper mentor Tom Flanagan's proposal to legislate "extinguishment"[3];
· Initiating *Dawes Act*–style privatizing of tribal lands; and
· Offering individual cash buyouts for Aboriginal rights and title both which Flanagan has also proposed.

Much will depend on the extent to which Flanagan has his hand on the Conservative policy pen. Flanagan, Harper's campaign manager and former chief of staff, is also the author of the book *First Nations:*

Second Thoughts.[4] His bluntly assimilationist agenda has made him Public Enemy Number 1 among First Nation leaders. However, as long as he is the leader of a minority government, the new prime minister will likely listen instead to the kinder and gentler voice of Minister Prentice.

When the very conservative B.C. Liberal Party won the 2001 provincial election, many First Nations were worried. Between 2001 and 2005, however, Liberals in Victoria shifted from defending provincial sovereignty against Aboriginal claims to defending treaties as good for business. The four First Nation agreements in principle reached during the B.C. Liberals' tenure accept that certain First Nation law-making powers will be constitutionally entrenched in the final agreements. Attorney General Geoff Plant took office as an articulate defender of settler imperatives, but even his toughest critics credit him with bringing intellectual clarity to the public debates and being determined to provide concrete "deliverables" from the treaty process in the form of interim or economic measures. With Plant's retirement from politics at the time of the 2005 election, leadership on the Aboriginal-policy file shifted to the premier's office.

No one expected a great leap forward under the leadership of Gordon Campbell. Yet in the spring of 2005, during the run-up to the provincial election, Campbell's office began to discuss a "New Relationship" accord with British Columbia's First Nations leaders. Negotiated with the First Nations Summit, the Union of B.C. Indian Chiefs, and the regional office of the Assembly of First Nations, the province's unsigned five-page accord proposes replacing conflict and litigation with a new relationship based on sharing resource revenues, shared provincial-Aboriginal decision making, and provincial recognition of Aboriginal rights and title. This remarkable accord also contemplates measures to address Aboriginal deficits in health, education, and economic development. According to the accord's Statement of Vision:

We are all here to stay. We agree to a new government-to-government relationship based on respect, recognition and accommodation of aboriginal title and rights. Our shared vision includes respect for our respective laws and responsibilities. Through this new relationship, we commit to reconciliation of Aboriginal and Crown titles and jurisdictions.

We agree to establish processes and institutions for shared decision-making about the land and resources and for revenue and benefit sharing, recognizing, as has been determined in court decisions, that the right to aboriginal title "in its full form", including the inherent right for the community to make decisions as to the use of the land and therefore the right to have a political structure for making those decisions, is constitutionally guaranteed by Section 35. These inherent rights flow from First Nations' historical and sacred relationship with their territories.

The historical Aboriginal-Crown relationship in British Columbia has given rise to the present socio-economic disparity between First Nations and other British Columbians.[5]

Upon his re-election, Premier Campbell created a Ministry of Aboriginal Relations and Reconciliation and re-established a Ministry of Environment. As news of the New Relationship accord spread, First Nations leaders could hardly contain their delight. Chief Stewart Phillip, president of the Union of B.C. Indian Chiefs, was quoted as saying, "There's a very public commitment made by the newly elected government of British Columbia and an evident willingness on the part of unified First Nations leadership to come to the table and work... with the government and the opposition to learn from the mistakes of the past, take instructions from the courts, and get on with the business of reconciling aboriginal and Crown title interests in B.C."[6] Grand Chief Edward John observed: "We may yet bury Joseph Trutch's denial of aboriginal rights and title legacy... which this

province has hung onto like a colonial security blanket."[7] Campbell
has created extraordinary expectations.

Of course, the specifics of the new "government-to-government
relationship" with First Nations are vague. For instance, no one could
say exactly how this New Relationship might inform the province's
posture on Aboriginal self-government. "Shared decision-making"
sounds admirable, but its resemblance to the "co-management" of
the northern treaties or the "co-jurisdiction" ambitions of many First
Nations might only emerge with time.

In 2001 Campbell and Plant sent provincial negotiators to the
treaty tables as representatives of non-Indians, defenders of settler
interests. When the Yukon government adopted such a posture in
the eighties, the Council for Yukon Indians rejected government offers, and negotiations broke down. A new territorial administration
took a different position; it argued that the territorial government
represented all Yukoners, Aboriginal and non-Aboriginal. The duty
of government negotiators was therefore to advance the broad public
interest, settling treaties not just in the Aboriginal interest but also for
the common good. That attitudinal shift marked the moment that
Yukon treaties became possible. Is B.C.'s New Relationship accord
such a moment? We shall see.

For months in 2005, First Nations had also been engaged in dialogue with the government of Prime Minister Paul Martin. These
talks led to a First Nations–Federal Crown Political Accord on the
Recognition and Implementation of First Nations Governments,
signed in Ottawa on May 31, 2005. Phil Fontaine, national chief of the
Assembly of First Nations, called the accord a "historic step forward
for First Nations in their relationship with the federal government"[8]
and an opportunity to give life to the inherent Aboriginal and treaty
rights of First Nations, as recognized in Section 35 of Canada's constitution. None of the accord items had become concrete by the time
of Martin's defeat, however.

On November 25, 2005, a federal-provincial-Aboriginal leaders summit at Kelowna, British Columbia, announced $5 billion worth of new economic development, education, health, housing, and infrastructure programs for First Nation, Inuit, and Métis, as well as for indigenous people in urban centres. The federal Conservative government elected in 2006 has already indicated that it might "renegotiate" these agreements. Although critics outside the conference protested that the politicians were using money to mask their failure to deal with Aboriginal rights and treaty issues, most observers praised the announcement and credited Campbell, the host premier, with playing a constructive role in creating the commitment to reduce Aboriginal poverty. Clearly, Campbell had come a long way from his rhetoric about "race-based" government during the 2002 treaty referendum. Yet as recently as May 2005, some critics were still accusing him of hating Aboriginal people.[9] So, what cued this dramatic conversion?

First, there was the educational experience of the treaty negotiation and the inescapable failings of that sluggish process. Second, the courts had laid down the law. Third, the Business Council of British Columbia had convinced the premier that, without certainty over land and resource ownership in the province, many foreign investment opportunities would be lost. Fourth, the presence in the premier's office of an experienced Aboriginal advisor, in the person of Allen Edzerza, obviously made a difference. Finally, political realities took hold. In the 2005 election, Campbell's Liberals lost thirty seats in the legislature. Of ten provincial constituencies in which Aboriginal people make up more than 10 per cent of the population, the Liberals won four seats and the NDP six.[10] In 2001 Campbell's party had taken all ten.

Campbell's 2005 accord suggests the possibility of new forms of reconciliation, and of different kinds of accommodation agreements and political accords. Will this stunning shift in public policy produce more treaties, though? Curiously, the word "treaty" appears nowhere in the New Relationship's text.

Aboriginal-rights lawyer Art Pape participated in the New Relationship negotiations. He is enthusiastic about the accord but sounds a cautionary note about treaty making: "In most cases it has proved to be too big a leap to go from colonial status directly to treaties and self-government agreements in British Columbia, and until 2004 governments felt little pressure to achieve reconciliation through treaties, since business could usually obtain the short-term certainty they required without treaties being concluded."[11] The *Taku* and *Haida* decisions in November of 2004 meant that economic certainty required a new relationship between government and First Nations, Pape says, and the negotiation of the accord itself proves the potential of the new relationship's political and legal foundations.

Pape sits on the Aboriginal side of the table; Thomas Isaac represents corporate interests. In reflecting on the *Haida* decision, Isaac and his colleagues have written that the Supreme Court ruling might "allow for more comprehensive, fair agreements. Conversely, there also exists the possibility that the need for treaties will subside, as many Aboriginal rights claims could be dealt with at the consultation and accommodation level. The ability of the Crown to engage in 'hard bargaining' may lead to an understanding that consultation and any resulting agreements may prove more efficient than the treaty negotiation process."[12] Of course, "efficient accommodation" will not be to everybody's liking.

Does the New Relationship imply that treaties are not a Campbell priority in the near term? At this point, nobody seems to know. By September 2005, Robert Morales, chief negotiator of the Hul'qumi'num Treaty Group of Vancouver Island's Cowichan Valley, had already said, "The treaty table is where we want to see the new relationship begin to materialize."[13] Certainly, this "new relationship" would not encourage "business as usual" at the B.C. Treaty Commission. The June 2005 edition of the treaty commission's *Update* newsletter reported: "Progress slow as talks continue. Negotiations are continuing for three First Nations closest to a treaty, and hope remains high that agreements are possible this year."

WHETHER OR NOT the Campbell Liberals ever intend to fast-track final agreements under the New Relationship, they must realize that the treaty process needs renovating. For the Assembly of First Nations, negotiation is still the right path to reconciliation and rehabilitation for Aboriginal communities, but those negotiations have to be fair:

> Existing policies assume an equality of bargaining position. They do not take into account in their design or policy framework the actual power imbalance between the parties and how this affects both process and outcomes. The slow progress of negotiations is a symptom of this fundamental problem.[14]

Apologists have often said that treaty making takes so long because governments are building a new relationship with First Nations. In light of the New Relationship accord, the B.C. government clearly believes that this relationship should not depend on treaties alone. One way or another, however, all three parties seem to accept that, if Canada is to complete treaty making in British Columbia, the current operation needs retooling.

To review, here are a few suggestions about how that might happen.

1. MANDATES

Rather than negotiating under mandates based on a collation of departmental agendas, both the federal and the provincial governments should begin with a statement of the Crown's broad principles for treaty making—a statement of the public interest in reconciliation. Mandates should be organic, growing out of the negotiations at hand. For without genuine efforts at reconciliation, the courts could eventually decide questions of Aboriginal title and Aboriginal governance, and their rulings could produce outcomes unsatisfactory to any party.

Governments could afford to adopt more flexible mandates, reflecting regional and cultural realities, if they sent the country's best negotiators to treaty tables.

2. NEGOTIATORS

One of the best ways for government to signal seriousness about treaty negotiations would be to hire the strongest professional negotiators available and reward them financially for concluding agreements. In short, Canada and the provinces should be employing closers. Generally, career civil servants do not make great negotiators, but there are obvious exceptions to that rule, including those who helped complete the Nisga'a, Nunavut, and Yukon treaties. Whatever their backgrounds, chief negotiators must have access to their ministers and first ministers, and the authority to craft a deal, whether it is a final agreement or an interim measure.

3. INTERIM MEASURES

The B.C. Claims Task Force recommended the negotiation of interim measures to balance the interests of the parties while treaty talks are under way. In its *Delgamuukw* decision, the Supreme Court of Canada urged consultation and compensation. In *Haida*, the Supreme Court ruled that government should consult and accommodate First Nations when developments are contemplated on their traditional territory. The most common form of accommodation, as outlined earlier, is the interim measure.

Lawyer, constitutionalist, and Maa-nulth chief negotiator Gary Yabsley points out an interesting difference between compensation and accommodation: compensation suggests a final resolution; accommodation implies a continuing process.[15] Yabsley's observation provides a reminder that, while the B.C. treaty process has produced hundreds of them, the interim measure is an evolving instrument. My fear has been that the province views interim measures as a cheap and easy substitute for treaties. If this is the case, then it is making a mistake. Although interim measures can expedite treaty negotiations, they cannot settle either of the two fundamental questions, land and governance. Even if the New Relationship led to bigger and better interim measures, these two central issues would remain unresolved.

A First Nation may see ongoing interim measures or accommodation agreements as a better alternative than a land-selection treaty, at least in the short term. However, the Finance and Justice departments will likely tally those benefits one way or the other and count them against a potential treaty settlement. Worse, a judge may decide at some point in the future that the First Nation's interests have been fully accommodated by interim measures, leaving nothing to be negotiated at a treaty table. An unlikely scenario? Perhaps. But delayed resolution invites such speculation. If a treaty is the shared goal of all three parties, then interim measures negotiations may represent a diversion, rather than progress.

4. DISPUTE RESOLUTION

As outlined in Chapter 17, one way to understand why treaty making takes so long is to compare labour and treaty negotiations. Collective agreements last for one, two, or more years. Treaties are supposed to last "as long as the sun shall shine." Collective bargaining normally involves two parties, an employer and a union; treaty negotiations in British Columbia are tripartite. Collective bargaining usually occurs in private. In theory, treaty negotiations go on in public; in fact, public sessions are infrequent and inaccessible, and they rarely involve any negotiating.

Employers and employees normally close gaps in measured steps, interrupted occasionally by lockouts and strikes. It is a game of checkers motivated by economic fear: lost profits versus lost wages. Treaty negotiations are complex chess games, frequently interrupted by caucuses, consultations, elections, and cabinet shuffles—sometimes by litigation and civil disobedience. Caucusing by either side during collective bargaining usually involves going off to a separate room for an hour or a day. For First Nations and governments, internal consultations can last weeks or months.[16] Treaty negotiators on all sides are careerists or hourly paid professionals. They have no fear of unemployment or bankruptcy. They have no financial incentive to settle. Indeed, their incentives are perverse.

In comparing labour and treaty negotiations, Tom Molloy, the federal government's chief negotiator at the Nisga'a table, writes: "Unlike a collective agreement... a treaty is forever. The parties will not be able to revisit its provisions in two or three years. There are no labour relations boards to act as adjudicators, no amendments except in accordance with strict provisions that must themselves be negotiated."[17]

As stated, unlike Molloy, I think the B.C. treaty process could use mediators to help negotiators unblock troubled talks. These dispute-resolution professionals bring fresh eyes and ears to the table and often suggest novel solutions to seemingly intractable problems. Indeed, former Indian Affairs Deputy Minister Scott Serson says that Regional Director John Watson played exactly this kind of go-between role in the final stages of the Nisga'a negotiations. For years, I have strongly recommended building this capacity at the B.C. Treaty Commission. The New Relationship accord seems to signal that the B.C. government is ready to change its mind on this point.

It is worth restating also that, although treaties normally contain dispute-resolution chapters, the agreed procedures should be tested during negotiations; otherwise, they may not work later, when the parties really need them. If we were truly committed to treaties, the parties at a particular table might even allow mediators or professionals skilled in alternative dispute resolution to redesign their table to improve the chances of agreement.

5. CERTAINTY

Treaties have been described as a search for certainty, and that theme runs through the Nisga'a treaty. The Nisga'a final agreement lays out the constitutional rights the Nisga'a enjoy, the lands on which these rights apply, and the limits of these rights. According to federal negotiator Molloy, "It does so by modifying any Aboriginal rights the Nisga'a may have and by clearly defining any other rights the Parties have agreed the Nisga'a should exercise."[18] Certainty comes when all parties know who owns which lands and what everyone's rights and responsibilities are.

Continued uncertainty has measurable economic costs, and governments are not prepared to buy certainty at any price. They will pay only what the tax-paying public will accept as fair.

Apparently, taxpayers want fairness and finality. Fearing that capital transfers might be squandered like lottery winnings, they want to know that capital transfer will be deposited in Aboriginal community trust funds for the benefit of future generations. This paternalism will surprise no one who has probed public opinion. Canadians do not want to face the prospect of renegotiating a modern treaty a decade or a century after its signing. Also, if Canadians want finality and certainty, treaties must be fair to First Nations.

6. SELF-GOVERNMENT

As I write, the B.C. government finally seems poised to respect the First Nation right to self-government, and it has begun to focus on working out practical arrangements for the exercise of these rights. Treaties will give birth to new forms of tribal governments, but intergovernmental agreements with Canada and the province should give these new governments the means to grow and function properly. Negotiations should, therefore, concentrate less on ideology and more on the practicalities of institution building, economic service delivery or aggregation, and funding arrangements. First Nations want to be partners, not subjects of the provincial government. There is every indication that, given the relevant information, the public will support the desire of Aboriginal peoples to retake control of their own lives.

7. COMMUNICATIONS

The 1763 Royal Proclamation required that negotiations should take place "in publick," but for the most part B.C. treaty negotiations occur in private. Nevertheless, the public is entitled to know what happens at treaty tables, and communicating with citizens is the responsibility of all parties. Modern treaties are complex, the issues often controversial. In my view, nobody should be allowed to negotiate for government unless she or he has the skills to explain the issues to citizens outside the negotiating room. In a modern democracy, if you cannot sell an agreement to the majority of citizens, it won't stick. All parties to agreements, negotiators and politicians, must share in this difficult but essential task.

I believe, in fact, that communicating with outside parties is the negotiator's second most important job. Yukon negotiators had to think constantly about what the mineworker needed to know and which issues the Chamber of Commerce really cared about. The chamber wanted an end to the Indian tax exemption. Municipalities wanted to know that Aboriginal self-government would not apply to individual Indian properties within city limits. We understood that the most skeptical audience for treaties was the working-class, white male. The "average working man" wanted assurance that, after the treaty, he would still have his job, his cabin by the lake, and a chance to hunt a moose. Of course, explaining all this would be made a lot easier if treaties were written in plain English.

The communications challenges for Aboriginal communities are as complex as those for government, especially since the members of a First Nation are rarely unanimous in supporting the particulars of a treaty. If a community is seriously divided and internal communications are stunted, a treaty will be impossible.

On September 17, 2004, I attended a "public negotiation meeting" at the Gitksan treaty office in Hazelton. The Supreme Court's 1997 decision on the Gitksan's *Delgamuukw* action had confirmed the existence of Aboriginal title in British Columbia, and in 2001 the Gitksan entered the B.C. treaty process. By 2004, however, in part because of internal divisions, there had been very little progress.

Although the B.C. Claims Task Force had recommended a public negotiating process, public meetings like the one in Hazelton are carefully controlled events with the three chief negotiators giving brief reports and answering selected questions from the audience. A B.C. treaty commissioner normally chairs such meetings. At Hazelton, commissioner Jody Wilson chaired the session.

As they entered the meeting room, audience members were handed an agenda and a sheet called "Guidelines for Observers." Those attending were required to sign an attendance sheet and forbidden from taping the proceedings. The guidelines made the position of audience members clear: "You are being permitted as an observer, not as a participant... The Chair will not recognize any speakers from the floor during the meeting. Talking or disruptions are not allowed during the proceedings. The Chair reserves the right to ask anyone who does not respect these rules to leave."[19]

Sitting at the back of the room, I tried to imagine how a local union's rank-and-file members, at a meeting called to report on progress in collective bargaining, might receive such instructions. Not well, I thought. In the midst of this reverie, I noticed someone come to the doorway with an RCMP officer and point out a tiny Aboriginal woman sitting quietly just in front of me. The officer came into the room and told the woman she would have to leave. "This is a public meeting," she protested quietly. The officer said, "I'm just doing my job." "Who told you to do this?" she asked. The officer refused to say, and a moment later he handcuffed the woman. She fell to the floor and started crying.

None of the three treaty commission negotiators came over to ask why someone would be dragged out of a public meeting, but two old women came over to comfort her. The woman's male seatmate asked the RCMP officer, "Why are you doing this? Aren't you an Aboriginal person?"

Clearly embarrassed, the officer answered, "Yes, I'm Coast Salish."

The scene was totally unsettling. For a moment, I thought I was in the pre–civil rights U.S. South or apartheid-era South Africa. Apparently, part of the tension in the community arises from the tribal negotiators' failure to get consensus on a negotiating mandate, and dissidents allege that millions of dollars have been spent on or borrowed for negotiations that have gone nowhere. Whatever the merits of the arguments on either side, it is outrageous that the B.C. Treaty Commission would hold a public meeting about Gitksan treaty negotiations in a building from which certain beneficiaries had been barred (as I learned later) and that the RCMP would be used to enforce such a ban.[20]

8. B.C. TREATY COMMISSION

Even with the energy invested by the province in accommodation agreements and the New Relationship accord, the B.C. treaty process risks being sidelined unless the parties change the way it operates. In particular, the parties need to review the way the B.C. Treaty Commission carries out its facilitation, funding, and communication mandates. As early as 2002, Edward John was saying he felt the treaty commission had too narrowly interpreted its facilitation role to mean merely the convening of meetings: "The treaty commission needs to take a look at its mandate and its interpretation of the word 'facilitate.' Short of that, the treaty commission would be of limited value."[21] Former chief federal negotiator Robin Dodson conceded the parties sometimes need neutral participants to assist the negotiation of particular issues: "We used to talk about a British Columbia Treaty Commission with teeth, and I think that is the same idea."[22] In response, treaty commissioner Jack Weisgerber has joked, "I think that everyone wants the commission to have more teeth and believes that somebody else needs to be bitten."[23] In order to fully play its facilitation role, the commission obviously requires a degree of independence from the three parties involved in negotiations.

The commission's website proudly declares: "The Treaty Commission is the independent and neutral body responsible for facilitating treaty negotiations."[24] But how much independence does the commission really enjoy? Both New Democrat and Liberal governments have threatened to cut the commission's funding, clearly signalling who was boss. The 1991 task force report noted that the "impartiality" of the commission depended on both Ottawa and Victoria contributing to its operating costs: "Secure long-term funding for the operations of the Commission and First Nations participation in the process will give all the parties confidence in the commission and the process."[25] The key word here is "security." Financial insecurity would render the BCTC continually dependent, rather than guaranteeing it the kind of independence Canadian judges enjoy.

The established procedure for selecting B.C. treaty commissioners also challenges the commission's claim of independence. The task force report recommended that the commission be "accountable" to all three parties, but to be independent and yet accountable is a precarious balancing act. The tripartite agreement setting up the commission reads: "Decisions of the Commission shall be made by agreement of at least one Commissioner nominated by each Principal."[26] This triple-majority rule offers some protection for both government and Aboriginal sides at treaty tables, but it could also compromise the commission's independence. For example, it would probably prevent the commission from providing truly neutral "dispute resolution services" if one of the three parties were to become obstructionist.

To achieve greater independence, the commission might need, at a minimum, full-time commissioners jointly appointed by all parties, or commissioners appointed for longer terms, say six years rather than two, and unshakeably reliable long-term funding.

The task force spoke brave words about the need for public information and education, but neither the commission nor the parties involved have done a great job on this score. Successful negotiations depend upon an atmosphere conducive to building new relationships among the parties' constituents, and, as the task force observed, "[I]n large measure the atmosphere... depend[s] on the public awareness and the understanding of the history of British Columbia, and the dissemination of accurate information about the negotiations."[27] The B.C. government's 2002 province-wide referendum became a vivid demonstration of the need for public education on the land-claims question; the public deserved an independent source of factual information about treaty making, and the B.C Treaty Commission should have provided that. The commission does publish a newsletter called *Update*, a "Why Treaties?" pamphlet, annual reports, videos, and curriculum materials. All are informative and readable, but the circulation of these publications is consistently under ten thousand. At present, the commission is a quiet voice.

One treaty negotiator has likened the B.C. Treaty Commission to Canada's governor general, a public figure with mainly ceremonial duties. For want of independence in the areas of facilitation, funding, and communication, the commission currently acts only as the manager, not the governor, of the treaty process. Nevertheless, BCTC still has unrealized potential—potential that can be realized only by the treaty commission becoming a truly independent authority. Thus reformed, it could open up policy tables on challenging ideas like co-jurisdiction, develop lists of mediators, widely communicate the hard truths about treaties, and start to act as an implementation tribunal.

The three B.C. parties should think seriously about giving the treaty commission an adjudicative role for future treaty-implementation issues. The commission was created on the assumption that it would be wound up when all of the treaties were settled. The question is not yet urgent, but the parties might want to consider anew the advantages of an independent local body that could hear and resolve disputes about the implementation of B.C. treaties.

THE B.C. TREATY process suffers from a lack of creativity: what University of Toronto scholar Thomas Homer-Dixon calls an "ingenuity gap."[28] Escaping the bog of bureaucratic inertia and passive-aggressive behaviours requires imagination: strong negotiators, flexible mandates, and creative problem solving. Treaty tables need to experiment. Not all of their solutions will work, but some might represent breakthroughs. Arriving at different solutions for different First Nations need not be a problem as long as these solutions are generally equitable. Some bands might get more land, others more money, resources, or jurisdiction.

North America has gone from making treaties in days to taking decades, from *Indian Act* colonialism to Aboriginal self-government, from reserves to titled land in tribal hands, but the issues of Aboriginal rights and title remain. Some say that First Nations without treaties have benefited from the delays; others argue that the Supreme Court of Canada is closing the box of rights, and that settlements will not get much better than they are now. What can be improved, without a doubt, is the process. Achieving that will require, above all, political will.

No treaty will ever be concluded until political leaders—federal, provincial, and territorial—get personally involved. This is borne out by looking at Quebec minister John Ciacca's role in the 1975 James Bay treaty, federal Indian Affairs minister Ron Irwin's commitment to the Nunavut agreement, minister Bill McKnight's key part in completing the Yukon settlement, and the contributions of premiers Bill Vander Zalm, Mike Harcourt, and Glen Clark to the Nisga'a agreement. Treaty making depends on political leadership—Aboriginal and non-Aboriginal. When Robert Kennedy became attorney general of the United States in 1961, he hired more lawyers and gave them mere months to settle hundreds of outstanding land claims.[29] Kennedy showed political will. So did Gordon Campbell when he sponsored the New Relationship accord. Nobody has ever demonstrated political will quite like the Nisga'a. For a century they banged the same drum, demanding a treaty to settle the "land question." But no other First Nation should have to face such a struggle.

Treaties will come when and if federal and provincial first ministers develop a commitment to more than rhetorical accommodation and reconciliation. Peacemaking requires a different mindset than the normal competitions of economic and political life. To make peace—to make a treaty—takes the courage to make compromises and to surrender thoughts of total victory or total defeat.

Statistics show that life is slowly improving for Aboriginal Canadians. Treaties cannot meet every need, but they can contribute to community health, social peace, and economic prosperity. Thanks to significant federal expenditures over the last few decades, Aboriginal health outcomes are improving, but the rates for diabetes and suicide remain disturbingly high. In fact, the suicide rate on reserves is twice that of the rest of the country. Suicide accounts for a large percentage of the deaths of Indian young people on reserves.[30] M.J. Chandler and C. Lalonde's study "Cultural Continuity as a Hedge against Suicide in Canada's First Nations" showed that First Nations communities with high levels of self-government had low suicide rates, a hopeful message for treaty makers.[31]

The failure to make timely treaties eventually comes to the city. Census data show that half of Canada's Aboriginal population now live in urban settings. For many young people, the city represents an escape from poverty and boredom.[32] Ottawa has long argued that it has few responsibilities for urban Aboriginal populations and that its constitutional duty extends to "Indians *and* Lands reserved for the Indians." First Nations respond that the constitution does not say "Indians *on* Lands reserved for Indians" and that Ottawa makes an argument of financial convenience. In 1997 the federal government adopted an "urban aboriginal strategy" with no funding attached. In 2001 the strategy received funding.[33]

Bradley Regehr, an Aboriginal lawyer from Winnipeg, sees urban reserves not only as economic opportunities but also as the embodiment of the inherent right to self-government: "Existing reserves have become crowded, and migration to urban areas has greatly increased the First Nation population in such areas. First Nations want to be able to interact and to service their members living in urban areas, and the establishment of an urban reserve can help."[34]

Neither the provinces nor the cities will be quick to welcome new reserves within municipal borders, but even if governments seriously address the poverty and powerlessness of life in rural Aboriginal communities, Aboriginal migration to the cities will continue. In the big city, the challenges for treaty makers get really complex. Nobody yet has even begun to sort out the questions of tax collection, land-use planning, and dispute resolution in the urban treaty environment.[35] In Powell River, Prince George, and Osoyoos, municipal and Aboriginal governments have found reasons to cooperate. Things are not so positive in the big cities of B.C.'s Lower Mainland. By refusing to cooperate on service issues, the municipality of Delta could scuttle the efforts of the Tsawwassen Nation to get a treaty.[36]

It is time for Canada and Canadians to get serious about treaty negotiations. Reconciliation requires a larger, more open-minded view than that demonstrated by most political partisans. Treaties are a solution to a problem, and that problem is colonization, not judicial activism, as conservative commentators sometimes seem to believe. Why have we not yet made treaties with the Aboriginal peoples of British Columbia? The long answer lies in our colonial history. The short answer is that contemporary premiers and prime ministers have not wanted them. This failure could become our Balkans, our Beirut, our Belfast. An alternative future of reconciliation through just treaties is ours to debate and to choose.

APPENDIX

TEN RECOMMENDATIONS FOR POLICY MAKERS

1. Bury colonial attitudes about Aboriginal institutions with a new commitment to accommodation, reconciliation, and treaties.
2. Open up negotiations by tabling government land-and-money negotiating mandates.
3. Hire creative negotiators and give them incentives to settle.
4. Do not use interim measures as substitutes for treaties.
5. Use alternative dispute resolution techniques and bring mediators to treaty tables. Allow First Nations to litigate disputes when necessary.
6. Respect the Aboriginal right to self-government, but invest in aggregation: democratic, efficient, and effective institutions of governance.
7. Build a truly independent British Columbia Treaty Commission to fund negotiations, fully inform citizens, and adjudicate implementation issues.
8. Create options with fast-track treaties and high-level dialogues on co-jurisdiction.
9. Write treaties in plain language, as principled agreements and constitutional documents, with the details attached in appendices.
10. Show the political will to complete Canada's reconciliation with its Aboriginal peoples through treaties and other agreements.

ENDNOTES

INTRODUCTION

1. Arthur Manuel, "Chief Calls on First Nations to Walk Away from the B.C. Treaty Process—Open Letter to All of the Aboriginal Nations and Communities Participating in the British Columbia Treaty Commission Process," February 15, 2000.
2. Royal Commission on Aboriginal Peoples, *Report of the Royal Commission on Aboriginal Peoples, Vol. 5—Renewal: A Twenty-Year Commitment* (Ottawa: Indian and Northern Affairs Canada, 1996).
3. Anatol Rapoport, "Debates," *Peace and Change: A Journal of Peace Research* 13 (1988): 44.

A NOTE ON TERMINOLOGY

1. *Delgamuukw v. Attorney General of British Columbia*, (1997) 3 S.C.R. 45.
2. Royal Commission on Aboriginal Peoples.

CHAPTER 1: COLONIAL ATTITUDES

1. Sean Clarke, "Europe United in the Magdalenian Era," *Guardian Weekly*, April 22–28, 2003, 8.
2. Adam Kuper, "Men's Work," *London Review of Books*, June 24, 2004, 37.
3. Kuper, "Men's Work."
4. Bartolomé de Las Casas, *In Defense of the Indians*. Translated by Stafford Poole (DeKalb, IL: Northern Illinois University Press, 1992), 271.
5. Christopher Columbus, *The Four Voyages*. Translated and edited by J.M. Cohen (London: Penguin, 1969), 70.
6. Columbus, *The Four Voyages*, 71.
7. Columbus, *The Four Voyages*, 16.
8. Daniel Francis, *The Imaginary Indian: The Image of the Indian in Canadian Culture* (Vancouver: Arsenal Pulp Press, 1995), 7–8.
9. Alfred W. Crosby, *The Columbian Exchange: Biological and Cultural Consequences of 1492* (New York: Praeger, 2003).
10. Pope Alexander VI, The Bull *Inter Caetera*, May 4, 1493.
11. Bartolomé de Las Casas, *The Devastation of the Indies: A Brief Account*, Translated by Herma Briffault (Baltimore and London: Johns Hopkins University Press, 1974), 27–28.
12. Bartolomé de Las Casas, *History of the Indies*. Translated and edited by Andrée M. Collard (New York, Evanston and London: Harper and Row). 68.
13. Las Casas, *History of the Indies*, 33.
14. Las Casas, *History of the Indies*, 35.

15. Juan López de Palacios Rubios, Requerimiento (Council of Castille, 1510).
16. Rubios, Requerimiento.
17. Hernán Cortés, *Letters from Mexico*, revised ed. Translated and edited by A. Pagden (New Haven and London: Yale University, 1986), 59.
18. Cortés, *Letters from Mexico*, 61.
19. Las Casas, *The Devastation of the Indies*, 59–60.
20. Hugh Thomas, *Rivers of Gold: The Rise of the Spanish Empire, from Columbus to Magellan* (New York: Random House, 2003), 490.
21. James Wilson, *The Earth Shall Weep: A History of Native America* (New York: Grove Press, 1998), 35.
22. Ronald Wright, *Stolen Continents: The "New World" Through Indian Eyes* (Toronto: Penguin, 1992), 47.
23. Wright, *Stolen Continents*, 47.
24. Juan Ginés de Sepúlveda, *Democrates Alter, or, On the Just Causes for War Against the Indians*, 1547.
25. Lewis Hanke, *All Mankind is One* (DeKalb, IL: Northern Illinois University Press, 1974), 93.

CHAPTER 2: LAND CLAIMS

1. John Locke, "Of Property." Second Treatise, 1689.
2. John C. Weaver, *The Great Land Rush and the Making of the Modern World, 1650–1900* (Montreal and Kingston: McGill-Queen's University Press, 2003).
3. Weaver, *The Great Land Rush and the Making of the Modern World, 1650–1900*, 13.
4. Weaver, *The Great Land Rush and the Making of the Modern World, 1650–1900*, 137.
5. Weaver, *The Great Land Rush and the Making of the Modern World, 1650–1900*, 149.
6. Adam Smith, "Private Law," in R.L. Meek, D.D. Raphael, and P.G. Sten, eds., *Adam Smith: Lectures on Jurisprudence* (Oxford: Clarendon Press, 1978), 459–60.
7. Smith, "Private Law," 459–60.
8. Smith, "Private Law," 459–60.
9. David Christian, *Maps of Time: An Introduction to Big History* (Berkeley and Los Angeles: University of California Press, 2005), 222.
10. Georges Erasmus and Joe Sanders, "Canadian History: An Aboriginal Perspective," in John Bird, ed., *Nation to Nation: Aboriginal Sovereignty and the Future of Canada* (Toronto: Irwin Publishing, 2002), 5.
11. Catherine McClellan, et al., *Part of the Land, Part of the Water: A History of Yukon Indians* (Vancouver: Douglas & McIntyre, 1987).
12. Henry Reynolds, *The Law of the Land* (Victoria, Australia: Penguin Books Australia, 1992), 65.

13. John Richards, *Creating Choices: Rethinking Aboriginal Policy* (Toronto: C.D. Howe Institute, 2006), 10.
14. Charles C. Mann, "The Pristine Myth," *Atlantic Unbound*, March 7, 2002, www.theatlantic.com/unbound/ interviews/int2002-03-07.htm.
15. Mann, "The Pristine Myth."
16. Colin G. Calloway, *One Vast Winter Count: The Native American West Before Lewis and Clark* (Lincoln and London: University of Nebraska Press, 2003), 308.
17. Hugh Brody, *The Other Side of Eden* (Vancouver and Toronto: Douglas & McIntyre, 2001), 7.
18. James Wilson, *The Earth Shall Weep: A History of Native America* (New York: Grove Press, 1998), 249.

CHAPTER 3: PONTIAC'S PROCLAMATION

1. Colin G. Calloway, *One Vast Winter Count: The Native American West Before Lewis and Clark.* (Lincoln and London: University of Nebraska Press, 2003), 215.
2. James Wilson, *The Earth Shall Weep: A History of Native America* (New York: Grove Press, 1998), 77.
3. Wilson, *The Earth Shall Weep*, 62.
4. Wilson, *The Earth Shall Weep*, 62.
5. John Brewer, "The Irish Indian Chief," *New York Review of Books*, December 1, 2005.
6. Calloway, *One Vast Winter Count*, 349.
7. Francis Parkman, *The Conspiracy of Pontiac and the Indian War After the Conquest of Canada, Volume 1* (Lincoln and London: University of Nebraska Press, 1994), 2.
8. Parkman, *The Conspiracy of Pontiac and the Indian War After the Conquest of Canada, Volume 1*, 206–7.
9. Francis Parkman, *The Conspiracy of Pontiac and the Indian War After the Conquest of Canada, Volume 2*, (Lincoln and London: University of Nebraska Press, 1994), 39.
10. Parkman, *The Conspiracy of Pontiac and the Indian War After the Conquest of Canada, Volume 2*, 40.
11. Charles C. Mann, "The Pristine Myth," *Atlantic Unbound*, March 7, 2002, www.theatlantic.com/unbound/ interviews/int2002-03-07.htm.
12. Mann, "The Pristine Myth."
13. George III, Royal Proclamation, 1763.
14. John C. Weaver, *The Great Land Rush and the Making of the Modern World, 1650–1900* (Montreal and Kingston: McGill-Queen's University Press, 2003), 136.
15. Calloway, *One Vast Winter Count*, 355.
16. Thomas Jefferson, *The Declaration of Independence*. In Congress, July 4, 1776.
17. Calloway, *One Vast Winter Count*, 350.

CHAPTER 4: CHEROKEE SELFISHNESS

1. Thomas Berger, *A Long and Terrible Shadow: White Values, Native Rights in the Americas, 1492–1992* (Vancouver: Douglas & McIntyre, 1991), xi.

2. Dee Brown, *Bury My Heart at Wounded Knee* (New York: Holt, 1970); and Vine Deloria, Jr., *Custer Died for Your Sins* (New York: Macmillan, 1969).

3. Angie Debo, *A History of the Indians of the United States* (Norman: University of Oklahoma Press, 1970).

4. Debo, *A History of the Indians of the United States*, 311.

5. Jill Norgren, *The Cherokee Cases: Two Landmark Federal Decisions in the Fight for Sovereignty* (New York: McGraw-Hill, 1996), 80.

6. Norgren, *The Cherokee Cases*, 63.

7. Norgren, *The Cherokee Cases*, 81.

8. Gore Vidal, *Inventing a Nation: Washington, Adams, Jefferson* (New Haven: Yale University Press, 2003).

9. Thomas Jefferson, The Declaration of Independence. In Congress, July 4, 1776.

10. Vidal, *Inventing a Nation*, 177.

11. Vidal, *Inventing a Nation*, 182.

12. *Cherokee Nation v. Georgia* 30 U.S. 1 (1831).

13. *Worcester v. Georgia* 31 U.S. 515 (1832).

14. Andrew Jackson, 7th Congress, Debates, 1830.

15. Norgren, *The Cherokee Cases*, 136.

16. Henry Dawes, quoted in Gloria Steinem, *Revolution from Within* (New York: Little Brown, 1992), 179.

17. Debo, *A History of the Indians of the United States*, 300.

18. Debo, *A History of the Indians of the United States*, 311.

19. Theodore Roosevelt, First Annual Message, December 3, 1901.

20. Chris Stainbrook, presentation to EcoTrust Foundation Conference, Tofino, B.C., June 6–8, 2002.

21. Debo, *A History of the Indians of the United States*, 309.

22. "Into Oklahoma at Last: Thousands Wildly Dashing in for Homes—The Scramble of Settlers, Boomers and Speculators," *New York Times*, April 23, 1889.

23. "Into Oklahoma at Last," *New York Times*.

24. Brown, *Bury My Heart at Wounded Knee*, 414–18.

CHAPTER 5: MONEY MATTERS

1. Harry Swain, presentation to Treasury Board, Ottawa, June 25, 1992.

2. Samuel B. Steele, *Forty Years in Canada: Reminiscences of the Great North-West, with Some Account of His Service in South Africa* (Toronto: Coles Publishing Co., 1915), 104.

3. Peter Erasmus, *Buffalo Days and Nights* (Calgary: Fifth House, 1999), 237.

4. Deanna Christensen, *Ahtahkakoop* (Shell Lake, SK: Ahtahkakoop Publishing, 2000), 155.

5. Erasmus, *Buffalo Days and Nights*, 238.
6. Alexander Morris, *The Treaties of Canada with the Indians of Manitoba and the North-West Territories Including the Negotiations on Which They Were Based* (Toronto: Coles, 1880, reprinted 1971), 182.
7. Erasmus, *Buffalo Days and Nights*, 139.
8. Morris, *The Treaties of Canada with the Indians of Manitoba and the North-West Territories*, 32.
9. Morris, *The Treaties of Canada with the Indians of Manitoba and the North-West Territories*, 197–98.
10. Christensen, *Ahtahkakoop*, 236
11. Erasmus, *Buffalo Days and Nights*, 240.
12. Morris, *The Treaties of Canada with the Indians of Manitoba and the North-West Territories*, 199.
13. Morris, *The Treaties of Canada with the Indians of Manitoba and the North-West Territories*, 204–6.
14. Morris, *The Treaties of Canada with the Indians of Manitoba and the North-West Territories*, 206–7.
15. Morris, *The Treaties of Canada with the Indians of Manitoba and the North-West Territories*, 207–8.
16. Erasmus, *Buffalo Days and Nights*, 244
17. Morris, *The Treaties of Canada with the Indians of Manitoba and the North-West Territories*, 195.
18. J.R. Miller, *Lethal Legacy: Current Native Controversies in Canada* (Toronto: McClelland and Stewart, 2004), 142 .
19. John Richards, *Creating Choices: Rethinking Aboriginal Policy* (Toronto: C.D. Howe Institute, 2006), 3.
20. Sheila Fraser, presentation to Assembly of First Nations, Indigenous Bar Association and Law Commission of Canada, Hull, Quebec, April 24, 2003.

CHAPTER 6: THE BERGER-SMITH DEBATE

1. Government of British Columbia, *Your Guide to the Nisga'a Treaty* (Victoria: Ministry of Aboriginal Affairs, 1998).
2. Thomas Berger, *A Long and Terrible Shadow: White Values, Native Rights in the Americas, 1492–1992* (Vancouver: Douglas & McIntyre, 1991), 183.
3. Melvin Smith, *Our Home or Native Land: What Governments' Aboriginal Policy Is Doing to Canada* (Victoria: Crown Western, 1995).
4. George Vancouver, *A Voyage of Discovery to the North Pacific Ocean and Round the World* (Originally published 1792; republished Amsterdam: N. Israel, 1967), 259.
5. Berger, *A Long and Terrible Shadow*, 143.
6. Robin Fisher, *Contact and Conflict* (Vancouver: University of British Columbia Press, 1992), 66.
7. Smith, *Our Home or Native Land*, 76.

8. Fisher, *Contact and Conflict*, 160.
9. Fisher, *Contact and Conflict*, 55.
10. Fisher, *Contact and Conflict*, 57.
11. Fisher, *Contact and Conflict*, 61.
12. Smith, *Our Home or Native Land*, 76.
13. Smith, *Our Home or Native Land*, 76.
14. Smith, *Our Home or Native Land*, 76.
15. Berger, *A Long and Terrible Shadow*, 143.
16. Berger, *A Long and Terrible Shadow*, 144.
17. Berger, *A Long and Terrible Shadow*, 144.
18. Smith, *Our Home or Native Land*, 79.
19. Smith, *Our Home or Native Land*, 79.
20. Smith, *Our Home or Native Land*, 79.
21. David Mills, Minister of the Interior, letter to Gilbert Sproat, Indian Land Commissioner, Kamloops, August 3, 1877.
22. Berger, *A Long and Terrible Shadow*, 146.
23. Berger, *A Long and Terrible Shadow*, 147.
24. Berger, *A Long and Terrible Shadow*, 147.
25. Berger, *A Long and Terrible Shadow*, 147
26. Smith, *Our Home or Native Land*, 80.
27. Smith, *Our Home or Native Land*, 81.
28. Berger, *A Long and Terrible Shadow*, 140.
29. Thomas Berger, "The Importance of the Nisga'a Treaty to Canadians," Corry Lecture, Queen's University, Kingston, February 10, 1999.
30. Pierre Trudeau, speech, Seaforth Armories, Vancouver, August 8, 1969.
31. Smith, *Our Home or Native Land*, 9
32. Smith, *Our Home or Native Land*, 81–82.
33. Berger, *A Long and Terrible Shadow*, 141.
34. Smith, *Our Home or Native Land*, 266.

CHAPTER 7: CROSSROADS: TABLES, COMMISSIONS, AND COURTS

1. Imperial measurements are cited in Parts I and II, appropriate to historical references; Part III uses the metric system.
2. British Columbia Treaty Commission Agreement, 1992, 7 (1) (iii) B (h).
3. Jack Weisgerber, presentation to the Continuing Legal Education Society of British Columbia, June 11, 2004.
4. Thomas Jefferson, "INDIANS, American Nations and," *The Jeffersonian Cyclopedia* (Charlottesville, VA: University of Virginia Library, Electronic Text Centre) http://etext.lib.virginia.edu/etcbin/foley-entry?id=JCE3903.
5. Jill Norgren, *The Cherokee Cases: Two Landmark Federal Decisions in the Fight for Sovereignty* (New York: McGraw-Hill, 1996), 206.
6. *St. Catherine's Milling and Lumber Company v. Regina* (1888), 13 S.C.R., 577.
7. *Calder v. Attorney General of British Columbia*, (1973) S.C.R. 313.

8. *R. v. Sparrow*, (1990) 1 S.C.R. 1075.
9. *R v. Van der Peet*, (1996) 2 S.C.R. 507.
10. *Van der Peet.*
11. Russell L. Barsh and James Y. Henderson, "The Supreme Court's Van der Peet Trilogy: Naïve Imperialism and Ropes of Sand," *McGill Law Journal*, 1997, 993.
12. *R v. Gladstone*, (1996) 2 S.C.R. 723.
13. *Delgamuukw v. The Queen* (1991) 3W.W.R.97 (B.C.S.C.)
14. *Delgamuukw.*
15. *Delgamuukw.*
16. *Delgamuukw.*
17. John J.L. Hunter, "Judicial Recognition of Aboriginal Self-Government: Where Do We Stand?" Presentation to Canadian Bar Association 2002 Aboriginal Law Conference, Victoria, April 27–28, 2002.
18. Jim Aldridge, e-mail message to the author, April 17, 2005.
19. Ian Mulgrew, "Second Chilcotin War, Justice Southin Says," *Vancouver Sun*, January 11, 2006.
20. Bruce Clark, *Justice in Paradise* (Montreal and Kingston: McGill-Queen's University Press, 1999), 254.
21. Clark, *Justice in Paradise*, 89–98.
22. Clark, *Justice in Paradise*, 91
23. Russell L. Barsh, "Evaluating the Quality of Justice," *Justice as Healing*, Spring 1995, 180.

CHAPTER 8: NORTHERN TREATIES

1. Felipe Fernández-Armesto, *The Americas: A Hemispheric History* (New York: Modern Library, 2003), 23.
2. Donald C. Mitchell, *Take My Land, Take My Life: The Story of Congress's Historic Settlement of Alaska Native Claims, 1960–1971* (Fairbanks: University of Alaska Press, 2001), 493.
3. Niilo Koponen, letter to the author, July 8, 2002.
4. Ken Coates, *Best Left as Indians: Native-White Relations in the Yukon Territory, 1840–1973* (Montreal and Kingston: McGill-Queen's University Press, 1991), 356.
5. *Calder v. Attorney General of British Columbia*, (1973) S.C.R. 313.
6. Umbrella Final Agreement between the Government of Canada, the Council for Yukon Indians and the Government of the Yukon, http://www.ainc-inac.gc.ca/pr/agr/umb/index_e.html.
7. Steven Smyth, "Colonialism and Language in Canada's North: A Yukon Case Study," *Arctic*, June 1996, 155–61.
8. Joyce Green, "The Challenge of the 21st Century: Setting the Real Bottom Line," Saskatchewan Institute of Public Policy, Armchair Discussion Series, Regina, March 18, 2003.
9. Preston Manning, *The Nisga'a Final Agreement* (Ottawa: Official Opposition, 1999).

10. Thomas Berger, *Northern Frontier, Northern Homeland: The Report of the Mackenzie Valley Pipeline Inquiry*. (Ottawa: Minister of Supply and Services Canada, 1977).

11. Fernández-Armesto, *The Americas*, 147.

12. Ted Moses, keynote speech to Redefining Relationships conference, Ottawa, November 13, 2003.

13. Moses, keynote speech to Redefining Relationships conference.

14. Moses, keynote speech to Redefining Relationships conference.

15. Lloyd Axworthy, *The Northern Dimension of Canada's Foreign Policy* (Ottawa: Department of Foreign Affairs and International Trade, 2000), http://www.dfait-maeci.gc.ca/circumpolar/seco6_ndfp_rpt-en.asp.

16. René Fumoleau, *As Long as This Land Shall Last* (Calgary: University of Calgary Press, 2003).

CHAPTER 9: HUNTING GROUNDS

1. Harold Innis, *The Fur Trade in Canada* (Toronto: University of Toronto Press, 1930, reprinted in 1970), 419.

2. Peter Newman, *Caesars of the Wilderness* (Markham, ON: Penguin Books, 1987), 378–80.

3. Robert McCandless, *Yukon Wildlife: A Social History* (Edmonton: University of Alberta Press, 1985), 59–60.

4. *Yukon Act*, 1898, http://www.pco-bcp.gc.ca/aia/default.asp?Language=E&page=federation&sub=Actsestablishingtheprovi&Doc=yukon_e.htm.

5. First Nations of British Columbia, Government of British Columbia, and Government of Canada, *The Report of the British Columbia Claims Task Force*, June 28, 1991, http://www.bctreaty.net/files_2/pdf_documents/bc_claims_task_force_report.pdf.

6. Jeffrey Simpson, "Trolling for Trouble on Fishery Rights," *Globe and Mail*, July 2003.

7. Simpson, "Trolling for Trouble on Fishery Rights."

8. Stephen Hume, "A Double Standard on Salmon," *Vancouver Sun*, June 26, 2003.

9. Thomas Isaac, "No End in Sight," *Globe and Mail*, September 19, 2000.

10. Peter Pearse and Donald McRae, *Treaties and Transition: Towards a Sustainable Fishery on Canada's Pacific Coast* (Vancouver: Fisheries and Oceans Canada, 2004).

11. Pearse and McRae, *Treaties and Transition*, 2.

12. Pearse and McRae, *Treaties and Transition*, 11.

13. Geoff Meggs, e-mail message to the author, September 12, 2004.

14. Pearse and McRae, *Treaties and Transition*, 56.

15. Terry Glavin, "A Radical Solution to the Salmon Crisis: A (Gasp) Free-Market Quota Fishery," *Vancouver Sun*, May 2, 2005.

CHAPTER 10: THE NISGA'A REFERENDUM

1. Joseph Gosnell, "The Nisga'a Treaty" (speech to British Columbia legislature, December 2, 1998), *BC Studies: The British Columbia Quarterly* (120, Winter 1998–99), 6.
2. Thomas Berger, "I Won't Be Voting in Premier Campbell's Referendum," *Vancouver Sun*, April 15, 2002.
3. Gordon Campbell, "Referendum Will Spur Treaty Process," *National Post*, April 27, 2002.
4. *Campbell et al. v. British Columbia*, (2000), 4 C.N.L.R. 1.
5. Preston Manning, *The Nisga'a Final Agreement* (Ottawa: Official Opposition, 1999).
6. Gordon Gibson, "A Principled Analysis of the Nisga'a Treaty," *Inroads* 8 (1999): 165.
7. Neil Sterritt, "The Nisga'a Treaty: Competing Claims Ignored," *BC Studies: The British Columbia Quarterly* (120, Winter 1998–99), 73.
8. Campbell, "Referendum Will Spur Treaty Process."
9. Raif Mair, "Editorial," CKNW, Vancouver, December 14, 1998.
10. Geoff Plant, speech to Aboriginal Law Section, Canadian Bar Association, Vancouver, October 18, 2001.
11. Plant, speech to Aboriginal Law Section.
12. Government of British Columbia, *Your Guide to the Nisga'a Treaty* (Victoria: Ministry of Aboriginal Affairs, 1998).
13. Tony Penikett, "Treaty Questions Falsely Simplistic," *Vancouver Sun*, March 6, 2002.
14. Geoff Plant, CKNW interview, Vancouver, October 29, 2001.
15. Norman Spector, "Ten Comments on the Treaty Referendum," *Vancouver Sun*, April 22, 2002.
16. Campbell, "Referendum Will Spur Treaty Process."
17. Berger, "I Won't Be Voting in Premier Campbell's Referendum."
18. Berger, "I Won't Be Voting in Premier Campbell's Referendum."
19. Berger, "I Won't Be Voting in Premier Campbell's Referendum."

CHAPTER 11: CONSULTATION

1. Government of British Columbia, "Consultation Guidelines," September 1998.
2. *Delgamuukw v. Attorney General of British Columbia*, (1997) 3 S.C.R. 1010.
3. *Taku River Tlingit First Nation v. Ringstad et al.*, (2002) B.C.C.A. 59.
4. *Taku River Tlingit*, 4.
5. *Taku River Tlingit*, 109.
6. Art Pape, presentation to Canadian Bar Association, Aboriginal Law Section, Vancouver, April 23, 2002.
7. Randal Kaardal, presentation to Canadian Bar Association, Aboriginal Law Section, Vancouver, April 23, 2002.

8. *Haida Nation v. B.C. and Weyerhaeuser*, (2002) B.C.J. 147.

9. *Haida Nation*, 29.

10. John Hunter, "Recent Developments in the Duty to Consult with First Nations" (presentation to Pacific Business and Law Institute, Vancouver, May 1, 2002).

11. Jeffrey Simpson, "A Right That Walks, Talks and Smells Like a Veto," *Globe and Mail*, May 1, 2002.

12. Simpson, "A Right That Walks, Talks and Smells Like a Veto."

13. "Consultation After the *Taku River Tlingit* and *Haida* Decisions," conference organized by the Pacific Business and Law Institute, Vancouver, May 1, 2002.

14. Hunter, "Recent Developments in the Duty to Consult with First Nations."

15. Louise Mandel, presentation to Pacific Business and Law Institute, Vancouver, May 1, 2002.

16. Denis de Keruzec, presentation to Pacific Business and Law Institute, Vancouver, May 1, 2002.

17. Government of British Columbia, Provincial Policy on Consultation with First Nations, October 2002.

18. Government of British Columbia, Operational Guidelines.

19. Edward John, "Treaty Negotiations: What Works, What Doesn't—A Negotiators' Dialogue" (panel discussion, Morris J. Wosk Centre for Dialogue, Vancouver, November 22, 2002), http://www.sfu.ca/dialogue/publications/Treaty_What_Works.pdf.

20. Thomas Isaac, presentation to Cordilleran Roundup Mining Conference, Vancouver, January 27, 2003.

21. Business Council of British Columbia, *The British Columbia Treaty Process: A Road Map for Further Progress* (Vancouver: Business Council of British Columbia, May 2004).

22. Business Council, *The British Columbia Treaty Process*, 13.

23. Business Council, *The British Columbia Treaty Process*, 16–17.

24. *Haida Nation*, 33.

25. *Haida Nation*, 37.

26. Doug Caul, in discussion with the author, 2002.

CHAPTER 12: RENTED CERTAINTY: INTERIM MEASURES

1. John Walsh, e-mail message to the author, January 15, 2004.

2. Arthur Manuel, "Chief Calls on First Nations to Walk Away from the B.C. Treaty Process—Open Letter to All of the Aboriginal Nations and Communities Participating in the British Columbia Treaty Commission Process," February 15, 2000.

3. J. Woodward, in discussion with the author, August 14, 2002.

4. Louise Mandell, Garry Wouters, Thomas Isaac, Michael Hudson, Doug Caul, Randy Brant, Gary Yabsley, Jack Weisgerber, Lydia Hwitsum,

Kathryn Teneese, and Jim Aldridge, "Treaty Negotiations: Key Questions (panel discussion, Morris J. Wosk Centre for Dialogue, Vancouver, April 16, 2003), http://www.sfu.ca/dialogue/publications/Treaty_Key_Questions.pdf.

CHAPTER 13: MANIPULATIVE MANDATES

1. Douglas McArthur, "Treaty Negotiations: What Works, What Doesn't—A Negotiators' Dialogue" (panel discussion, Morris J. Wosk Centre for Dialogue, Vancouver, November 22, 2002), http://www.sfu.ca/dialogue/publications/Treaty_What_Works.pdf.
2. McArthur, "Treaty Negotiations: What Works, What Doesn't."
3. Robin Dodson, "Treaty Negotiations: What Works, What Doesn't."
4. Edward John, "Treaty Negotiations: What Works, What Doesn't."
5. Lydia Hwitsum, "Treaty Negotiations: Key Questions" (panel discussion, Morris J. Wosk Centre for Dialogue, Vancouver, April 16, 2003), http://www.sfu.ca/dialogue/publications/Treaty_Key_Questions.pdf.
6. Improving the Treaty Process—Report of the Tripartite Working Group, B.C. Treaty Commission, February 25, 2002, 12.
7. Jim Barkwell, "Treaty Negotiations: Key Questions."
8. Thomas Isaac, "Treaty Negotiations: Key Questions."
9. Jim Aldridge, "Treaty Negotiations: Key Questions."
10. Barkwell, "Treaty Negotiations: Key Questions."
11. Lorne Brownsey, "Treaty Negotiations: Key Questions."
12. Robin Dodson, "Treaty Negotiations: Key Questions."
13. Barkwell, "Treaty Negotiations: Key Questions."
14. Aldridge, "Treaty Negotiations: Key Questions."
15. Barry Stuart, e-mail message to the author, November 9, 2005.
16. Barkwell, "Treaty Negotiations: Key Questions," paraphrasing Roger Fisher and William Ury in *Getting to Yes: Negotiating without Giving In* (London: Penguin Books, 1991).
17. Doug Caul, "Treaty Negotiations: Key Questions."
18. Manny Jules, in discussion at "Planning for Prosperity: First Nations, Intergovernmental Cooperation and Treaties," Morris J. Wosk Centre for Dialogue, Vancouver, September 9, 2004, http://www.sfu.ca/dialogue/pdf/Planning_for_Prosperity.pdf.
19. Douglas McArthur, "Planning for Prosperity."
20. McArthur, "Planning for Prosperity."
21. John Files, "U.S. Is Ordered to Tell Indians Before Selling Trust Property," *New York Times*, October 4, 2004.
22. Files, "U.S. Is Ordered to Tell Indians Before Selling Trust Property."
23. Umbrella Final Agreement between the Government of Canada, the Council for Yukon Indians and the Government of the Yukon, http://www.ainc-inac.gc.ca/pr/agr/umb/index_e.html.
24. Nisga'a Final Agreement, http://www.ainc-inac.gc.ca/pr/agr/nsga/index_e.html.

25. Dodson, "Treaty Negotiations: What Works, What Doesn't."

26. John, "Treaty Negotiations: What Works, What Doesn't."

27. Grant Thornton LLP, *An Update to the Financial and Economic Analysis of Treaty Settlements in British Columbia* (Vancouver: B.C. Treaty Commission, March 12, 2004).

28. Felipe Fernández-Armesto, *The Americas: A Hemispheric History* (New York: Modern Library, 2003), 149.

29. Raymond Hernandez, "Trump Among Those Named in Inquiry into Bankrolling of Would-Be Tribes," *New York Times*, May 6, 2004.

30. Barbara Yaffe, "A Big-Picture Perspective on Meeting Our Aboriginal Woes," *Vancouver Sun*, November 8, 2005.

31. Dodson, "Treaty Negotiations: What Works, What Doesn't."

32. David Joe, "Treaty Negotiations: What Works, What Doesn't."

33. Harry Swain, in discussion with the author, May, 2003.

34. B.C. Treaty Commission, *Looking Back, Looking Forward: A Review of the B.C. Treaty Process* (Vancouver: B.C. Treaty Commission, 2001), 5.

35. Barry Stuart, *The Big Picture: Yukon Self-Government Justice Negotiations: Preliminary Observations and Suggestions* (draft report prepared for the federal government, Vancouver, 2004).

36. John, "Treaty Negotiations: What Works, What Doesn't."

CHAPTER 14: MORE BROKEN PROMISES? IMPLEMENTATION ISSUES

1. Implementation Review Working Group, *Five-Year Review of the Umbrella Final Agreement Implementation Plan and Yukon First Nation Final Agreement Implementation Plans for the Four Yukon First Nations* (Ottawa: Indian and Northern Affairs Canada, 2000).

2. Barry Stuart, in discussion with the author, June 1992.

3. Lesley McCullough, in discussion with the author, September 18, 2002.

4. Tim Koepke, in discussion with the author, September 19, 2002.

5. Ed Schultz, speech to Redefining Relationships conference, Ottawa, November 12, 2003.

6. Terry Fenge, "Inuit Self-Determination: Implementing the Nunavut Land Claims Agreement" (unpublished, 2003).

7. Nunavut Implementation Panel, *Implementation of the Nunavut Land Claims Agreement: An Independent 5-Year Review, 1993–1998* (Ottawa: Indian and Northern Affairs Canada, 2000).

8. Nunavut Implementation Panel, *Implementation of the Nunavut Land Claims Agreement.*

9. Fenge, *Inuit Self-Determination*, 22.

10. Sheila Fraser, "Chapter 8: Indian and Northern Affairs Canada—Transferring Federal Responsibilities to the North," in 2003 *Report of the Auditor General of Canada* (Ottawa: Office of the Auditor General of Canada, 2004), http://www.oag-bvg.gc.ca/domino/reports.nsf/html/20031108ce.html.

11. Fraser, "Chapter 8: Indian and Northern Affairs Canada—Transferring Federal Responsibilities to the North."

12. Joe Gosnell, speech to Redefining Relationships conference, Ottawa, November 12, 2003.

13. Andrew Gamble, presentation of working group's recommendations, Redefining Relationships conference, Ottawa, November 13, 2003.

14. Ron Doering, presentation of working group's recommendations, Redefining Relationships conference, Ottawa, November 13, 2003.

15. Land Claim Agreement Coalition, letter to Prime Minister Paul Martin, March 24, 2004.

CHAPTER 15: REBUILDING NATIONS: SELF-GOVERNMENT

1. Indian and Northern Affairs Canada, *Federal Policy Guide: The Government of Canada's Approach to Implementation of the Inherent Right and the Negotiation of Aboriginal Self-Government* (Ottawa: Indian and Northern Affairs Canada, 1995).

2. Royal Commission on Aboriginal Peoples, *Report of the Royal Commission on Aboriginal Peoples, Volume 5: Renewal: A Twenty-Year Commitment* (Ottawa: Indian and Northern Affairs Canada, 1996).

3. Indian and Northern Affairs Canada, "Gathering Strength: Canada's Aboriginal Action Plan" (Ottawa: Indian and Northern Affairs Canada, 1998).

4. "Gathering Strength," Statement of Renewal.

5. "Brainstorming Governance" (panel discussion, Morris J. Wosk Centre for Dialogue, Vancouver, July 2, 2003), http://www.sfu.ca/dialogue/pdf/Brainstorming_Governance.pdf

6. The Harvard Project on American Indian Economic Development, http://www.ksg.harvard.edu/hpaied/people/cornell.htm.

7. Neil Sterritt, *First Nations Governance Handbook: A Resource Guide for Effective Councils* (Ottawa: Minister of Public Works and Government Services, 2002).

8. Peter W. Hogg and Mary Ellen Turpel, "Implementing Aboriginal Self-Government: Constitutional and Jurisdictional Issues," Royal Commission on Aboriginal Peoples Paper Number 93, 1994, 417.

9. Thomas Courchene, "Aboriginal Self-Government in Canada," Australian Senate Occasional Lecture Series, April 19, 1993, 19.

10. M.J. Chandler and C. Lalonde, "Cultural Continuity as a Hedge Against Suicide in Canada's First Nations," *Journal of Transcultural Psychiatry* (35), 191.

11. J.R. Miller, *Lethal Legacy: Current Native Controversies in Canada* (Toronto: McClelland and Stewart, 2004), 101.

12. In discussion with the author, February 15, 2005.

CHAPTER 16: HAIDA FORESTS: A NEW MODEL

1. Nancy Turner, *Plants of Haida Gwaii* (Winlaw, BC: Sono Nis Press, 2004).
2. E.D.K. and K.M. Porterfield, *Encyclopedia of American Indian Contributions to the World* (New York: Facts on File, 2001), 49.
3. Gordon Hamilton, "Mutiny in the Woods Could Change the Face of Logging on the B.C. Coast," *Vancouver Sun*, July 25, 2002.
4. Robert Davidson, in *The Abstract Edge*, edited by Karen Duffek (Vancouver: Museum of Anthropology at the University of British Columbia in association with the National Gallery of Canada, 2004), 36.
5. Haida Nation, Statement of Intent filed with B.C. Treaty Commission, Vancouver, December 15, 1993.
6. *Haida Nation v. B.C. and Weyerhauser*, (2002) B.C.J. 147.
7. Louise Mandell, in discussion with the author, Vancouver, September 26, 2002.
8. Guujaaw, "Voices of Haida Gwaii," *Vancouver Sun*, March 16, 2002. D3
9. Thomas Isaac, *Aboriginal Title* (Saskatoon: Native Law Centre, University of Saskatchewan, 2006), 3.
10. Mandell, in discussion with the author.
11. Guujaaw, in discussion with the author, October 30, 2002.
12. Guujaaw, in discussion with author, October 30, 2002.
13. Garry Wouters, in discussion with the author, April 4, 2006.
14. Vaughn Palmer, "The Liberals' Bottom Line on Forest Reform," *Vancouver Sun*, April 18, 2002.
15. Stephen Hume, "Do We Want the Vast Majority of Our Old-Growth Forests, the Inventory of High-Value Wood They Contain and the Complex Ecosystems They Sustain Simply Liquidated to Make Way for Genetically Engineered Tree Plantations," *Vancouver Sun*, April 18, 2002.
16. Ken Drushka, "Old Misguided Forest Policies Set Stage for Current Dispute," *Business in Vancouver*, April 23–29, 2002.
17. Tony Penikett, "The Haida Don't Let Go Easily," *Globe and Mail*, September 9, 2003.
18. Guujaaw, interview on CBC, *B.C. Almanac*, September 4, 2003.
19. E. Wright, "Planning for Prosperity: First Nations, Intergovernmental Cooperation and Treaties" (panel discussion, Morris J. Wosk Centre for Dialogue, Vancouver, September 9, 2004), http://www.sfu.ca/dialogue/pdf/Planning_for_Prosperity.pdf.
20. Guujaaw, in discussion with the author, October 30, 2002.
21. Forest (First Nations Development) Amendment Act, 2002, http://www.legis.gov.bc.ca/37th3rd/3rd_read/gov41-3.htm.
22. British Columbia Ministry of Forests, *Forestry Revitalization Plan*, http://www.for.gov.bc.ca/mof/plan/frp/pdf.htm.
23. Business Council of British Columbia, *The British Columbia Treaty Process: A Road Map for Further Progress* (Vancouver: Business Council of British Columbia, May 2004), 9.

24. Michael de Jong, Minister of Forests, letter to Guujaaw, President, Haida Nation, May 29, 2003.

25. Guujaaw, President, Haida Nation, letter to Michael de Jong, Minister of Forests, June 4, 2003.

26. Larry Pynn, "Decision Will Shape B.C.'s Future: Natives, Industry," *Vancouver Sun*, November 17, 2004.

27. Mike Harcourt, *Vancouver Sun*, November 17, 2004.

28. *Haida Nation v. British Columbia (Minister of Forests)*, (2004) 3 s.c.r. 511.

29. Guujaaw, e-mail message to the author, April 14, 2005.

30. Guujaaw, e-mail message to the author, July 1, 2005.

31. Jessica Clogg, "Recognition of Aboriginal Title in B.C.: A Legally and Morally Defensible Foundation for Tenure Reform," *Ecoforestry* 16(3):4.

CHAPTER 17: MEDIATION WORKS

1. Sheila Fraser, "Chapter 8: Indian and Northern Affairs Canada—Transferring Federal Responsibilities to the North," in 2003 *Report of the Auditor General of Canada* (Ottawa: Office of the Auditor General of Canada, 2004), http://www.oag-bvg.gc.ca/domino/reports.nsf/html/20031108ce.html.

2. John Calvert, e-mail message to the author, September 10, 2004.

3. First Nations of British Columbia, Government of British Columbia, and Government of Canada, *The Report of the British Columbia Claims Task Force*, June 28, 1991, http://www.bctreaty.net/files_2/pdf_documents/bc_claims_task_ force_report.pdf, 46.

4. Definition of "facilitate," *Oxford English Dictionary* (Oxford: Oxford University Press, 1984), http://www.oed.com/.

5. Business Council of British Columbia, *The British Columbia Treaty Process: A Road Map for Further Progress* (Vancouver: Business Council of British Columbia, May 2004).

6. Assembly of First Nations, "Negotiations Background Paper," Calgary, January 12–13, 2005.

CHAPTER 18: FAST-TRACK TREATIES

1. First Nations of British Columbia, Government of British Columbia, and Government of Canada, *The Report of the British Columbia Claims Task Force*, June 28, 1991, http://www.bctreaty.net/files_2/pdf_documents/bc_claims_task_ force_report.pdf, 46.

2. Tim Koepke, in discussion with the author, August 19, 2002.

3. B.C. Treaty Commission, *Tripartite Review of the B.C. Treaty Process: Report of the Working Group*, January 26, 1999, 3.

4. B.C. Treaty Commission, *Tripartite Review of the B.C. Treaty Process*, 7.

CHAPTER 19: UNITED NATIONS

1. Thomas L. Sever, *Validating Prehistoric and Current Social Phenomena upon the Landscape, Peten, Guatemala*, special publication of the National Academy of

Sciences/National Research Council on "People and Pixels: Linking Remote Sensing and Social Science" (Washington: National Academy Press, 1998), 145–63.

2. Commission for Historical Clarification, "Caso Ilustrativo No. 31: Masacre de Las Dos Erres," *Guatemala: Memoria del Silencio* (Guatemala: Commission for Historical Clarification, 1999), Anexo 1, Volumen 1.

3. Peter Goodspeed, "Bolivia May Just Be the Start—Much of Central and South America Ripe for Leftist Revolutions," *National Post*, October 21, 2003.

4. Niall Ferguson, "Who Lost Latin America?" *National Post*, February 15, 2006, A15.

5. Jean Chrétien, Prime Minister, letter to Tony Penikett, MLA, July 16, 1975.

6. Ferguson, "Who Lost Latin America?"

7. Juan Forero and Larry Rohter, "Bolivia's Leader Solidifies Region's Leftward Tilt," *New York Times*, January 22, 2006.

8. Ferguson, "Who Lost Latin America?"

9. Miguel Alfonso Martinez, *Study on Treaties, Agreements and Other Constructive Arrangements between States and Indigenous Populations* (in United Nations Commission on Human Rights Sub-commission on Prevention of Discrimination and Protection of Minorities, 51st session, item 7 of provisional agenda, New York, June 22, 1999).

10. Martinez, *Progress Report* (1992), point 109.

11. Martinez, point 100.

12. Martinez, points 64 and 146.

13. Martinez, point 46.

14. Martinez, points 307 and 307.

15. Bruce Clark, *Justice in Paradise* (Montreal and Kingston: McGill-Queen's University Press, 1999), 210.

16. Clark, *Justice in Paradise*, 224.

17. Wendy Sawatsky, "J.J. Harper: 15 Years Later," CBC Manitoba, March 7, 2003, http://www.cbc.ca/manitoba/features/harper/.

18. Waitangi Tribunal, http://www.waitangi-tribunal.govt.nz/.

19. Martinez, points 45 and 46.

20. James Dao, "Drums and Bells Open Indian Museum," *New York Times*, September 22, 2004.

21. John Pilger, "Paradise Cleansed—Our Deportation of the People of Diego Garcia Is a Crime That Cannot Stand," *The Guardian*, October 2, 2004.

22. Neal Acherson, "The Breaking of the Mau Mau," *New York Review of Books*, April 7, 2005.

23. Barack Obama, *Dreams from My Father* (New York: Three Rivers Press, 2004), 350.

24. Martinez, point 47.

25. Arctic Council, http://www.arctic-council.org.

26. Beverley McLachlin, "Aboriginal Rights: International Perspectives"

(speech to Order of Canada luncheon, Canadian Club of Vancouver, Vancouver, February 8, 2002).

27. Martinez, *Study on Treaties, Agreements and Other Constructive Arrangements between States and Indigenous Populations.*

28. Joseph Gosnell, "The Nisga'a Treaty" (speech to British Columbia Legislature, December 2, 1998), *BC Studies: The British Columbia Quarterly* (120, Winter 1998–99).

CHAPTER 20: POLITICAL WILL

1. Charles Campbell, "Mike Harcourt's Bold Predictions," *The Tyee*, December 7, 2004.

2. John Richards, e-mail message to the author, March 16, 2005.

3. Tom Flanagan, "Transcending the B.C. Treaty Process," *National Post*, November 5, 2001.

4. Tom Flanagan, *First Nations, Second Thoughts* (Montreal and Kingston: McGill-Queen's University Press, 2000).

5. Government of British Columbia, "The New Relationship with Aboriginal People," May 4, 2006, http://www.gov.bc.ca/arr/popt/the_new_relationship.htm.

6. Richard Chu, "Native Chiefs Welcome New Reconciliation," *Vancouver Sun*, June 17, 2005.

7. Edward John, e-mail message to the author, July 13, 2005.

8. Phil Fontaine, "First Nations-Federal Crown Political Accord and Cabinet Retreat Signal Steps Towards Self-Determination and Self-Government for First Nations," http://www.afn.ca/article.asp?id=1218.

9. Raymond Tomlin, "Gordon Campbell: British Columbia's Premier Hates Women and: Children, Aboriginals, Seniors, the Disabled and the Poor," May 8, 2005, http://www.vanramblings.com/bc-politics/gordon-campbell-british-c.html.

10. B.C. Stats, *Infoline Report*, Issue 05-17, April 29, 2005.

11. Art Pape, e-mail message to the author, August 3, 2005.

12. Tom Isaac, Tony Knox, and Sarah Bird, "The Crown's Duty to Consult and Accommodate Aboriginal Peoples: The Supreme Court of Canada Decision in *Haida*," *The Advocate*, September 2005.

13. Mark Hume, "Treaty Commission Predicts Progress," *Globe and Mail*, September 28, 2005.

14. Assembly of First Nations, "Negotiations Background Paper," Calgary, January 12–13, 2005.

15. Gary Yabsley, in discussion with the author, October 9, 2004.

16. Tom Molloy, *The World Was Our Witness: The Historic Journey of the Nisga'a into Canada* (Calgary: Fifth House, 2000), 43.

17. Molloy, *The World Was Our Witness*, 43.

18. Molloy, *The World Was Our Witness*, 61–62.

19. B.C. Treaty Commission, "Guidelines for Observers," Gitxsan Treaty Negotiations: Public Main Table Meeting, September 17, 2004, Hazelton, B.C.

20. Norman Stephens, e-mail message to the author, September 23, 2004.
21. Edward John, "Treaty Negotiations: What Works, What Doesn't—A Nego-
    tiators' Dialogue" (panel discussion, Morris J. Wosk Centre for Dialogue,
    Vancouver, November 22, 2002), http://www.sfu.ca/dialogue/publications/Trea-
    ty_What_Works.pdf.
22. Robin Dodson, "Treaty Negotiations: What Works, What Doesn't."
23. Jack Weisgerber, "Treaty Negotiations: What Works, What Doesn't."
24. B.C. Treaty Commission, *Annual Report 2004: Consider. . . a New
    Relationship* (Vancouver: B.C. Treaty Commission, 2004).
25. First Nations of British Columbia, Government of British Columbia, and
    Government of Canada, *The Report of the British Columbia Claims Task Force*,
    June 28, 1991, http://www.bctreaty.net/files_2/pdf_documents/bc_claims_task_
    force_report.pdf, 15.
26. B.C. Treaty Commission, *Tripartite Review of the BC Treaty Process: Report of
    the Working Group*, January 26, 1999.
27. First Nations of British Columbia, Government of British Columbia,
    and Government of Canada, *The Report of the British Columbia Claims Task
    Force*, 24.
28. Thomas Homer-Dixon, *The Ingenuity Gap: Can We Solve the Problems of the
    Future?* (Toronto: Vintage Canada, 2001), 395–96.
29. Arthur M. Schlesinger, *Robert Kennedy and His Times* (New York: Ballantine
    Books, 1978), 439–40.
30. Health Canada, *A Statistical Profile on the Health of First Nations in Canada*
    (Ottawa: Health Canada, 2003), 34.
31. M.J. Chandler and C. Lalonde, "Cultural Continuity as a Hedge Against
    Suicide in Canada's First Nations," *Journal of Transcultural Psychiatry* (35).
32. Statistics Canada, "About One-Half of Aboriginal People Lived in Urban
    Areas," in *2001 Census: Aboriginal Peoples of Canada: A Demographic Profile*,
    (Ottawa: Statistics Canada, 2002).
33. Indian and Northern Affairs Canada, "Urban Aboriginal Strategy,"
    http://www.ainc-inac.gc.ca/interloc/uas_e.html.
34. Bradley Regehr, "Urban Reserves in Manitoba: New Relationships from
    Old Promises" (presentation, Manitoba Bar Association mid-winter meeting,
    Winnipeg, January 30, 2004).
35. P. McNeil, in discussion at "Planning for Prosperity: First Nations, Inter-
    governmental Cooperation and Treaties," Morris J. Wosk Centre for
    Dialogue, Vancouver, September 9, 2004, http://www.sfu.ca/dialogue/pdf/
    Planning_for_Prosperity.pdf.
36. Mike Harcourt, in discussion at "Planning for Prosperity: First Nations,
    Intergovernmental Cooperation and Treaties," Morris J. Wosk Centre for
    Dialogue, Vancouver, September 9, 2004, http://www.sfu.ca/dialogue/pdf/
    Planning_for_Prosperity.pdf.

∇

ACKNOWLEDGMENTS

FIRST AMONG THE many persons I would like
to acknowledge for their support are the board
chair, Hugh Segal, and the trustees of the Walter and Duncan Gordon
Foundation, without whose financial support this book would have
remained just an idea. Thanks also go to the Gordon Foundation's
staff: Brenda Lucas, Patrick Johnston, and James Stauch, with special
gratitude to the foundation's former executive director, Christine
Lee, who made the hospitable arrangements to house this project
at West Coast Environmental Law and the Morris J. Wosk Centre
for Dialogue at Simon Fraser University's Harbour Centre campus
in Vancouver.

Dozens of others shared their opinions or offered editorial suggestions. Of this number, I am most grateful to the informal advisory
group with whom I met regularly at the Beijing Restaurant on Hornby
Street in Vancouver. Depending on the day, this group included
Karen Campbell, Jessica Clogg, Thomas Isaac, Dave Joe, Wendy
Grant John, Dennis Patterson, Miles Richardson, Garry Wouters,
and Gary Yabsley.

During my two years as a fellow at Simon Fraser University I
convened four roundtable discussions on treaty issues at the Wosk

Centre for Dialogue. The principal participants were senior negotiators from all three sides of the treaty tables, plus treaty commissioners, as well as chiefs and councillors, federal and provincial ministers and deputy ministers, mayors and municipal officials, entrepreneurs, and, of course, scholars. All brought insights to these dialogues based on their experience and expertise and, one way or another, each has influenced my thinking, some more than they could know.

My thanks go to Jim Aldridge, Stewart Alsgard, Gerald Amos, Robert S. Anderson, Martha Anslow, Jo-ann Archibald, Kim Baird, Jim Barkwell, Ian Batey, Mel Bevan, Nancy Bircher, Kevin Blaney, the late Randy Brant, Lyn Brown, Lorne Brownsey, Cheryl Casimer, Doug Caul, Stephen Cornell, Robin Dodson, Jack Ebbels, Dave Formosa, Mike Furey, Leonard George, Debra Hanuse, Mike Harcourt, L. Maynard Harry, Michael Hudson, Lydia Hwitsum, Thomas Isaac, Dave Joe, Edward John, Manny Jules, Stephen Kelleher, Chris Kelly, Colin Kinsley, Rick Krehbiel, Stan Lanyon, Louise Mandell, Tom Mann, Douglas McArthur, Rick McDougall, Alison McNeil, Stephen Owen, Arthur C. Pape, Sophie Pierre, Clarence Pennier, Marino Piombini, Kirsteen Pirie, Murray Rankin, Tim Raybould, Miles Richardson, Lloyd Roberts, Barry Seymour, Finlay Sinclair, John Slater, Jerome Slavick, Dan Smith, Ken Smith, Philip Steenkamp, Neil Sterritt, Harold Steves, Barry Stuart, Kathryn Teneese, Maureen Thomas, Sandi Tremblay, Michael Uehara, Bill Wareham, John Watson, Hal Weinberg, Edmond Wright, Garry Wouters, Jack Weisgerber, and Gary Yabsley.

Others who proved very helpful include James Beebe, Thomas Berger, Colin Braker, Peter Cameron, Linda Coady, Nellie Cournoyea, John Crump, Terry Fenge, Jim Fulton, Guujaaw, Adele Hurley, Dave Kennedy, Tim Koepke, Guuduniia LaBoucan, Lesley McCullough, Geoff Meggs, Mike M'Gonigle, Yasmin Miller, Vince Ready, Debbie Seto-Kitson, Scott Serson, Ralph Sultan, Rodion Sulyandziga, Charles and Mary Ungerleider, Saeko Usukawa, Marilyn Van Bibber, John Walsh, John Ritter, Lennard Sillanpaa, and Jack Woodward. West

Coast Environmental Law staff members Lawrence Alexander, Ceceline Goh, Alexandra Melnyk, Linda Nowlan, Ian Reid, and Chris Rolfe helped me get started. SFU colleagues, particularly Joanna Ashworth, Ann Cowan, Patricia Graca, Mark Winston, and Nicole Mah, aided me in numerous ways. British Columbia Treaty Commission staff Isabel Budke, Peter Colenbrander, Brian Mitchell, Nancy Olding, and Lloyd Roberts were always ready to answer my questions. Several government officials who prefer not to be named also spoke frankly to me about their challenges.

For thirty years my children's extended family in the Upper Tanana communities of Alaska and Yukon provided me with a continuing education in Aboriginal-settler relations. To them I want to say, *Tsin'ii choh.*

Finally, notes of gratitude go to Scott McIntyre, who agreed to publish this book, and my editor, Barbara Pulling, who made it fit to print.

Needless to say, none of the above can be held responsible for my interpretation of events and policies or my conclusions about the treaty processes in British Columbia and Canada.

INDEX

Italicized page numbers refer to maps.

Photo: Jane Weitzel

TONY PENIKETT, *currently a Vancouver-based mediator, was deputy minister of negotiations for the British Columbia government and, later, deputy minister of labour. A former Yukon premier, Penikett has been involved in Aboriginal rights negotiations for over twenty years. He also teaches courses in negotiation in Simon Fraser University's Dialogue and Master of Public Policy programs.*